ARCO

PRACTICE FOR CLERICAL, TYPING, AND STENOGRAPHIC TESTS

Maryhelen H. Paulick Hoffman

Prentice Hall
New York • London • Toronto • Sydney • Tokyo • Singapore

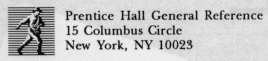 Prentice Hall General Reference
15 Columbus Circle
New York, NY 10023

An Arco Book

Arco, Prentice Hall, and colophons are
registered trademarks of Simon & Schuster, Inc.

Library of Congress Cataloging-in-Publication Data

Hoffman, Maryhelen H. Paulick.
    Practice for clerical, typing, and stenographic tests / Maryhelen H.
Paulick Hoffman. —8th ed.
    p. cm.
ISBN 0-671-84668-X
    1. Civil service—United States—Examinations. 2. Clerical ability and
aptitude tests. 3. Stenographers. 4. Typewriting—Examinations,
questions, etc. I. Title.
JK716.H353   1992   91-42085
651.3'741—dc20   CIP

Manufactured in the United States of America

1 2 3 4 5 6 7 8 9 10

CONTENTS

PRETEST

PRACTICE ON PRETEST SUBJECTS

TYPING

SHORTHAND

INTRODUCTION

How This Book Will Help You

As you apply for an examination, you may ask, "How will this book help me?" or "What will I gain from it?" If you use it correctly, this book will:

- Show you what to expect, and
- Give you a speedy brush-up on the subjects tested in examinations.

Some of these topics are not taught in a formal classroom at all. Even if your study time is very limited, you should:

Become familiar with the various types of examinations you may have.

Improve your general examination-taking skill.

Improve your skill in analyzing and answering questions involving reasoning, judgment, comparison, and evaluation.

Improve your speed and skill in reading and understanding of what you read. This is an important part of your ability to learn and an important part of most examinations.

Applying for Public and Private Sector Positions

Employment opportunities include practically every skill and profession in our complex world. Every year thousands of new jobs are created and tens of thousands of replacements are needed to fill vacancies.

Employers in both public and private sectors have recruitment procedures for filling positions.

In the public sector, information may be obtained from:

1. *The offices of the State Employment Services.* There are many located throughout the country. These offices are administered by the states in which they are located. You will find the address of the one nearest you in your local telephone directory.

2. *Your state Civil Service Commission.* Look in your local telephone directory and then address your inquiries to the proper authority. If no address is available, address your inquiry to the capital city of your state.

3. *Your city Civil Service Commission.* If you live in a large city, contact the Commission. The Commission often is called by another name, such as the Department of Personnel. You will be able to iden-

tify it in your telephone directory by looking under the listing of city departments.

4. *Your municipal building and your local library.*

5. *Local newspapers.* Many local newspapers run a section on civil service news.

6. *School Boards and Boards of Education.* Ask for information about job openings.

7. *Job Opportunity Bulletins.* The bulletins are available at various public buildings throughout individual states, in libraries, and in Employment Security Offices. Announcements of some examinations are advertised in appropriate newspapers as well.

In the private sector, you can obtain information by the following means:

1. *Read occupational literature.* Among these books are the *Occupational Outlook Handbook* and *Dictionary of Occupational Titles.* These books are distributed by the U.S. Department of Labor. Other books are: *Guide to Career Information, Bibliography of Current Occupational Literature,*

Business Periodicals Index, and *Vocational and Professional Monographs*.

2. *Depend upon your friends and relatives.* Ask them if they know of any possible openings; let them know you are job hunting; and tell them in what area(s) of employment you are interested.

3. *Read newspaper advertisements, professional journals, and trade magazines.* If you are willing to relocate, read newspapers from other areas and newspapers and magazines that carry national advertising.

4. *Contact private and state operated employment agencies.* Try to find an agency that charges the employer rather than you, the employee. Do your homework, and ask questions.

5. *Contact the personnel office in large companies.* Check in your local library for these names and addresses.

The Job Announcement

What It Contains

When a position is open, whether it be in the private or public sector, a job announcement is drawn up. This announcement contains just about everything you have to know about the job.

Each announcement contains such information as: job title, location, jurisdiction, salary, residence requirements, short definition of duties, minimum education and/or experience requirements, type of examination, system of rating, veterans preference, and other pertinent data. It tells which application form you fill out, where to get the form, and where and when to file it.

Study the job announcement carefully. It will answer many of your questions and help you decide whether you might like the position and if you are qualified for it.

Where the Job Is Located

Be sure you are willing to work in the area noted on the job announcement. There is no point in applying for a position and in taking the examination if you do not want to move.

A civil service job close to your home has an additional advantage. At times, local residents receive preference in appointments.

The Duties

Often a job title does not accurately describe the job, so read the description of duties carefully. Sometimes the words *Optional Fields* head up a list of other occupations covered by the same announcement.

Not every announcement has options, but if it does, the precise duties are described in detail, usually under the heading *Description of Work*. Make sure these duties come within the range of your experience and ability, if the options appeal to you.

The Deadline

Most job requirements give a deadline for filing an application. Others bear the words *No Closing Date*, at the top of the first page. This means your application will be accepted until the needs of the agency are met. In some cases a public notice is issued when a certain number of applications have been received.

No application mailed past the deadline date will be considered.

Education and Experience

Every announcement has a detailed section on education and experience requirements for the particular job and for the optional fields. Make sure you meet the minimum qualifications in both education and experience. If you do not meet the given standards for one job, there may be others open where you stand a better chance of making the grade.

Veterans Preference

If the job announcement does not mention veterans preference, inquire if there is such a provision. In the public sector (federal, state, county, or local jurisdiction), there is usually such a provision, however, there may be none or it may be limited to disabled veterans. In some jurisdictions, preference is given to the surviving spouses of deceased veterans. Obtain all such information through the agency that issues the job announcement.

Bilingual Testing and Certification Programs

Some jurisdictions provide BICAT (Bilingual Communicative Ability Testing). This program has two objectives:

1. To make it easier for individuals with bilingual skills to obtain employment; and

2. To make it easier for employers to hire qualified bilingual employees.

Check with the testing agency to determine if there is such a program available.

The Test

Examinations are developed by trained individuals in the field concerned. These individuals know how to phrase questions so the problem is clearly stated. Ethics do not permit "trick" or "catch" questions. It is important, however, that you *read* each question thoroughly. Often, if a person "half" reads a question, a wrong answer may seem right.

The announcement describes the kind of examination given for a particular position. It tells what areas are to be covered in the examination and lists the specific subjects on which questions will be asked. Sometimes sample questions are given.

In order to prepare for these examinations, you should know how they differ from other examinations you may have taken. The examination determines your current ability to perform the duties of a position, as well as your potential to learn to perform these duties. In other words, an examination attempts to determine how successful you will be on the job.

Usually the announcement states whether the examination is *assembled* or *unassembled*. In an assembled examination, you and other test-takers gather in the same place at the same time to take a written or performance examination. In the unassembled examination, you do not take an examination; instead you are rated on your education, experience, and whatever records of past achievement you provide.

In the public sector, similar kinds of positions are placed under a specific title. All positions in the group are paid according to the salary range for that group or job title. One title covers all the positions in the group, and all the positions are tested for by the same examination.

How to Get an Application Form

After you have studied the job announcement, have decided that you want the position, and are qualified for it, your next step is to get an application form. The job announcement tells you where to get it.

The Application Form

Most application forms are similar. The questions are generally simple and direct and are designed to obtain a maximum of information about you.

Many prospective employees did not get a job because of erroneous, incomplete, misleading, or untruthful answers. Give the application the serious attention it deserves as the first step toward getting the job you want. The application form is your first introduction and a major impression to a prospective employer.

The following list, along with some helpful comments, contains the questions usually asked on the average application form, although not necessarily in this order.

Filling Out Forms

Upon receipt of an application form and/or job announcement, do the following:

1. Read the job announcement thoroughly to familiarize yourself with the specific requirements listed. Also check the column labeled "Open To Residents Of." You may file an application for any examination if by the closing date for accepting applications you are a resident of the governmental jurisdiction (state, county, or municipality) for which the examination is being offered. Read the announcement so you know what subjects to

study. Learn as much as possible about the class of positions for which you have applied. The examination will test the knowledge, skills, and abilities needed to do the work.

2. Begin the process of completing the form by remembering the following general guidelines:

   a. Use a typewriter. If this is not possible, print or write neatly and clearly in ink. *Follow the directions on the form.*

   b. Make an original copy and *do not sign and date it.* Then photocopy additional copies and sign and date each copy when necessary for distribution (unless directions specify that you file an original).

   c. Review your life experiences, especially those which can enhance the position for which you are applying before you prepare your form. Make a list of specific activities, duties, skills, and work experiences.

3. You must furnish all requested information. The information you provide will be used to determine your qualifications for employment. *Do not send a resume instead of completing this form.* However, you may attach a resume for additional information. [*Note*: Some offices state, "If you are submitting your application with any documents which are to be returned, please enclose a self-addressed stamped envelope."]

4. So it is clearly *understood* you did not omit an item, write the letters "N/A" (Not Applicable) beside those items that do not apply to you, unless instructions say otherwise.

5. Be sure to sign your name and double check everything before sending in your application form.

6. All applications **must** be postmarked or delivered to the agency before the "Last Date for Filing Applications." Once the last date for filing applications has passed, you may not add anything to your application. So be sure it is complete and correct before you send it in.

7. If your address changes after filing, notify the agency immediately by writing to them. Include the job title and your social security number with your new address.

The Questions

1. *Name of examination or kind of position applied for.* This information appears in large type on the first page of the job announcement. Fill in the position category or name and announcement number or title, symbol, and code supplied on the job announcement.

2. *Optional job* (if mentioned in the job announcement). If you wish to apply for an option, simply copy the title from the job announcement. If you are not interested in an option, write "None." Or fill in "Any job for which qualified."

3. *Primary place of employment applied for.* The location of the position is probably contained in the job announcement. You must consider whether you want to work there. The job announcement may list more than one location where the job is open. If you would accept employment in any of the places, list them all; otherwise, list the specific place or places where you would like to work. Do not check those sections where you have no intention of working.

4. *Name and address.* Give in full, including your middle and/or maiden name and previous married names. Fill in every block completely. If your name or address changes after you have applied for a job, be sure to inform the hiring agency.

5. *Home or office telephone.* Fill in your home telephone and work telephone number. If none, write "None."

6. *Legal or voting residence.* The state in which you vote is the one you list here. To be eligible for some positions, you must meet the residence requirement by the closing date for accepting applications.

7. *Married or single.* If you are a widow, widower, or are divorced, you are considered single.

8. *Birthplace.* Changes in the borders of European countries make it difficult for many foreign-born American citizens to know which country to list as the land of their birth. One suggestion is to write down the name of the town and country which now controls it, together with the name of the country to which it belonged at the time of your birth.

9. *Date of birth.* Give the exact day, month, and year of your birth.

10. *Lowest grade or pay you will accept.* Although the salary is clearly stated in the job announcement, there may be a quicker opening in the same occupation which carries less responsibility and thus a lower, basic entrance salary. You will not

be considered for a job paying less than the amount you give in answer to this question.

11. *Will you accept less than full-time employment?* Part-time work comes up now and then. Consider whether you want to accept such a position while waiting for a full-time appointment.

12. *Will you accept temporary employment if offered you for (a) one month or less, (b) one to four months, or (c) four to twelve months?* Temporary positions come up frequently and it is important to know whether you are available.

13. *Availability.* Put whatever date you expect to be available.

14. *Travel.* Check what is possible for you.

15. *Were you in active military service in the armed forces of the United States?* Veterans preference, if given, is usually limited to active service during certain periods. Check with the appointing authority.

16. *Do you claim disabled veterans credit?* If you do claim it, you have to show proof of a war-incurred disability. This is done through certification by the Veterans Administration.

    There may be specific sections for a wife of a disabled veteran, widow of a disabled veteran, widow of a veteran who died in service, widow of a veteran who did not die in the service, or gold star mother.

17. *Past employment.* Examiners check all responses closely. Do not falsify your record. If you were ever fired, say so. It is better for you to state this openly than for the examiners to find out the truth from your former employer. State when, where, and how long you were employed.

    You will be asked if personnel staff may contact your present employer. If you do not wish your present employer to know that you are "looking," answer "No" and provide some form of evaluation, such as a performance evaluation or letter of recommendation.

    In describing your duties:
    — Use the word "I" instead of "the incumbent" or "she/he." Use "I" sparingly by listing your responsibilities, i.e., "Was directly responsible for . . ."
    — Use "active" verbs (a verb with a direct object is an active verb.) Example: "I typed letters."
    — Be complete. Use all the lines allotted to each job and write more if you need to on plain white paper. Be sure to number the attachments with your complete name, the item number, your social security number, and your date of birth.
    — Include all major duties of each job.
    — Use your own words, not words from position descriptions.
    — Be specific about what tasks you performed; do not summarize; explain fully.
    — Include volunteer work.
    — List your present job first then the previous one, and so on. Experience gained more than 15 years ago may be summarized in one block if it is not applicable to the type of position you are applying for.
    — Write a draft of your experiences first. Then rewrite your draft as many times as is necessary to produce a complete, well-written description of duties.
    — Don't abbreviate. Don't use acronyms unless you explain the meaning in the first use.
    — Include brief excerpts from official or unofficial letters in which your work was praised. Mention job-related awards.
    — Don't type your material into one long, unending paragraph. Break up your description into short sentences or paragraphs and use headings.

18. *Previous federal employment.* State on the form, where, when, and how long you were employed. Experience requirements for each examination announced are usually included in the job announcement. The information you provide on your application form must state clearly that you meet all minimum requirements of the examination for which you are applying. When you list your past work experience, be sure to include all experience which qualifies you for the examination.

19. *Special qualifications and skills.* Even though not directly related to the position for which you are applying, include such information as licenses and certificates obtained for teachers, pilots, registered nurses, counselors, and real estate agents. List experience in the use of machines and equipment, and other skills you have gained. List your published and unpublished writings, public speaking experience, membership in professional societies, relevant hobbies and typing and/or shorthand skills.

    Honors and awards don't have to be earth-shaking to be included. Cite scholarships, letters of commendation from your supervisor, safety awards, suggestion awards (describe the suggestion and its benefits briefly), community awards and nominations, election to honorary societies or groups, and fellowships. Your most recent awards are usually the most important. However, if you received only a few awards, list them all—even if they were presented some years ago.

20. *Education*. List your entire educational history, including name of school, location, dates attended, subjects studied, number of classroom or credit hours received, all diplomas, degrees, and all special courses taken in any accredited or Armed Forces school. Also give your credits toward a college or a graduate degree (credit hours refer to the number of units you earned for a college course). As in other items, you may have to add separate sheets. If possible, include a college transcript.

    Note: Include service workshops, seminars, professional conferences, private study, correspondence courses, leadership orientation, career speciality training, and others. Be sure to give all the details requested, including time involved, so it may be properly rated.

    If you were educated outside the United States, you must submit an evaluated transcript with your application.

21. *References*. Give the names of people who can give information about you, their occupations, business, and home addresses. Use people who know you and your work.

    Don't list people who are out of the country, have no phone, or whose whereabouts are unknown to you. Ask your references for permission to use their names.

22. *Your health*. Questions are often asked about your medical record. You are expected to have the physical and psychological capacity to perform the job for which you are applying. Standards vary, of course, depending on the requirements of the position. A physical handicap will not bar you from a job you can perform adequately.

23. *Foreign language*. Any familiarity with a foreign language should also be stated on the form. Be honest in evaluating your abilities.

24. *Social security number*. Be sure your number is correct.

25. *Have you failed an examination for the title applied for?* This may be limited to a time period.

26. *Have you ever been dismissed from a position?* If so, give date and reason for each dismissal.

27. *Handicap section*. If you are physically or mentally handicapped (blind, learning disabled, etc.) and need assistance in taking an examination, let the agency know what type of assistance you will require (reader, marker, deaf interpreter, other). This information is used to provide those applicants accommodations so they can compete in the testing process on an equal basis.

The Examinations

When you have filled out the application as completely as possible, sign it and send it to the address given on the form. If your examination includes a written test, you must wait until this test is scheduled. Shortly before it is to be held, you will be notified where and when to report.

You Are Tested

Sometimes the date of the written examination appears on the job announcement; sometimes it does not. You must simply wait until you receive notification of the time and place.

The most important step you can take in preparing for your examination is to study questions similar to the ones in this book. The purpose of this book is to acquaint you with the kinds of questions that will be asked and to provide you with review material in the subjects that will be covered. A thorough knowledge of the form of the actual examination as well as of the subject matter will give you an advantage. There are no substitutes for experience and familiarity.

Reference Sources

For information on careers in secretarial work, write to:

Professional Secretaries International
10502 NW Ambassador Drive
Kansas City, MO 64153-1289

U.S. Department of Labor
Bureau of Labor Statistics
441 G Street NW
Washington, DC 20212-0001

We would also like to thank the U.S. Department of Labor, Bureau of Labor Statistics, for all the up-to-date information used in this book.

PREPARING YOURSELF FOR YOUR EXAMINATION

How To Study

Outlined below are a few of the steps you can take in preparing for an examination:

1. *Study the announcement*. The examination will test the knowledge, skills, and abilities needed to do the work. Often the brief description of the position in the examination announcement offers some idea about the subjects to be covered. Think about the job itself. Review the duties in your mind. Can you perform them or are there some areas in which you need help or review? Attempt to fill in the blank spots in your preparation.

2. *Review your own background*. Once you learn what the position is all about and what you need to know to do the work, ask yourself which subject areas you already know fairly well and which you need to improve. The pretest will aid you in this determination.

3. *Determine the level of the position*. Another way to tell how you should prepare is to understand the level of the job for which you are applying. Is it entry, senior (intermediate), or principal (advanced) level? Often this is noted by such words as ''Trainee'' or ''Senior'' or ''Supervisor.'' If the level is not stated in the title, check the description of duties. Will you be working under very close supervision or will you have responsibility for independent decisions in this work?

4. *Choose appropriate study materials*. When you have an idea about the subject areas to be examined and the relative importance of each, you can choose suitable study materials. If you have any weakness in some aspects of your training, read an *up-to-date* textbook or handbook in that field. For entry-level positions, questions of appropriate difficulty are chosen; they are neither too advanced nor too simple. Such questions require careful thought but not advanced training.

Some Abilities Which Are Often Tested

Examinations are used for purposes other than measuring knowledge and ability to perform specified duties. For some positions it is equally important to test the ability to make adjustments to new situations or to profit from training. In others, basic mental abilities not dependent upon special information are essential. Questions which test skills and abilities may not appear as pertinent for a given position as those questions which test for knowledge and information. Yet, they are highly important parts of a fair examination. For very general questions, it is almost impossible to help you direct your study efforts. What we can do is to point out some of the most common general abilities needed and to describe some typical questions:

1. *Verbal ability*. The ability to use and to understand words is typically measured with vocabulary and grammar examinations. ''Reading comprehension'' or ''paragraph interpretation'' questions are also common. You are given a paragraph of written material and are asked to interpret its meaning.

2. *Numerical ability*. Number skills may be tested by arithmetic problems or by charts and graphs, printed in the examination booklet for you to use as the basis for answering questions.

3. *Following directions*. In many positions, the employee must be able to carry out written instructions accurately. You may be given a chart with several columns, each listing a variety of information. The questions require you to carry out directions involving the information given in the chart.

4. *Manual skills and abilities*. Performance tests effectively measure some manual skills and abilities. When the skill is one in which you are trained, such as typing or shorthand, you can practice. These examinations are often very much like those given in business schools, colleges, or high school courses. For many of the other skills and aptitudes, however, no short-term preparation is possible. Skills and abilities natural to you or those which you have developed throughout your lifetime are being tested.

Many of the general questions provide the information you need in order to respond, and merely require that you use your reasoning ability to find the answers. The best preparation for these examinations, as well as for tests of facts and ideas, is to be at your physical and mental peak. You, no doubt, have your own methods of getting into an examination-taking mood and of keeping ''in shape.'' The next section includes some ideas which occur to us on this subject.

Taking the Examination

Probably the most important single strategy you can learn is to do the easy questions first. Read and postpone the very hard questions. Identify them with a dot (if you are allowed) and return to them later. Here are a few additional hints:

1. Answer all the questions you are sure of so you can get credit.

2. By reading and delaying the tough questions, you give your subconscious a chance to work on them.

3. Don't get caught by the time limit. Use your time wisely.

4. Relax occasionally. Stretch your legs, shift your body, rest your eyes, take deep breaths, and get back to the job.

5. Edit, check, and proofread all the answers.

Testing Tips

1. *Cue words*. Pay special attention to qualifying words or phrases in the directions. Such words as "one," "best reason," "surest," "mean most nearly the same as," "preferable," "least correct," etc., all show that one response is called for. Select the response which best fits the qualifications in the question.

2. *Time*. Sometimes a time limit is set for each section of the examination. If that is the case, follow the time instructions carefully. The card notifying you of the place and the time of the examination will usually advise you whether you are required to bring a watch. Even if you haven't finished a section when the time limit is up, go on to the next section. The examinations are planned according to the time schedule. If the examination paper says "Do not turn over page until signal is given," or "Do not start until signal is given," follow the instructions. Otherwise, you may be disqualified.

3. *Watch your "weights."* If the examination is "weighted," it means some parts of the examination are more important than others and rated more highly.

Types of Examination Questions

Examinations are usually of the short answer type. Full instructions for answering these questions will be given to you at the examination. General instructions are usually on the examination booklet. Here is what you need to know:

1. *Multiple-choice questions*. In these questions you will be given a question or statement and several possible answers. Sometimes you will be asked to give the best answer or the worst. In some questions which call for the exercise of judgment, one statement and several reasons are given; you must select the best reason. Sometimes questions are included to be marked partly right or partly wrong, so be sure you understand the *directions*. In this type of question, look for words such as "always," "never," "sometimes," which qualify the statements, and for a suggested answer which is fairly close in meaning.

Use these methods to answer multiple-choice questions correctly:

- Read the item closely to see what the examiner is after.
- Mentally reject answers that are clearly wrong.
- Suspect as being wrong any of the choices which contain broad statements hinging on "clue" words like:

absolute	often
absolutely	one
all	positive
always	preferable
completely	quite
doubtless	self-evident
entirely	some
every	surest
forever	totally
frequently	unchangeable
indefinitely	unchallenged
inevitable	undeniable
inflexible	unequivocal
invariably	unexceptionable
least correct	unimpeachable
many	unqualified
nearly	wholly
never	

- A well-constructed multiple-choice item will avoid obviously incorrect choices. The good examiner will try to write a cluster of answers, all of which are plausible. Use the clue words to help you select the *most* correct answer.
- When in doubt, try to review the information you have gained from previous study. This

knowledge might be sufficient to show that some of the suggested answers are not so plausible. Eliminate such answers from further consideration.

- If the item is in the form of an incomplete statement, try to complete the statement before you look at the suggested answers.

2. *Completion questions*. These are usually in the form of a sentence from which key words are missing, and you must supply the missing item. There is no way to guess. If you think you have the correct answer, put it down. If you have an idea you think may be right, put it down and make a check on the margin of the paper. Then, if you have time later on, return to it and give the question a little more thought.

   Occasionally, you may get a clue to the answer by noting whether it should be *singular* or *plural*. The article "a" or "an" means one item; often the form of the sentence will show that a plural answer is called for. It may be possible to arrive at a correct answer by taking the original question and turning it around in your mind and rephrasing it. However, do not spend too much time on any one question of this type.

3. *True-false questions*. True-false questions may appear on your examination. Because they are easier to answer they are used less frequently than multiple-choice questions. However, here are some suggestions to help you answer them correctly:

- Suspect the truth of broad statements hinged on those all or nothing "clue" words previously listed.

- Watch out for "spoilers." These are words or phrases which negate an otherwise true statement.
- Statements containing such modifiers as *generally, usually, most*, and similar words are usually true.
- Your first hunch is usually best. Unless you have a very good reason to do so, don't change your mind.

Follow Directions Carefully

In answering questions on the objective or short-form examination, it is most important to follow all instructions carefully.

On most examinations you will be given an example with the correct answer. Avoid the temptation to skip the directions and begin working just from reading the example. Even though you may be familiar with that particular type of question, the directions may be different from those which you had followed previously. If the type of question is new to you, work through the example until you understand it perfectly.

If the directions for the examination are written, read them carefully, at least twice. If the directions are given orally, listen attentively and then follow them precisely.

Mark all symbols legibly and make sure they have been placed in the proper answer space.

The Answer Sheet

Most employment examinations use separate answer sheets that are scored by machine. You must be careful to mark your answers correctly so as to get credit. Avoid making any stray marks on the paper.

If you are instructed to mark your answers in the question booklet, be careful that no other marks interfere with the legibility of the answers.

Summary

There are many factors that will contribute to your success in passing examinations. Your own determination, ability to follow directions carefully, and steady practice all work toward your final goal of successfully passing the examination of your choice.

We have provided you with enough practice material to help you achieve your desired goal. Now that you have read this introductory section, let's begin. The rest is up to you. Good luck!

PRETEST

PRETEST

Introduction

In making up this Pretest, we tried to prepare questions with the same difficulty level you will meet on your examination. The various subjects are represented by separate parts, and each part is timed accordingly. Some parts may have about the same number of questions you may find on the actual examination, while others do not.

If possible, proceed through the entire Pretest without pausing after each part. Imagine you are taking this test under actual conditions. Do not stop until the total time limit is up. However, if you want to break up this Pretest into several convenient sessions, keep a record of your time. Use the following chart to gauge your time for each part.

Don't lose time by trying to score each part as you complete it. You will be able to score yourself when time is up for the entire Pretest.

The answer key appears at the end of the Pretest. Don't cheat yourself by looking at these answers while taking the Pretest. They are to be compared with your own answers after the time limit is up.

Since the number of questions for each part may vary on different forms of the actual examination, the time allotments below are flexible.

Subjects Tested	Time Allowed
VOCABULARY	4 MINUTES
VERBAL ANALOGIES	4 MINUTES
SPELLING & WORD USAGE	4 MINUTES
ENGLISH GRAMMAR	4 MINUTES
READING COMPREHENSION	5 MINUTES
FILING/RECORDS MANAGEMENT	4 MINUTES
OFFICE PROCEDURES AND TERMINOLOGY	8 MINUTES
MATHEMATICS REVIEW	5 MINUTES
CLERICAL PERFORMANCE ABILITY	2 MINUTES
TYPING FORMAT QUESTIONS	2 MINUTES
TYPING PERFORMANCE TEST	5 MINUTES
SHORTHAND FORMAT QUESTIONS	2 MINUTES
SHORTHAND DICTATION	3 MINUTES
SHORTHAND PERFORMANCE TRANSCRIPTION	30 MINUTES

Total Time Allowed For Pretest: 82 Minutes

An Introduction To Determine Weak Areas

The first step in your preparation is to take the Pretest. The Pretest will help you determine your weak areas. When you look at the "Weak Area Determination Guide" at the end of this section, it will tell you:

- Which subjects of this book you need to review,
- Which subjects of this book you are strong in, and
- Which subjects of this book you need to concentrate on the most.

On the following chart, keep a record of your scores.

Pretest Score Chart

Subject Topics	Total Questions	Number Wrong	Score
Vocabulary	10		
Verbal Analogies	10		
Spelling and Word Usage	10		
English Grammar	10		
Reading Comprehension	10		
Filing/Records Management	18		
Office Procedures and Terminology	18		
Mathematics Review	10		
Clerical Performance Ability	21		
Typing Format Questions	5		
Typing Performance Test (wpm)			
Shorthand Format Questions	5		
Shorthand Performance Test	98		
TOTAL	225		

Answer Sheet For Pretest

PART I

Vocabulary

1 Ⓐ Ⓑ Ⓒ Ⓓ Ⓔ   3 Ⓐ Ⓑ Ⓒ Ⓓ Ⓔ   5 Ⓐ Ⓑ Ⓒ Ⓓ Ⓔ   7 Ⓐ Ⓑ Ⓒ Ⓓ Ⓔ   9 Ⓐ Ⓑ Ⓒ Ⓓ Ⓔ
2 Ⓐ Ⓑ Ⓒ Ⓓ Ⓔ   4 Ⓐ Ⓑ Ⓒ Ⓓ Ⓔ   6 Ⓐ Ⓑ Ⓒ Ⓓ Ⓔ   8 Ⓐ Ⓑ Ⓒ Ⓓ Ⓔ   10 Ⓐ Ⓑ Ⓒ Ⓓ Ⓔ

Verbal Analogies

11 Ⓐ Ⓑ Ⓒ Ⓓ Ⓔ   13 Ⓐ Ⓑ Ⓒ Ⓓ Ⓔ   15 Ⓐ Ⓑ Ⓒ Ⓓ Ⓔ   17 Ⓐ Ⓑ Ⓒ Ⓓ Ⓔ   19 Ⓐ Ⓑ Ⓒ Ⓓ Ⓔ
12 Ⓐ Ⓑ Ⓒ Ⓓ Ⓔ   14 Ⓐ Ⓑ Ⓒ Ⓓ Ⓔ   16 Ⓐ Ⓑ Ⓒ Ⓓ Ⓔ   18 Ⓐ Ⓑ Ⓒ Ⓓ Ⓔ   20 Ⓐ Ⓑ Ⓒ Ⓓ Ⓔ

Spelling and Word Usage

21 Ⓐ Ⓑ Ⓒ Ⓓ Ⓔ   23 Ⓐ Ⓑ Ⓒ Ⓓ Ⓔ   25 Ⓐ Ⓑ Ⓒ Ⓓ Ⓔ   27 Ⓐ Ⓑ Ⓒ Ⓓ Ⓔ   29 Ⓐ Ⓑ Ⓒ Ⓓ Ⓔ
22 Ⓐ Ⓑ Ⓒ Ⓓ Ⓔ   24 Ⓐ Ⓑ Ⓒ Ⓓ Ⓔ   26 Ⓐ Ⓑ Ⓒ Ⓓ Ⓔ   28 Ⓐ Ⓑ Ⓒ Ⓓ Ⓔ   30 Ⓐ Ⓑ Ⓒ Ⓓ Ⓔ

English Grammar

31 Ⓐ Ⓑ Ⓒ Ⓓ Ⓔ   33 Ⓐ Ⓑ Ⓒ Ⓓ Ⓔ   35 Ⓐ Ⓑ Ⓒ Ⓓ Ⓔ   37 Ⓐ Ⓑ Ⓒ Ⓓ Ⓔ   39 Ⓐ Ⓑ Ⓒ Ⓓ Ⓔ
32 Ⓐ Ⓑ Ⓒ Ⓓ Ⓔ   34 Ⓐ Ⓑ Ⓒ Ⓓ Ⓔ   36 Ⓐ Ⓑ Ⓒ Ⓓ Ⓔ   38 Ⓐ Ⓑ Ⓒ Ⓓ Ⓔ   40 Ⓐ Ⓑ Ⓒ Ⓓ Ⓔ

Reading Comprehension

41 Ⓐ Ⓑ Ⓒ Ⓓ Ⓔ   43 Ⓐ Ⓑ Ⓒ Ⓓ Ⓔ   45 Ⓐ Ⓑ Ⓒ Ⓓ Ⓔ   47 Ⓐ Ⓑ Ⓒ Ⓓ Ⓔ   49 Ⓐ Ⓑ Ⓒ Ⓓ Ⓔ
42 Ⓐ Ⓑ Ⓒ Ⓓ Ⓔ   44 Ⓐ Ⓑ Ⓒ Ⓓ Ⓔ   46 Ⓐ Ⓑ Ⓒ Ⓓ Ⓔ   48 Ⓐ Ⓑ Ⓒ Ⓓ Ⓔ   50 Ⓐ Ⓑ Ⓒ Ⓓ Ⓔ

Filing/Records Management

51 Ⓐ Ⓑ Ⓒ Ⓓ Ⓔ   55 Ⓐ Ⓑ Ⓒ Ⓓ Ⓔ   59 Ⓐ Ⓑ Ⓒ Ⓓ Ⓔ   63 Ⓐ Ⓑ Ⓒ Ⓓ Ⓔ   66 Ⓐ Ⓑ Ⓒ Ⓓ Ⓔ
52 Ⓐ Ⓑ Ⓒ Ⓓ Ⓔ   56 Ⓐ Ⓑ Ⓒ Ⓓ Ⓔ   60 Ⓐ Ⓑ Ⓒ Ⓓ Ⓔ   64 Ⓐ Ⓑ Ⓒ Ⓓ Ⓔ   67 Ⓐ Ⓑ Ⓒ Ⓓ Ⓔ
53 Ⓐ Ⓑ Ⓒ Ⓓ Ⓔ   57 Ⓐ Ⓑ Ⓒ Ⓓ Ⓔ   61 Ⓐ Ⓑ Ⓒ Ⓓ Ⓔ   65 Ⓐ Ⓑ Ⓒ Ⓓ Ⓔ   68 Ⓐ Ⓑ Ⓒ Ⓓ Ⓔ
54 Ⓐ Ⓑ Ⓒ Ⓓ Ⓔ   58 Ⓐ Ⓑ Ⓒ Ⓓ Ⓔ   62 Ⓐ Ⓑ Ⓒ Ⓓ Ⓔ

Office Procedures and Terminology

69 Ⓐ Ⓑ Ⓒ Ⓓ Ⓔ   73 Ⓐ Ⓑ Ⓒ Ⓓ Ⓔ   77 Ⓐ Ⓑ Ⓒ Ⓓ Ⓔ   81 Ⓐ Ⓑ Ⓒ Ⓓ Ⓔ   84 Ⓐ Ⓑ Ⓒ Ⓓ Ⓔ
70 Ⓐ Ⓑ Ⓒ Ⓓ Ⓔ   74 Ⓐ Ⓑ Ⓒ Ⓓ Ⓔ   78 Ⓐ Ⓑ Ⓒ Ⓓ Ⓔ   82 Ⓐ Ⓑ Ⓒ Ⓓ Ⓔ   85 Ⓐ Ⓑ Ⓒ Ⓓ Ⓔ
71 Ⓐ Ⓑ Ⓒ Ⓓ Ⓔ   75 Ⓐ Ⓑ Ⓒ Ⓓ Ⓔ   79 Ⓐ Ⓑ Ⓒ Ⓓ Ⓔ   83 Ⓐ Ⓑ Ⓒ Ⓓ Ⓔ   86 Ⓐ Ⓑ Ⓒ Ⓓ Ⓔ
72 Ⓐ Ⓑ Ⓒ Ⓓ Ⓔ   76 Ⓐ Ⓑ Ⓒ Ⓓ Ⓔ   80 Ⓐ Ⓑ Ⓒ Ⓓ Ⓔ

Mathematics

87 Ⓐ Ⓑ Ⓒ Ⓓ Ⓔ   89 Ⓐ Ⓑ Ⓒ Ⓓ Ⓔ   91 Ⓐ Ⓑ Ⓒ Ⓓ Ⓔ   93 Ⓐ Ⓑ Ⓒ Ⓓ Ⓔ   95 Ⓐ Ⓑ Ⓒ Ⓓ Ⓔ
88 Ⓐ Ⓑ Ⓒ Ⓓ Ⓔ   90 Ⓐ Ⓑ Ⓒ Ⓓ Ⓔ   92 Ⓐ Ⓑ Ⓒ Ⓓ Ⓔ   94 Ⓐ Ⓑ Ⓒ Ⓓ Ⓔ   96 Ⓐ Ⓑ Ⓒ Ⓓ Ⓔ

Clerical Performance Ability

97 _____   98 _____   99 _____   100 _____

101 Ⓐ Ⓑ Ⓒ Ⓓ Ⓔ   105 Ⓐ Ⓑ Ⓒ Ⓓ Ⓔ   109 Ⓐ Ⓑ Ⓒ Ⓓ Ⓔ   112 Ⓐ Ⓑ Ⓒ Ⓓ Ⓔ   115 Ⓐ Ⓑ Ⓒ Ⓓ Ⓔ
102 Ⓐ Ⓑ Ⓒ Ⓓ Ⓔ   106 Ⓐ Ⓑ Ⓒ Ⓓ Ⓔ   110 Ⓐ Ⓑ Ⓒ Ⓓ Ⓔ   113 Ⓐ Ⓑ Ⓒ Ⓓ Ⓔ   116 Ⓐ Ⓑ Ⓒ Ⓓ Ⓔ
103 Ⓐ Ⓑ Ⓒ Ⓓ Ⓔ   107 Ⓐ Ⓑ Ⓒ Ⓓ Ⓔ   111 Ⓐ Ⓑ Ⓒ Ⓓ Ⓔ   114 Ⓐ Ⓑ Ⓒ Ⓓ Ⓔ   117 Ⓐ Ⓑ Ⓒ Ⓓ Ⓔ
104 Ⓐ Ⓑ Ⓒ Ⓓ Ⓔ   108 Ⓐ Ⓑ Ⓒ Ⓓ Ⓔ

PART II

Typing Format

118 Ⓐ Ⓑ Ⓒ Ⓓ Ⓔ   119 Ⓐ Ⓑ Ⓒ Ⓓ Ⓔ   120 Ⓐ Ⓑ Ⓒ Ⓓ Ⓔ   121 Ⓐ Ⓑ Ⓒ Ⓓ Ⓔ   122 Ⓐ Ⓑ Ⓒ Ⓓ Ⓔ

Typing Performance

Number of WPM Typed _____
Number of Errors _____

PART III

Shorthand Format

123 Ⓐ Ⓑ Ⓒ Ⓓ Ⓔ   124 Ⓐ Ⓑ Ⓒ Ⓓ Ⓔ   125 Ⓐ Ⓑ Ⓒ Ⓓ Ⓔ   126 Ⓐ Ⓑ Ⓒ Ⓓ Ⓔ   127 Ⓐ Ⓑ Ⓒ Ⓓ Ⓔ

Shorthand

128 Ⓐ Ⓑ Ⓒ Ⓓ Ⓔ   148 Ⓐ Ⓑ Ⓒ Ⓓ Ⓔ   168 Ⓐ Ⓑ Ⓒ Ⓓ Ⓔ   188 Ⓐ Ⓑ Ⓒ Ⓓ Ⓔ   207 Ⓐ Ⓑ Ⓒ Ⓓ Ⓔ
129 Ⓐ Ⓑ Ⓒ Ⓓ Ⓔ   149 Ⓐ Ⓑ Ⓒ Ⓓ Ⓔ   169 Ⓐ Ⓑ Ⓒ Ⓓ Ⓔ   189 Ⓐ Ⓑ Ⓒ Ⓓ Ⓔ   208 Ⓐ Ⓑ Ⓒ Ⓓ Ⓔ
130 Ⓐ Ⓑ Ⓒ Ⓓ Ⓔ   150 Ⓐ Ⓑ Ⓒ Ⓓ Ⓔ   170 Ⓐ Ⓑ Ⓒ Ⓓ Ⓔ   190 Ⓐ Ⓑ Ⓒ Ⓓ Ⓔ   209 Ⓐ Ⓑ Ⓒ Ⓓ Ⓔ
131 Ⓐ Ⓑ Ⓒ Ⓓ Ⓔ   151 Ⓐ Ⓑ Ⓒ Ⓓ Ⓔ   171 Ⓐ Ⓑ Ⓒ Ⓓ Ⓔ   191 Ⓐ Ⓑ Ⓒ Ⓓ Ⓔ   210 Ⓐ Ⓑ Ⓒ Ⓓ Ⓔ
132 Ⓐ Ⓑ Ⓒ Ⓓ Ⓔ   152 Ⓐ Ⓑ Ⓒ Ⓓ Ⓔ   172 Ⓐ Ⓑ Ⓒ Ⓓ Ⓔ   192 Ⓐ Ⓑ Ⓒ Ⓓ Ⓔ   211 Ⓐ Ⓑ Ⓒ Ⓓ Ⓔ
133 Ⓐ Ⓑ Ⓒ Ⓓ Ⓔ   153 Ⓐ Ⓑ Ⓒ Ⓓ Ⓔ   173 Ⓐ Ⓑ Ⓒ Ⓓ Ⓔ   193 Ⓐ Ⓑ Ⓒ Ⓓ Ⓔ   212 Ⓐ Ⓑ Ⓒ Ⓓ Ⓔ
134 Ⓐ Ⓑ Ⓒ Ⓓ Ⓔ   154 Ⓐ Ⓑ Ⓒ Ⓓ Ⓔ   174 Ⓐ Ⓑ Ⓒ Ⓓ Ⓔ   194 Ⓐ Ⓑ Ⓒ Ⓓ Ⓔ   213 Ⓐ Ⓑ Ⓒ Ⓓ Ⓔ
135 Ⓐ Ⓑ Ⓒ Ⓓ Ⓔ   155 Ⓐ Ⓑ Ⓒ Ⓓ Ⓔ   175 Ⓐ Ⓑ Ⓒ Ⓓ Ⓔ   195 Ⓐ Ⓑ Ⓒ Ⓓ Ⓔ   214 Ⓐ Ⓑ Ⓒ Ⓓ Ⓔ
136 Ⓐ Ⓑ Ⓒ Ⓓ Ⓔ   156 Ⓐ Ⓑ Ⓒ Ⓓ Ⓔ   176 Ⓐ Ⓑ Ⓒ Ⓓ Ⓔ   196 Ⓐ Ⓑ Ⓒ Ⓓ Ⓔ   215 Ⓐ Ⓑ Ⓒ Ⓓ Ⓔ
137 Ⓐ Ⓑ Ⓒ Ⓓ Ⓔ   157 Ⓐ Ⓑ Ⓒ Ⓓ Ⓔ   177 Ⓐ Ⓑ Ⓒ Ⓓ Ⓔ   197 Ⓐ Ⓑ Ⓒ Ⓓ Ⓔ   216 Ⓐ Ⓑ Ⓒ Ⓓ Ⓔ
138 Ⓐ Ⓑ Ⓒ Ⓓ Ⓔ   158 Ⓐ Ⓑ Ⓒ Ⓓ Ⓔ   178 Ⓐ Ⓑ Ⓒ Ⓓ Ⓔ   198 Ⓐ Ⓑ Ⓒ Ⓓ Ⓔ   217 Ⓐ Ⓑ Ⓒ Ⓓ Ⓔ
139 Ⓐ Ⓑ Ⓒ Ⓓ Ⓔ   159 Ⓐ Ⓑ Ⓒ Ⓓ Ⓔ   179 Ⓐ Ⓑ Ⓒ Ⓓ Ⓔ   199 Ⓐ Ⓑ Ⓒ Ⓓ Ⓔ   218 Ⓐ Ⓑ Ⓒ Ⓓ Ⓔ
140 Ⓐ Ⓑ Ⓒ Ⓓ Ⓔ   160 Ⓐ Ⓑ Ⓒ Ⓓ Ⓔ   180 Ⓐ Ⓑ Ⓒ Ⓓ Ⓔ   200 Ⓐ Ⓑ Ⓒ Ⓓ Ⓔ   219 Ⓐ Ⓑ Ⓒ Ⓓ Ⓔ
141 Ⓐ Ⓑ Ⓒ Ⓓ Ⓔ   161 Ⓐ Ⓑ Ⓒ Ⓓ Ⓔ   181 Ⓐ Ⓑ Ⓒ Ⓓ Ⓔ   201 Ⓐ Ⓑ Ⓒ Ⓓ Ⓔ   220 Ⓐ Ⓑ Ⓒ Ⓓ Ⓔ
142 Ⓐ Ⓑ Ⓒ Ⓓ Ⓔ   162 Ⓐ Ⓑ Ⓒ Ⓓ Ⓔ   182 Ⓐ Ⓑ Ⓒ Ⓓ Ⓔ   202 Ⓐ Ⓑ Ⓒ Ⓓ Ⓔ   221 Ⓐ Ⓑ Ⓒ Ⓓ Ⓔ
143 Ⓐ Ⓑ Ⓒ Ⓓ Ⓔ   163 Ⓐ Ⓑ Ⓒ Ⓓ Ⓔ   183 Ⓐ Ⓑ Ⓒ Ⓓ Ⓔ   203 Ⓐ Ⓑ Ⓒ Ⓓ Ⓔ   222 Ⓐ Ⓑ Ⓒ Ⓓ Ⓔ
144 Ⓐ Ⓑ Ⓒ Ⓓ Ⓔ   164 Ⓐ Ⓑ Ⓒ Ⓓ Ⓔ   184 Ⓐ Ⓑ Ⓒ Ⓓ Ⓔ   204 Ⓐ Ⓑ Ⓒ Ⓓ Ⓔ   223 Ⓐ Ⓑ Ⓒ Ⓓ Ⓔ
145 Ⓐ Ⓑ Ⓒ Ⓓ Ⓔ   165 Ⓐ Ⓑ Ⓒ Ⓓ Ⓔ   185 Ⓐ Ⓑ Ⓒ Ⓓ Ⓔ   205 Ⓐ Ⓑ Ⓒ Ⓓ Ⓔ   224 Ⓐ Ⓑ Ⓒ Ⓓ Ⓔ
146 Ⓐ Ⓑ Ⓒ Ⓓ Ⓔ   166 Ⓐ Ⓑ Ⓒ Ⓓ Ⓔ   186 Ⓐ Ⓑ Ⓒ Ⓓ Ⓔ   206 Ⓐ Ⓑ Ⓒ Ⓓ Ⓔ   225 Ⓐ Ⓑ Ⓒ Ⓓ Ⓔ
147 Ⓐ Ⓑ Ⓒ Ⓓ Ⓔ   167 Ⓐ Ⓑ Ⓒ Ⓓ Ⓔ   187 Ⓐ Ⓑ Ⓒ Ⓓ Ⓔ

PRETEST

Allow 82 Minutes For This Complete Pretest

Part I (For All Clerks, Typists, and Stenographers)

Vocabulary

Allow 4 minutes for this part of the test.

Directions: For each question in this test, select the appropriate letter preceding the word which is most nearly the same in meaning as the capitalized word. Mark the answer sheet with the letter of that answer.

1. FORTITUDE
   - (A) wealth
   - (B) courage
   - (C) honesty
   - (D) loudness
   - (E) luck

2. ABOLITION
   - (A) retirement
   - (B) disgust
   - (C) enslavement
   - (D) unrestricted power
   - (E) complete destruction

3. LABYRINTH
   - (A) pool
   - (B) maze
   - (C) formula
   - (D) monster
   - (E) song

4. MAIM
   - (A) heal
   - (B) disable
   - (C) outwit
   - (D) murder
   - (E) bury

5. CRESTFALLEN
   - (A) haughty
   - (B) dejected
   - (C) fatigued
   - (D) disfigured
   - (E) impolite

6. CUISINE
   - (A) headdress
   - (B) game of chance
   - (C) leisurely voyage
   - (D) artistry
   - (E) style of cooking

7. CENSURE
   - (A) erase
   - (B) build up
   - (C) criticize adversely
   - (D) charm
   - (E) help

8. DEVIATE
   - (A) destroy
   - (B) lower in value
   - (C) invent
   - (D) stray
   - (E) depress

9. SWARTHY
    (A) dark-complexioned
    (B) slender
    (C) grass-covered
    (D) springy
    (E) rotating

10. MERCENARY
    (A) poisonous
    (B) unworthy
    (C) serving only for pay
    (D) luring by false charms
    (E) showing pity

END OF TEST

CONTINUE TO THE NEXT PART OF THIS PRETEST AS YOU WOULD BE
EXPECTED TO DO ON THE ACTUAL EXAMINATION. HOWEVER, IF YOU
HAVE ANY AVAILABLE TIME LEFT FOR THIS PART, YOU MAY USE IT
TO MAKE SURE YOU HAVE MARKED YOUR ANSWER SHEET
PROPERLY.

Verbal Analogies

Allow 4 minutes for this part of the test.

Directions: In these test questions, the two CAPITAL-
IZED words have a certain relationship to each other. Following the capitalized words are other pairs of words, each
designated by a letter (A) to (E). Select the lettered pair
that is related in the same way as the two CAPITALIZED
words are related to each other. Mark the answer sheet
with the letter of that answer.

11. SMILE : AMUSEMENT
    (A) yell : game
    (B) guffaw : laughter
    (C) yawn : ennui
    (D) wink : vulgarity
    (E) cry : havoc

12. MINK : LION
    (A) chicken : wolf
    (B) tiger : zebra
    (C) farm : zoo
    (D) lady : gentleman
    (E) timidity : daring

13. DREDGE : SILT
    (A) tug : gravel
    (B) train : plane
    (C) scoop : ice cream
    (D) distance : sequence
    (E) drudge : sludge

14. LETTER : WORD
    (A) page : book
    (B) club : people
    (C) homework : school
    (D) product : factory
    (E) picture : crayon

15. WAVE : CREST
    (A) pinnacle : nadir
    (B) sea : ocean
    (C) mountain : peak
    (D) breaker : swimming
    (E) island : archipelago

16. 36 : 4
    (A) 3 : 27
    (B) 12 : 4
    (C) 5 : 2
    (D) 12 : 4
    (E) 9 : 1

17. MOLD : DIE
    (A) cast : stamp
    (B) fungus : death
    (C) form : destroy
    (D) hold : defeat
    (E) imprison : execute

18. DOOR : PORTAL
    (A) opening : closing
    (B) doorway : living room
    (C) house : ship
    (D) knob : key
    (E) porch : portico

19. GERM : DISEASE
    (A) trichinosis : pork
    (B) men : women
    (C) doctor : medicine
    (D) biologist : cell
    (E) war : destruction

20. DUNCE : CLEVER
    (A) idiot : stupid
    (B) help : weak
    (C) courageous : fearful
    (D) worry : poor
    (E) cucumber : soft

END OF TEST

CONTINUE TO THE NEXT PART OF THIS PRETEST AS YOU WOULD BE
EXPECTED TO DO ON THE ACTUAL EXAMINATION. HOWEVER, IF YOU
HAVE ANY AVAILABLE TIME LEFT FOR THIS PART, YOU MAY USE IT
TO MAKE SURE YOU HAVE MARKED YOUR ANSWER SHEET
PROPERLY.

Spelling and Word Usage

Allow 4 minutes for this part of the test.

Spelling

Directions: In this test all words but one of each group are spelled correctly. Indicate the misspelled word in each group. Mark the answer sheet with the letter of that answer.

21. (A) afford
    (B) closeing
    (C) latter
    (D) headache

22. (A) gravel
    (B) artifishal
    (C) lodge
    (D) lilies

23. (A) document
    (B) handsome
    (C) frighten
    (D) incorect

24. (A) atached
    (B) flakes
    (C) distributed
    (D) continue

25. (A) conducter
    (B) choice
    (C) particular
    (D) streamline

Word Usage

Directions: In each of the following groups of sentences, select the one sentence where word usage is incorrect. Mark the answer sheet with the letter of that answer.

Example: Incorrect: The child's manor of behavior is very bad.
          Correct: The child's manner of behavior is very bad.

26. (A) Mark on your calendar the vacation week of June 2.
    (B) We had our house rewired in order to bring in more currency.
    (C) The census taker took all the information.
    (D) The cleaners had to dye the dress red to get the stain out.

27. (A) She is uninterested in the speech about stress.
    (B) That was a handsome costume he had on.
    (C) Send all outside correspondents to the attention of my secretary.
    (D) All these lessons are a great way to learn and to study.

28. (A) I work in the personnel office that reports directly to the Commissioner.
    (B) She has a voracious appetite when it comes to eating fish.
    (C) Separate the yolk from the white of the egg when you are making a chiffon cake.
    (D) That was a very shear blouse you wore to the office yesterday.

29. (A) You should take a peak through the hole in the fence the contracting company put up.
    (B) The whole staff was in mourning for the loss of their fellow employee.
    (C) We had to be sure the receptionist would not let visitors in unannounced.
    (D) All the supervisors canvassed the staff about the proposed new office layout.

30. (A) Mail the letter in the envelope that is attached to the report.
    (B) The publisher asked me to write the forward for the book *How To Improve Your Typing Skills*.
    (C) When our office moved, we had to haul all the supplies in boxes and large cartons.
    (D) We asked the assay office to prepare the report on the radon.

END OF TEST

CONTINUE TO THE NEXT PART OF THIS PRETEST AS YOU WOULD BE EXPECTED TO DO ON THE ACTUAL EXAMINATION. HOWEVER, IF YOU HAVE ANY AVAILABLE TIME LEFT FOR THIS PART, YOU MAY USE IT TO MAKE SURE YOU HAVE MARKED YOUR ANSWER SHEET PROPERLY.

English Grammar

Allow 4 minutes for this part of the test.

Directions: In each of the following groups of sentences, select the one sentence that is grammatically incorrect. Mark the answer sheet with the letter of that answer.

31. (A) Everybody should do the very best they can.
    (B) Many adverbs in English are formed by adding "ly" to the corresponding adjective.
    (C) Jane hurt herself when she fell on the floor.
    (D) That report is being prepared by them now.

32. (A) Two thirds of the employees are on vacation.
    (B) A large stock of pens, papers, ribbons, and paper clips are carried on hand.
    (C) That statement doesn't sound correct to me.
    (D) Copies of our correspondence with Mr. Wilson, our vice president, have been made.

33. (A) Now that the repairman has oiled the typewriter, it works as well as a new one.
    (B) The reason he retired is because he was over 65 years of age.
    (C) Speak to whom you see first.
    (D) Our vacation has come to an end, I am sorry to say.

34. (A) Much information on the subject is available.
    (B) Except when the student driver becomes nervous, he drives as good as the instructor.
    (C) When the baseball pitcher's hand had healed, he played the game as well as ever.
    (D) They collected many details about the matter.

35. (A) He would have liked to go to the theater with us.
    (B) The dairy business was incidental to the regular grocery business.
    (C) Many persons are guilty of traffic violations.
    (D) The Professional Secretaries International has published it's yearly magazine *The Secretary*.

36. (A) The stone made a very angry bruise on her forearm.
    (B) Mrs. Watson made less errors than the other typists.
    (C) All of us shall partake of the benefits of exercise.
    (D) In all likelihood we shall be unable to attend the conference.

37. (A) Please send our office and me your new address.
    (B) His precision resulted in a nice combination of their relative merits.
    (C) We shall attempt to ascertain whether there has been any tampering with the lock.
    (D) Margaret could of been chosen president this term, but she would not enter her name.

38. (A) Leave us face it—the jury cannot make a determination of the facts.
    (B) He carried out the order with great dispatch but with little effect.
    (C) The supervisor's overbearing manner overawed his employer.
    (D) Everyone shall enjoy the homemade apple pies.

39. (A) The roast beef sandwiches were made with pita bread.
    (B) Green vegetables are healthful foods.
    (C) The supervisor's words of praise sounded well to our ears.
    (D) Good housekeeping is as necessary in an office as it is at home.

40. (A) There will never be another secretary like her.
    (B) Neither of the individuals think they will be affected by the ruling.
    (C) The staff meeting this afternoon was very interesting.
    (D) I wish I knew more people like you.

END OF TEST

CONTINUE TO THE NEXT PART OF THIS PRETEST AS YOU WOULD BE EXPECTED TO DO ON THE ACTUAL EXAMINATION. HOWEVER, IF YOU HAVE ANY AVAILABLE TIME LEFT FOR THIS PART, YOU MAY USE IT TO MAKE SURE YOU HAVE MARKED YOUR ANSWER SHEET PROPERLY.

Reading Comprehension

Allow 5 minutes for this part of the test.

Directions: The reading passages given below are followed by questions based on their content. After reading the passages, choose the best answer to each question. The questions are to be answered on the basis of what is stated or implied in the passages only. Mark the answer sheet with the letter of that answer.

Reading Passage 1

Education was free. That subject my father had written about repeatedly, as comprising his chief hope for us children, the essence of American opportunity, the treasure that no thief could touch, not even misfortune or poverty. It was the one thing he was able to promise us when he sent for us, surer, safer than bread or shelter. On our second day, I was thrilled with the realization of what this freedom of education meant.

A little girl from across the alley came and offered to show us the way to school. My father was out, but we five between us had a few words of English by this time. We knew the word school. We understood. This child, who had never seen us till yesterday, who could not pronounce our names, who was not much better dressed than we, was able to offer us the freedom of the schools of Boston! The doors stood open for every one of us. The smallest child could show us the way. This incident impressed me more than anything I had heard in advance about the freedom of education in America. It was concrete proof—almost the thing itself. One had to experience it to understand it.

41. The title below that best expresses the main theme or subject of this selection is
    (A) My First Day in America.
    (B) The Schools of Boston.
    (C) My Father's Education.
    (D) Our Greatest Opportunity in America.
    (E) The Little Girl Next Day.

42. When the father sent for his children, the only thing he could surely promise them was
    (A) bread.
    (B) friends.
    (C) shelter.
    (D) schooling.
    (E) wealth.

43. The father believed
    (A) he should have stayed in Europe.
    (B) education was not worthwhile.
    (C) the children could not learn English.
    (D) he would always live in poverty.
    (E) education was one possession that could not be stolen.

44. The word school
    (A) was not known to the children.
    (B) frightened the children.
    (C) was one of the first English words the children had learned.
    (D) reminded the children of unhappy days in Europe.
    (E) was difficult for the children to understand.

45. The children fully realized the meaning of their father's words when they discovered that
    (A) the little girl across the way had better clothes than they did.
    (B) they could not understand the little girl.
    (C) the Boston schools didn't want them.
    (D) in America even a little girl could take them to school.
    (E) the little girl could not pronounce their names.

Reading Passage 2

Greece, whose shores are washed by the warm waters of the Mediterranean Sea, lies between the tropics of the south and the cold country of the north. Her climate, especially in summer, is usually mild and sunny. Sometimes in the winter the chill winds, which the poet Hesiod said were "a great trouble to mortals," blow over the land. However, the ancient Greeks were very well pleased with their climate. Herodotus wrote that it was "the lot of Hellas [the name which the Greeks gave to their country] to have its seasons far more tempered than other lands." Since it was almost always like summer in Greece, the men of ancient Greece were out-of-door people. Much of their business was transacted outside, and their public meetings were usually held in the open.

Though the highest mountains were too rocky to support vegetation, laurel, oleander, and myrtle were found at lower altitudes. When the plentiful rains clothed the uplands with rich, green grass, the shepherds allowed their sheep and goats to roam over the hillsides. On the more fertile lowlands, wheat, olives, and grapes could be raised without cultivation. These products were changed into the three articles which were essential to the ancient Greeks—bread, oil, and wine. The oil was used as butter for their bread and for lighting and cleaning purposes. Bread and wine were served at nearly every meal.

46. The Greeks are sometimes made uncomfortable by the
   (A) warm waters of the Mediterranean.
   (B) mild climate.
   (C) tropics.
   (D) central position of the country.
   (E) cold winds.

47. A person who praised Greece's climate was
   (A) an unknown poet.
   (B) Herodotus.
   (C) Hellas.
   (D) a shepherd boy.
   (E) Hesiod.

48. Men of ancient Greece lived out-of-door lives because
   (A) there was little rain.
   (B) they enjoyed public meetings.
   (C) their poets recommended outdoor life.
   (D) the weather was usually mild.
   (E) they were easygoing people.

49. The most fertile land in ancient Greece was located
   (A) in the lowlands.
   (B) where the laurel grew.
   (C) on the top of the highest mountains.
   (D) in the uplands.
   (E) where the sheep were pastured.

50. Which statement is TRUE according to this passage?
   (A) The ancient Greeks were dissatisfied with the climate of their homeland.
   (B) Even the highest mountains of Greece produced abundant vegetation.
   (C) The essential foods in ancient Greece were grown within the country.
   (D) Butter was an important commodity of ancient Greece.
   (E) The ancient Greeks had more troubles than other mortals.

END OF TEST

CONTINUE TO THE NEXT PART OF THIS PRETEST AS YOU WOULD BE EXPECTED TO DO ON THE ACTUAL EXAMINATION. HOWEVER, IF YOU HAVE ANY AVAILABLE TIME LEFT FOR THIS PART, YOU MAY USE IT TO MAKE SURE YOU HAVE MARKED YOUR ANSWER SHEET PROPERLY.

Filing/Records Management

Allow 4 minutes for this part of the test.

Methods

Directions: Consider each group as a unit. In each of the following groups, there is one selection followed by a series of four other selections in proper order. The spaces between are lettered (A), (B), (C), (D), and (E). Decide where the underlined selection belongs in the series and choose the letter identifying that space as the answer. Mark the answer sheet with the letter of that answer.

Alphabetic

51. *Hackett, Gerald*
    (A)---
        Habert, James
    (B)---
        Hachett, J. J.
    (C)---
        Hachetts, K. Larson
    (D)---
        Hachettson, Leroy
    (E)---

52. *Margenroth, Alvin*
    (A)---
        Margeroth, Albert
    (B)---
        Margestein, Dan
    (C)---
        Margestein, David
    (D)---
        Margue, Edgar
    (E)---

53. *Bobbitt, Olivier E.*
    (A)---
        Bobbitt, D. Olivier
    (B)---
        Bobbitt, Olive B.
    (C)---
        Bobbitt, Olivia H.
    (D)---
        Bobbitt, R. Olivia
    (E)---

Numeric

54. 82 37 02
    (A)--
        82 07 78
    (B)--
        82 36 01
    (C)--
        82 37 18
    (D)--
        82 37 78
    (E)--

55. 49 07 44
    (A)--
        13 53 56
    (B)--
        49 25 56
    (C)--
        49 25 16
    (D)--
        49 53 32
    (E)--

56. 32 25 39
    (A)--
        31 24 16
    (B)--
        32 24 42
    (C)--
        32 25 21
    (D)--
        32 25 44
    (E)--

Geographic

57. Linwood Steel Co.
     Athens, GA
     (A)--

             Miller Stone Co.
             Albany, GA
     (B)--

             Milton Quarry Inc.
             Albany, GA
     (C)--

             Rand Racers
             Alston, GA
     (D)--

             Schwartz Meats
             Alston, GA
     (E)--

58. Boxwood Shoe Repair Shop
     Norwood, MA
     (A)--

             Ventnor Pharmacy
             New Bedford, ME
     (B)--

             Homemade Candies
             Northwood, ME
     (C)--

             Pennington Road Farm
             Norwood, ME
     (D)--

             Airport Service
             Norwood, MA
     (E)--

Subject

Directions: One of the five classes of employment, lettered (A) to (E), may be applied to each of the individuals listed below. Choose as your answer letter of the class in which that name may best be placed. Mark the answer sheet with the letter of that answer.

CLASS OF WORK

(A) CLERICAL
(B) EDUCATIONAL
(C) INVESTIGATIONAL
(D) MECHANICAL
(E) ARTISTIC

59. John M. Devine   Stenographer
60. G. D. Wahl   Lawyer

Information and Procedures

Directions: For each of the following questions, select the choice which best answers the question or completes the statement. Mark the answer sheet with the letter of that answer.

61. When the files have numbered notations on the guides and folder tabs followed by an alphabetic name file, this is called
     (A) Alphabetic-Numerical.
     (B) Triple Check System.
     (C) Alpha-Numeric Subject.
     (D) Index to Subject Files.

62. When capital letters are used for the main headings of an outline, followed by numbers for the first division, and small letters for the subject divisions, this is called
     (A) Subject Filing.
     (B) Alpha-Numeric.
     (C) Duplex Alphabetic.
     (D) Duplex Numeric.

63. The best definition for chronological filing is
     (A) Filed according to the dates on the papers.
     (B) Filed by using a variety of color labels, folders, or tabs.
     (C) Filed by using one section of the file where all names sound alike.
     (D) Filed by final digit.

64. Chronological files are very helpful when used with other filing systems. Which of the following is *not* usually used in chronological filing?
     (A) Subject.
     (B) Geographic.
     (C) Numeric.
     (D) Accession.

65. The five basic methods of filing are: alphabetic, numeric, subject, geographic, and chronologic. Which one of the above five methods does not use alphabetic concepts?
     (A) Alphabetic.
     (B) Numeric.
     (C) Geographic.

(D) Subject.

(E) Chronologic.

66. The system that involves a set of activities for deciding how long records should be retained and in what locations they should be stored is called

    (A) Follow-Up Procedures.

    (B) Requisition.

    (C) Retention Control.

    (D) Disposal Control.

    (E) Inspecting.

67. Which of the following is *not* a proper filing step that is taken before a record can be placed in a file storage unit?

    (A) Indexing.

    (B) Coding.

(C) Sorting.

(D) Outlining.

(E) Inspecting.

68. Which of the following is *not* the responsibility of a records manager?

    (A) To examine and evaluate records management systems.

    (B) To review records and to determine which electronic process to use.

    (C) To keep records retention schedules and follow government regulations.

    (D) To evaluate and recommend necessary changes and up-to-date techniques.

    (E) To receive records, to do preliminary sorting, filing and finding, and to do other related reference services.

END OF TEST

CONTINUE TO THE NEXT PART OF THIS PRETEST AS YOU WOULD BE EXPECTED TO DO ON THE ACTUAL EXAMINATION. HOWEVER, IF YOU HAVE ANY AVAILABLE TIME LEFT FOR THIS PART, YOU MAY USE IT TO MAKE SURE YOU HAVE MARKED YOUR ANSWER SHEET PROPERLY.

Office Procedures and Terminology

Allow 8 minutes for this part of the test.

Directions: For each of the following questions, select the choice which best answers the question or completes the statement. Mark the answer sheet with the letter of that answer.

Business Terminology

69. The attribute of an office employee who knows what tasks are to be done and what responsibilities are to be assumed without being told what to do is

    (A) dependability.

    (B) effectiveness.

    (C) organizational ability.

    (D) initiative.

70. In today's automated office, the transmission of data, text, voice, or graphics electronically is termed

    (A) telecommunications.

    (B) teleconference.

    (C) records management.

    (D) demodulation.

Telephone Techniques

71. A LAN is a system that connects a variety of equipment or systems from one office building to another. LAN means

    (A) Large Area Numbers.

    (B) Local Area Network.

    (C) Local Average Numbers.

    (D) Large Access Network.

72. When an office sends a copy of an original document by way of electronic means, this is called

    (A) Telex.

    (B) Communicating Word Processors.

    (C) Remote Mail Service.

    (D) Facsimile.

Courtesies

73. If your supervisor is unable to keep a business appointment, it is your responsibility to
    - (A) cancel the appointment by sending the person a note.
    - (B) cancel the appointment by making a telephone call without any explanation.
    - (C) cancel the appointment by making a telephone call and giving a simple reason.
    - (D) cancel the appointment by making a telephone call and rescheduling the appointment.

74. In order to do a successful effective job as a receptionist, there are several techniques which will help you. Which of the following is *not* a good technique?
    - (A) Speak clearly.
    - (B) Be helpful and discreet.
    - (C) Repeat the callers name as many times as you can.
    - (D) Be sure to take messages very accurately and completely with the time and date listed.

Correspondence

75. In order to produce an effective letter for your supervisor, there are certain characteristics that are necessary. Which of the following is *not* one of the major characteristics?
    - (A) Current.
    - (B) Clear.
    - (C) Correct.
    - (D) Concise.

76. In a simplified (AMS or NOMA) letter style, usually two major parts of a letter are omitted. These parts are
    - (A) return address and date.
    - (B) date and salutation.
    - (C) salutation and complimentary close.
    - (D) salutation and signature line.

Judgment

77. In your job function, you are responsible for remembering many things. A smart secretary knows where to find information. If you were asked to find information about the United States Government, which publication would you go to?
    - (A) City directories.
    - (B) Monthly catalog of U.S. Government Publications.
    - (C) Rand McNally.
    - (D) Guide to American Directories.

78. Your supervisor is going on vacation and has asked you to take over the supervision of the other secretaries. One of the individuals is your friend, and you always go to lunch with her. Since you took over, she has been arriving late each morning. You should
    - (A) write her a note and tell her to stop it.
    - (B) write her a note and tell her the supervisor will reprimand her when he returns.
    - (C) talk to her about the problem it is causing both of you.
    - (D) ignore it.

Mail Services and Shipping

79. The fastest service that is provided by the U.S. Postal Service is
    - (A) Registered.
    - (B) Certified.
    - (C) Special delivery.
    - (D) Express mail.

80. The Postal Service has automated and established a system where messages are transmitted by computer. This system is called
    - (A) Mailgrams.
    - (B) Electronic computer originated mail.
    - (C) Electronic recall of mail.
    - (D) Special electronic delivery.

Equipment

81. As a result of reprographics in the modern office, the type of copier that sends an original document electronically from one office to another is called a
    (A) facsimile machine.
    (B) exactocopy machine.
    (C) duplicating machine.
    (D) photocopy machine.

82. Any form of taking a direct image of a document from the original involves photocopying. Which of the following is *not* a form of direct image reproduction?
    (A) Thermography.
    (B) Lasers.
    (C) Xerography.
    (D) Multilith.

Communications

83. Nonverbal signals are a large part of communications. Which of the following has no role in body language?
    (A) Arms.
    (B) Toes.
    (C) Eyes.
    (D) Walk.

84. Listening is an important communication skill, yet a very difficult one. Which of the following is *not* a listening technique?
    (A) Listening for facts.
    (B) Taking verbatim notes.
    (C) Filtering out listening blocks.
    (D) Preparing yourself mentally.

Procedures

85. An office team working together to meet an established goal consists of a supervisor and a support person. Which of the following is *not* an established element?
    (A) A group of people.
    (B) A group of people who work together.
    (C) A group of people with defined goals.
    (D) A group of people who want to succeed separately.

86. In many large organizations, clerical individuals are responsible for establishing agendas for their supervisors' meetings. Which of the following is *not* usually part of an agenda?
    (A) Call to order.
    (B) Committee reports.
    (C) Handling outside reservations.
    (D) Election and appointments of committees.

END OF TEST

CONTINUE TO THE NEXT PART OF THIS PRETEST AS YOU WOULD BE EXPECTED TO DO ON THE ACTUAL EXAMINATION. HOWEVER, IF YOU HAVE ANY AVAILABLE TIME LEFT FOR THIS PART, YOU MAY USE IT TO MAKE SURE YOU HAVE MARKED YOUR ANSWER SHEET PROPERLY.

Mathematics

Allow 5 minutes for this part of the test.

Directions: For each of the following questions, select the choice which best answers the question or completes the statement. Mark the answer sheet with the letter of that answer.

Computations

87. Add $43.69, $64.08, $22.64, and $13.86. From this subtract $5.87, $2.10, and $3.13. The answer would be
    (A) $144.27
    (B) $123.37
    (C) $133.17
    (D) $124.27

88. The average of 18, 25, 34, 46, 18, and 3 is
    (A) 23
    (B) 24
    (C) 144
    (D) 142

89. 1/3 of 600 is
    (A) 180
    (B) 300
    (C) 250
    (D) 200

90. 2.372 times .012 equals
    (A) 2.8464
    (B) 28.464
    (C) 7114.2
    (D) .028464

91. 162,330 divided by 5411 is
    (A) 30
    (B) 33
    (C) 32
    (D) 20

Word Problems

92. A high school cooperative student reports to you. She worked the following hours: Monday, 3 1/2 hours; Tuesday, 4 1/3 hours; Wednesday, 2 2/3 hours; Thursday, 4 hours; and Friday, 5 1/2 hours. She earns $4.10 an hour. How much do you owe her for the week?

(A) $81.13
(B) $81.14
(C) $83.20
(D) $82.00

93. You ordered 6 reams of paper @ $7.80 a ream; 10 gross of pens @ $13.25 a gross; 500 envelopes @ 2 cents each; and 100 stamps @ 25 cents each. What is your total order less 10 percent discount?
    (A) $214.30
    (B) $192.87
    (C) $201.30
    (D) $221.13

94. Your weekly salary is $190.57. Your deductions are: social security $3.05; pension, $5.68; bond, $5.00; and taxes, $8.22. What is the amount of your check after these deductions?
    (A) $168.62
    (B) $21.95
    (C) $173.62
    (D) $160.40

95. In order to become a senior typist, you must be able to type an average of 45 words per minute (wpm) or faster on 5 five-minute timings. You took five timed writings at 68 wpm, 32 wpm, 45 wpm, 52 wpm, and 83 wpm. You had a total of 18 errors to be subtracted from the average of all five timings. What is your average wpm less errors?
    (A) 56
    (B) 18
    (C) 38
    (D) 46

96. You have 15 clerks working for you in your office. They can file 480 letters in one day. If you add 7 more clerks, how many letters will all the clerks file in one day?
    (A) 840
    (B) 736
    (C) 604
    (D) 704

END OF TEST

CONTINUE TO THE NEXT PART OF THIS PRETEST AS YOU WOULD BE EXPECTED TO DO ON THE ACTUAL EXAMINATION. HOWEVER, IF YOU HAVE ANY AVAILABLE TIME LEFT FOR THIS PART, YOU MAY USE IT TO MAKE SURE YOU HAVE MARKED YOUR ANSWER SHEET PROPERLY.

Clerical Performance Ability

Allow 2 minutes for this part of the test.

Coding

Directions: In an office it was decided to change the code which had been used for the secret marks on the cost price from:

OLD CODE	h	a	n	g	s	b	r	u	k	e
	1	2	3	4	5	6	7	8	9	0

to

NEW CODE	c	o	m	p	l	e	x	i	t	y
	1	2	3	4	5	6	7	8	9	0

This entailed changing all the price tags. You have been given the following list of tag prices in the old code marks to change to new code marks. In the correspondingly numbered spaces on the answer sheet, write the letters called for in the new code. Be sure that you put each answer opposite the right number so that it will correspond with the old code it replaces.

OLD CODE	NEW CODE
97. nekku	_____
98. kraeb	_____
99. enauk	_____
100. reana	_____

Name and Number Comparisons

Directions: Each of the following questions consists of three names or numbers which are much alike. For each question compare the name or number to decide which ones, if any, are exactly alike. Mark the answer sheet with the letter of that answer.

(A) if *all three* are exactly *alike*.
(B) if only the *first* and *second* are exactly *alike*.
(C) if only the *first* and *third* are exactly *alike*.
(D) if only the *second* and *third* are exactly *alike*.
(E) if *all three* are *different*.

101.	5261383	103.	W. E. Johnston
	5261283		W. E. Johnson
	5261338		W. E. Johnson

102.	8125690	104.	Vergil L. Muller
	8126690		Vergil L. Muller
	8124509		Vergil L. Muller

Data Interpretation

Directions: Answer questions 105 to 109 using the information given in the following chart.

Age Composition In The Labor Force In City A (1980–1988)

	Age Group	1980	1984	1988
Men	14–24	8,430	10,900	14,340
	25–44	22,200	22,350	26,065
	45 +	17,550	19,800	21,970
Women	14–24	4,450	6,915	7,680
	25–44	9,080	10,010	11,550
	45 +	7,325	9,470	13,180

105. The greatest increase in the number of people in the labor force between 1980 and 1984 occurred among
    (A) Men between the ages of 14 and 24.
    (B) Men age 45 and over.
    (C) Women between the ages of 14 and 24.
    (D) Women age 45 and over.

106. If the total number of women of all ages in the labor force increases from 1988 to 1994 by the same number as it did from 1984 to 1988, the total number of women of all ages in the labor force in 1994 will be
    (A) 27,425
    (B) 29,675
    (C) 37,525
    (D) 38,425

107. The total increase in numbers of women in the labor force from 1980 to 1984 differs from the total increase of men in the same years by being
    (A) 770 less than that of men.
    (B) 670 more than that of men.
    (C) 770 more than that of men.
    (D) 1,670 more than that of men.

108. In the year 1980, the proportion of married women in each group was as follows: 1/5 of the women in the 14–24 age group, 1/4 of those in the 25–44 age group, and 2/5 of those 45 and over. How many married women were in the labor force in 1980
    (A) 4,625
    (B) 5,990
    (C) 6,090
    (D) 7,910

109. The age 14–24 age group of men in the labor force from 1980 to 1988 increased by approximately
    (A) 40 percent.
    (B) 65 percent.
    (C) 70 percent.
    (D) 75 percent.

Matching Letters and Numbers

Directions: In this test of clerical ability, Column I consists of sets of questions which you are to answer one at a time. Column II consists of possible answers to the set of questions in Column I. Select from Column II the one possible answer which contains only the numbers and letters, regardless of their order, which appear in the question in Column I. If none of the four possible answers is correct, mark E on your answer sheet.

COLUMN I: (Set of Questions)	COLUMN II: (Possible Answers)
110. 6 2 5 K 4 P T G	(A) = 4, 5, K, T
111. L 4 7 2 T 6 V K	(B) = 4, 7, G, K
112. 3 5 4 L 9 V T G	(C) = 2, 5, G, L
113. G 4 K 7 L 3 5 Z	(D) = 2, 7, L, T
	(E) = none of these

Letter Series

Directions: Each question consists of a series of letters or numbers (or both) which follow some definite order. Study each series to determine what the order is. Then look at the answer choices. Select the one answer that will complete the set in accordance with the pattern established.

114. 1 2 2 4 3 8
    (A) 5
    (B) 6
    (C) 10
    (D) 4

115. A 3 C 5 E
    (A) G
    (B) 7
    (C) H
    (D) 5

116. 32 16 8 4
    (A) 10
    (B) 30
    (C) 6
    (D) 2

117. A B D C E F H G I J L K M N
    (A) R P
    (B) P O
    (C) O P
    (D) P Q

END OF TEST

CONTINUE TO THE NEXT PART OF THIS PRETEST AS YOU WOULD BE
EXPECTED TO DO ON THE ACTUAL EXAMINATION. HOWEVER, IF YOU
HAVE ANY AVAILABLE TIME LEFT FOR THIS PART, YOU MAY USE IT
TO MAKE SURE YOU HAVE MARKED YOUR ANSWER SHEET
PROPERLY.

Part II (For Typists and Stenographers Only)

Typing

Typing Format Questions

Allow 2 minutes for this part of the test.

Directions: For each of the following questions, select the choice which best answers the question or completes the statement. Mark the answer sheet with the letter of that answer.

118. There are a number of correction tools available to assist you in making typographical corrections. Which of the following is *not* a correction tool?
    (A) Correction paper.
    (B) Correction fluid.
    (C) Correction tape.
    (D) Correction ink.

119. Typewriter ribbons vary according to the typewriter; however, there are standard types of ribbons available. Which of the following is *not* a common type of typewriter ribbon?
    (A) Fabric.
    (B) Film.
    (C) Bond.
    (D) Multistrike.

120. Typists use a variety of stationery. The type of paper that is treated with a special chemical to duplicate the original is called
    (A) NCR.
    (B) Onionskin.
    (C) Bond.
    (D) Watermark.

121. When preparing a letter for an envelope, if you place the letterhead face up, fold the bottom 1/3 up, and then the top 1/3 down, and insert the letter into an envelope, which of the following is the correct size envelope you would use?
    (A) No. 10.
    (B) No. 6 1/2 window.
    (C) No. 6 1/2.
    (D) No. 5 1/2.

122. There are standard parts of every letter. The part of a letter that may include the copy slogan and telephone number is which of the following?
    (A) Company signature line.
    (B) Subject line.
    (C) Inside address.
    (D) Postscript.

END OF TEST

CONTINUE TO THE NEXT PART OF THIS PRETEST AS YOU WOULD BE
EXPECTED TO DO ON THE ACTUAL EXAMINATION. HOWEVER, IF YOU
HAVE ANY AVAILABLE TIME LEFT FOR THIS PART, YOU MAY USE IT TO
MAKE SURE YOU HAVE MARKED YOUR ANSWER SHEET PROPERLY.

Typing Performance Test

Allow 5 minutes for this part of the test.

Directions: Type the copy exactly as it is given below. Spell, space, begin and end each line, paragraph, punctuate, and capitalize precisely as shown. Make no erasures, insertions, or other corrections. Errors are penalized whether they are erased or otherwise corrected. Keep on typing even though you detect an error in your copy. If you finish typing the exercise before the time limit is up, double space once and start typing from the beginning of the exercise. If you fill up one side of the paper, turn it over and continue typing on the other side.

Exercise	words a minute
In the field of public administration in the	1
narrower and more technical sense, significant	2
trends are observable. These are closely related to	3
the efficiency movement in modern business and the new	4
social background of administrative activity. The new	5
movement involves larger administrative areas, consol-	6
idation of authority at all levels, central control	7
over subordinate authorities in the region, a pro-	8
fessional personnel, and the application of new tech-	9
nical devices to the rationalization of the service.	10
These movements are especially apparent in the states	11
and in the special fields of education, highways,	12
health, and finance. Consolidation is also seen in	13
the cities, both under the council mayor and the coun-	14
cil administrator forms of government.	15
The federal government has established an impor-	16
tant form of administrative control by means of	17
grants-in-aid. At the same time, an important rela-	18
tionship has been developed in the cooperative ex-	19
change of administrative services between the United	20
States and the states and to a more limited extent	21
between the states and localities. The continuing	22
involvement of federal agencies in these matters is	23
a significant indicator of this new policy. It	24
augurs well for the future.	25

Each time you reach this point, double space
once and begin again.

END OF TEST

CONTINUE TO THE NEXT PART OF THIS PRETEST AS YOU WOULD BE EXPECTED TO DO ON THE ACTUAL EXAMINATION.

Part III (For Stenographers Only)

SHORTHAND

Shorthand Format Questions

Allow 2 minutes for this part of the test.

Directions: For each of the following questions, select the choice which best answers the question or completes the statement. Mark the answer sheet with the letter of that answer.

123. When a secretary prepares for dictation, there are certain supplies needed. Which of the following is not a needed item?
     (A) Notebook.
     (B) Stop watch.
     (C) Calendar.
     (D) Pens/Pencils.

124. There are several basic kinds of office dictation equipment. Which of the following is *not* one of these dictation items?
     (A) Portable units.
     (B) Desktop units.
     (C) Stenographic machine unit.
     (D) Centralized system.

125. What is the term used that means to refer to the arrangement on each page of the various parts of a message?
     (A) Format.
     (B) Content.
     (C) Technique.
     (D) Message layout.

126. Stationery comes in a variety of commonly found sizes. Which of the following is *not* a commonly found stationery size?
     (A) Office.
     (B) Baronial.
     (C) Monarch.
     (D) Standard.

127. To save the time of a recipient of a letter in locating previous correspondence on the same subject or from the same correspondent, a secretary will use a specific part of a letter to note this information. The correct name for this part is
     (A) Copy notation.
     (B) Inside address.
     (C) File reference.
     (D) Mailing instructions.

END OF TEST

CONTINUE TO THE NEXT PART OF THIS PRETEST AS YOU WOULD BE
EXPECTED TO DO ON THE ACTUAL EXAMINATION. HOWEVER, IF YOU
HAVE ANY AVAILABLE TIME LEFT FOR THIS PART, YOU MAY USE IT
TO MAKE SURE YOU HAVE MARKED YOUR ANSWER SHEET
PROPERLY.

Stenography Performance Test

Directions for the dictator: Dictate at the rate of 80 words a minute. Do not dictate the punctuation except for periods. Dictate with the expression the punctuation requires. Use a watch with a second hand or a stopwatch to maintain the proper speed.

Dictator is allowed 3 minutes 15 seconds for this part of the test.

Exactly on a minute, start dictating:

Finish reading each group of lines at the number of seconds indicated below.

The most important expansion of institutions of higher education in this country is the	
development of the university, which provides training of	15 seconds
the post-college level.(Period) The chief characteristic	30 seconds
which distinguishes the university from other institutions of	
higher education is devotion	45 seconds
to research and productive scholarship.(Period) A	
generation ago American students desiring	1 minute
training of university grade were compelled to go to	
Europe.(Period) The colleges of the United States did not	15 seconds
recognize cultivation of productive scholarship as an	
institutional duty.(Period) Within the past thirty	30 seconds
years, however, there has been a radical change in the	
conception of the functions of the university.(Period)	45 seconds
Productive scholarship has come to be considered a	
cardinal virtue in the individual members	2 minutes
of university faculties.(Period) Tremendous resources are	
devoted in state and endowed institutions	15 seconds
to stimulation and support of research.(Period) American	
students now find it possible to secure advanced	30 seconds
training in many universities in this country and the resort	
to European institutions for post-	45 seconds
graduate study is much less common than it was at the	
beginning of this century.(Period) Critics of American	3 minutes
university education are accustomed to scoff at the	
extensive expansions which recent years have	
witnessed.(Period)	15 seconds

After dictating the passage: Pause for 15 seconds to permit the stenographer to complete his/her notes. The stenographer should then proceed to follow the transcription instructions given next. She/he should not be permitted to look back at the dictated passage which you have just read.

Transcription

Directions for the stenographer: The transcript given below is part of the material that was dictated to you, except many of the words have been left out. From your notes you must decide what the missing words are. You are to do the following:

1. Compare your notes with the transcript. When you come to a blank space, decide what word belongs there.

2. Look at the alphabetic word list to find the missing word. If you find the missing word there, note what letter—A, B, C, or D—is printed beside it. Write that letter in the blank space in your transcript.

3. If the missing word does not appear in the alphabetic word list, mark E in the blank space on your transcript.

4. After you have marked all the blank spaces in the transcript, transfer your answers to the answer sheet provided.

Allow 30 minutes for this part of the test.

ALPHABETIC WORD LIST

Write E if the answer is *not* listed.

ago—B	higher—A
away—C	important—C
character—D	impotent—D
chief —B	institutes—A
compiled—C	institutions—D
country—B	ladder—B
county—D	level—C
desirous—B	other—B
destruction—A	post-college—A
distinguished—B	pre-college—D
distinguishes—D	procures—D
development—D	producing—B
educate—C	productive—D
education—B	reason—D
Europe—B	research—C
European—C	scholarship—B
extension—A	students—D
from—A	training—D
from other—C	to go—A
generate—D	to go to—C
generation—A	universe—C
grade—D	university—A
graduate—A	what—A
high—D	which—C

TRANSCRIPT

The most ___ ___ of ___ of ___ ___ in this ___ is
    128 129   130   131 132   133
the ___ of the ___, ___ ___ ___ of the ___ ___.
    134   135   136 137 138   139 140
The ___ ___ which ___ the university ___ ___ insti-
    141 142   143   144 145
tutions of ___ ___ is ___ to ___ and ___ ___. A
           146 147   148   149   150 151
___ ___ American ___ ___ ___ of university ___
152 153   154 155 156   157
were ___ ___ to ___.
     158 159   160

CONTINUE TO THE NEXT PAGE WITHOUT WAITING FOR A
SIGNAL.

ALPHABETIC WORD LIST

Write E if the answer is *not* listed.

carnal—D
change—D
colleges—B
come—D
considered—A
culture—D
denoted—B
devoted—C
did not—A
does not—D
duly—C
duty—B
endued—C
facilities—A
faculties—D
had been—A
has been—B
however—A
individual—C
institutional—A
institutions—D

last—C
members—A
membership—D
of the—D
of these—C
producing—B
productive—C
racial—A
recognize—C
research—C
resources—A
scholars—A
scholarship—D
state—A
stimulation—D
supportive—B
the factions—A
the functions—C
virtual—A
virtue—B
years—C

TRANSCRIPT

The ____ ____ United States ____ ____ ____ of ____ ____
     161 162   163 164 165   166 167
as an ____ ____. Within the ____ thirty ____, ____, there
      168 169   170   171   172
____ a ____ ____ in the ____ of ____ ____ university.
173   174 175   176   177 178
Productive ____ has ____ to be ____ a ____ ____ in the
           179   180   181   182 183
____ ____ of university ____. Tremendous ____ are ____
184 185   186   187   188
in ____ and ____ ____ to ____ and ____ of ____.
   189   190 191   192   193   194

CONTINUE TO THE NEXT PAGE WITHOUT WAITING FOR A
SIGNAL.

ALPHABETIC WORD LIST

Write E if the answer is *not* listed.

accusing—A

accustomed—B

advance—A

advanced—D

begin—A

beginning—B

centuries—A

common—B

country—B

educating—D

education—B

Europe—A

European—C

expansions—C

expensive—B

extensive—A

find—A

find it—C

higher—A

in these—D

in this—B

institutes—C

institutions—D

it was—A

less—A

lower—B

many—C

most—B

much—D

of—D

of our—C

post-graduate—C

pre-graduate—A

probable—D

recent—D

resource—D

scholars—A

scowl—C

secure—D

students—D

the—D

this—A

training—A

trying—C

wished—B

years—B

TRANSCRIPT

American ____ now ____ it ____ to ____ ____ ____ in
　　　　　195　　　196　　197　　198　199　200

____ universities ____ ____ and the ____ to ____ ____ for
201　　　　　　　202　203　　　　　　204　　205　206

____ ____ is ____ ____ ____ than ____ at the ____ of ____
207　208　　　209　210　211　　　212　　　　213　　214

____. Critics ____ ____ university ____ are ____ to ____
215　　　　　216　217　　　　　　218　　　219　　220

at the ____ ____ which ____ ____ have ____.
　　　221　222　　　　223　224　　　225

WHEN TIME IS UP, TRANSFER YOUR TRANSCRIPT
ANSWERS TO THE ANSWER SHEET.

END OF PRETEST

Weak Area Determination Guide

Vocabulary

1. B	3. B	5. B	7. C	9. A
2. E	4. B	6. E	8. D	10. C

Verbal Analogies

11. C	13. C	15. C	17. A	19. E
12. B	14. A	16. E	18. E	20. C

Spelling and Word Usage

21. B	23. D	25. A	27. C	29. A
22. B	24. A	26. B	28. D	30. B

English Grammar

31. A	33. B	35. D	37. D	39. C
32. B	34. B	36. B	38. A	40. B

Reading Comprehension

41. D	43. E	45. D	47. B	49. A
42. D	44. C	46. E	48. D	50. C

Filing/Records Management

51. E	55. B	59. A	63. A	66. C
52. A	56. D	60. C	64. D	67. D
53. D	57. E	61. C	65. E	68. E
54. C	58. E	62. B		

Office Procedures and Terminology

69. D	73. D	77. B	81. A	84. B
70. A	74. C	78. C	82. D	85. D
71. B	75. A	79. D	83. B	86. C
72. D	76. C	80. B		

Mathematics

87. C	89. D	91. A	93. B	95. C
88. B	90. D	92. D	94. A	96. D

Clerical Performance Ability

97. mytti	102. E	106. D	110. A	114. D
98. txoye	103. D	107. B	111. D	115. B
99. ymoit	104. A	108. C	112. E	116. D
100. xyomo	105. A	109. C	113. B	117. B
101. E				

Typing Format

118. D	119. C	120. A	121. A	122. A

Shorthand Format

123. B	124. C	125. D	126. A	127. C

Shorthand

128. C	148. E	168. A	188. C	207. C
129. E	149. C	169. B	189. A	208. E
130. D	150. D	170. E	190. E	209. D
131. A	151. B	171. C	191. D	210. A
132. B	152. A	172. A	192. D	211. B
133. B	153. B	173. B	193. E	212. A
134. D	154. D	174. E	194. C	213. B
135. A	155. E	175. D	195. D	214. A
136. C	156. D	176. E	196. A	215. E
137. E	157. D	177. C	197. E	216. D
138. D	158. E	178. D	198. D	217. E
139. A	159. A	179. D	199. D	218. B
140. C	160. B	180. D	200. A	219. B
141. B	161. B	181. A	201. C	220. E
142. E	162. D	182. E	202. B	221. A
143. D	163. A	183. B	203. B	222. C
144. A	164. C	184. C	204. E	223. D
145. B	165. E	185. A	205. C	224. B
146. A	166. C	186. D	206. D	225. E
147. B	167. D	187. A		

TYPING PERFORMANCE

SPEED IN WPM	40	42	44	47–49	52–54	56–59	61–64	66–68	71–73	76+
ERRORS PERMITTED	3	4	5	6	7	8	9	10	11	12

PRACTICE ON
PRETEST SUBJECTS

Vocabulary Answer Sheet

Pretest

1 Ⓐ Ⓑ Ⓒ Ⓓ	5 Ⓐ Ⓑ Ⓒ Ⓓ	9 Ⓐ Ⓑ Ⓒ Ⓓ	13 Ⓐ Ⓑ Ⓒ Ⓓ Ⓔ	17 Ⓐ Ⓑ Ⓒ Ⓓ Ⓔ
2 Ⓐ Ⓑ Ⓒ Ⓓ	6 Ⓐ Ⓑ Ⓒ Ⓓ	10 Ⓐ Ⓑ Ⓒ Ⓓ	14 Ⓐ Ⓑ Ⓒ Ⓓ Ⓔ	18 Ⓐ Ⓑ Ⓒ Ⓓ Ⓔ
3 Ⓐ Ⓑ Ⓒ Ⓓ	7 Ⓐ Ⓑ Ⓒ Ⓓ	11 Ⓐ Ⓑ Ⓒ Ⓓ Ⓔ	15 Ⓐ Ⓑ Ⓒ Ⓓ Ⓔ	19 Ⓐ Ⓑ Ⓒ Ⓓ Ⓔ
4 Ⓐ Ⓑ Ⓒ Ⓓ	8 Ⓐ Ⓑ Ⓒ Ⓓ	12 Ⓐ Ⓑ Ⓒ Ⓓ Ⓔ	16 Ⓐ Ⓑ Ⓒ Ⓓ Ⓔ	20 Ⓐ Ⓑ Ⓒ Ⓓ Ⓔ

Vocabulary Test 1

1 Ⓐ Ⓑ Ⓒ Ⓓ	3 Ⓐ Ⓑ Ⓒ Ⓓ	5 Ⓐ Ⓑ Ⓒ Ⓓ	7 Ⓐ Ⓑ Ⓒ Ⓓ	9 Ⓐ Ⓑ Ⓒ Ⓓ
2 Ⓐ Ⓑ Ⓒ Ⓓ	4 Ⓐ Ⓑ Ⓒ Ⓓ	6 Ⓐ Ⓑ Ⓒ Ⓓ	8 Ⓐ Ⓑ Ⓒ Ⓓ	10 Ⓐ Ⓑ Ⓒ Ⓓ

Vocabulary Test 2

1 Ⓐ Ⓑ Ⓒ Ⓓ	3 Ⓐ Ⓑ Ⓒ Ⓓ	5 Ⓐ Ⓑ Ⓒ Ⓓ	7 Ⓐ Ⓑ Ⓒ Ⓓ	9 Ⓐ Ⓑ Ⓒ Ⓓ
2 Ⓐ Ⓑ Ⓒ Ⓓ	4 Ⓐ Ⓑ Ⓒ Ⓓ	6 Ⓐ Ⓑ Ⓒ Ⓓ	8 Ⓐ Ⓑ Ⓒ Ⓓ	10 Ⓐ Ⓑ Ⓒ Ⓓ

Vocabulary Test 3

1 Ⓐ Ⓑ Ⓒ Ⓓ Ⓔ	3 Ⓐ Ⓑ Ⓒ Ⓓ Ⓔ	5 Ⓐ Ⓑ Ⓒ Ⓓ Ⓔ	7 Ⓐ Ⓑ Ⓒ Ⓓ Ⓔ	9 Ⓐ Ⓑ Ⓒ Ⓓ Ⓔ
2 Ⓐ Ⓑ Ⓒ Ⓓ Ⓔ	4 Ⓐ Ⓑ Ⓒ Ⓓ Ⓔ	6 Ⓐ Ⓑ Ⓒ Ⓓ Ⓔ	8 Ⓐ Ⓑ Ⓒ Ⓓ Ⓔ	10 Ⓐ Ⓑ Ⓒ Ⓓ Ⓔ

Vocabulary Test 4

1 Ⓐ Ⓑ Ⓒ Ⓓ Ⓔ	3 Ⓐ Ⓑ Ⓒ Ⓓ Ⓔ	5 Ⓐ Ⓑ Ⓒ Ⓓ Ⓔ	7 Ⓐ Ⓑ Ⓒ Ⓓ Ⓔ	9 Ⓐ Ⓑ Ⓒ Ⓓ Ⓔ
2 Ⓐ Ⓑ Ⓒ Ⓓ Ⓔ	4 Ⓐ Ⓑ Ⓒ Ⓓ Ⓔ	6 Ⓐ Ⓑ Ⓒ Ⓓ Ⓔ	8 Ⓐ Ⓑ Ⓒ Ⓓ Ⓔ	10 Ⓐ Ⓑ Ⓒ Ⓓ Ⓔ

Posttest

1 Ⓐ Ⓑ Ⓒ Ⓓ	5 Ⓐ Ⓑ Ⓒ Ⓓ	9 Ⓐ Ⓑ Ⓒ Ⓓ	13 Ⓐ Ⓑ Ⓒ Ⓓ Ⓔ	17 Ⓐ Ⓑ Ⓒ Ⓓ Ⓔ
2 Ⓐ Ⓑ Ⓒ Ⓓ	6 Ⓐ Ⓑ Ⓒ Ⓓ	10 Ⓐ Ⓑ Ⓒ Ⓓ	14 Ⓐ Ⓑ Ⓒ Ⓓ Ⓔ	18 Ⓐ Ⓑ Ⓒ Ⓓ Ⓔ
3 Ⓐ Ⓑ Ⓒ Ⓓ	7 Ⓐ Ⓑ Ⓒ Ⓓ	11 Ⓐ Ⓑ Ⓒ Ⓓ Ⓔ	15 Ⓐ Ⓑ Ⓒ Ⓓ Ⓔ	19 Ⓐ Ⓑ Ⓒ Ⓓ Ⓔ
4 Ⓐ Ⓑ Ⓒ Ⓓ	8 Ⓐ Ⓑ Ⓒ Ⓓ	12 Ⓐ Ⓑ Ⓒ Ⓓ Ⓔ	16 Ⓐ Ⓑ Ⓒ Ⓓ Ⓔ	20 Ⓐ Ⓑ Ⓒ Ⓓ Ⓔ

VOCABULARY

Introductory Pretest and Answers

Directions: Select the appropriate letter preceding the word which is most nearly the same in meaning as the capitalized word. Mark the answer sheet with the letter of that answer.

Allow 4 minutes for this pretest.

1. CLOSE
   - (A) shut
   - (B) find
   - (C) touch
   - (D) see

2. BELOW
   - (A) beside
   - (B) above
   - (C) under
   - (D) near

3. NOURISHMENT
   - (A) food
   - (B) medicine
   - (C) fresh air
   - (D) treatment

4. INCREDIBLE
   - (A) not clear
   - (B) unexpected
   - (C) beyond belief
   - (D) unfair

5. AVERT
   - (A) support
   - (B) overcome
   - (C) prevent
   - (D) deny

6. PLAUSIBLE
   - (A) ostensible
   - (B) earnest
   - (C) extraordinary
   - (D) clever

7. BYTE
   - (A) unit of information
   - (B) moveable marker
   - (C) list of choices
   - (D) unit of measure

8. FORMAT
   - (A) changing material
   - (B) layout or arrangement
   - (C) a program
   - (D) insurance

9. GREGARIOUS
   - (A) ready to support
   - (B) emotional
   - (C) communal
   - (D) transparent

10. TERSE
    - (A) concise
    - (B) powerful
    - (C) resentment
    - (D) dangerous

DIRECTIONS: For each of the following questions, select the appropriate letter preceding the word that is opposite in meaning to the capitalized word. Mark the answer sheet with the letter of that answer.

11. MEND
    - (A) give back
    - (B) pray
    - (C) change
    - (D) destroy
    - (E) clean

12. BRAVADO
    - (A) scrawny
    - (B) shortness
    - (C) humility
    - (D) bowleggedness
    - (E) discord

47

13. HUMANE
    (A) bestial
    (B) ill-mannered
    (C) ill-tempered
    (D) anthropomorphic
    (E) anti-vivisection

14. HARD
    (A) crisp
    (B) soft
    (C) wet
    (D) nut
    (E) weak

15. ACID
    (A) sweet
    (B) bitter
    (C) bland
    (D) alkaline
    (E) saline

16. BRUSQUE
    (A) patient
    (B) clean
    (C) dirty
    (D) dusty
    (E) dim

17. ALLY
    (A) fight
    (B) resist
    (C) separate
    (D) hate
    (E) win

18. ABSTRACT
    (A) art
    (B) absurd
    (C) sculpture
    (D) concrete
    (E) asphalt

19. ANOREXIA
    (A) brazenness
    (B) gluttony
    (C) disrespect
    (D) anarchy
    (E) performance

20. CEILING
    (A) roof
    (B) wall
    (C) cellar
    (D) floor
    (E) foundation

END OF PRETEST

Answer Key for Pretest

1. A	5. C	9. C	13. A	17. C
2. C	6. A	10. A	14. B	18. D
3. A	7. A	11. D	15. D	19. B
4. C	8. B	12. C	16. A	20. D

Study Hints

You need to increase your vocabulary if you want to read with understanding. The most efficient way in which you can build up your vocabulary is by a systematic study of the basic word and letter combinations which make up the greater part of the English language.

Following are steps you can take in order to build up your word power:

1. *Learn to use the dictionary*. Whenever you don't know the meaning of a word, make a note of it. Then, when you get to a dictionary, look up the meaning of the word. Keep a notebook of new words. Say the word aloud, and then try to make a sentence using the word. Use a dictionary for proper pronunciation or accent.

2. *Learn to use the thesaurus*. The thesaurus defines words by their synonyms. However, do not use it in place of a dictionary. Use it as a supplement to increase word development.

3. *Read as much as you can*. Don't confine yourself to one type of reading. Read all kinds of newspapers, magazines, books, advertisements, letters, etc. Seek variety in what you read. For example, read different newspapers, several types of magazines, and all types of books (novels, poetry, essays, plays, etc.). If you get into the habit of reading widely, your vocabulary will grow rap-

idly. You will learn the meanings of words by *context*.

4. *Vocabulary Activities*.

   a. Use flash cards, write the word, write the definition, use sentences with the word, learn the part of speech, its synonyms, etc.

   b. Learn the various forms of words you already know.

   c. Use both your active (writing and speaking) vocabulary as well as your passive (listening and reading) vocabulary.

   d. Study homonyms and other frequently confused words.

   e. Learn words that pertain to office work.

5. *Letter combinations*. *Etymology* is the science of the formation of words. This science can be of great help to you in learning new words and identifying words which may be unfamiliar to you.

   Many of the words which we use every day have come into our language from Latin and Greek. In the process of being absorbed into English, they appear as parts of words, many of which are related in meaning to each other. Latin and Greek syllables and letter combinations are categorized into three groups:

   a. *Prefixes*. Letter combinations which appear at the beginning of a word.

   b. *Suffixes*. Letter combinations which appear at the end of a word.

   c. *Roots or stems*. These carry the basic meaning and are combined with each other and with prefixes and suffixes to create other words with related meanings.

   Check with an up-to-date English or spelling textbook.

6. Separate and develop each of the following kinds of vocabulary:

   a. Reading

   b. Writing

   c. Speaking

   d. General recognition

Sample Question and Explanation

The questions may appear in one of several forms, but one of the most common is that of choosing a word which is most nearly the same in meaning as the question word. The example here has been chosen because it will help to illustrate the way in which vocabulary questions are answered.

Select the letter of the answer which is most nearly the same in meaning as the capitalized word.

Example: GARRULOUS
    (A) complaining
    (B) careless
    (C) overly talkative
    (D) defensive
    (E) dishonest

Notice that the instructions tell you to select the choice which is *most nearly* the same in meaning as the capitalized word.

First, examine the capitalized word. If you know its meaning, your task is fairly simple. But suppose you do not know what GARRULOUS means. Perhaps we can eliminate some of the choices by analyzing them.

(A) *Complaining*: Does *complaining* have any thing to do with GARRULOUS? It might. However, a synonym for *complaining* is *querulous*. In this case it is best to avoid *complaining* as a possibility, since it is probably there to confuse you.

(B) *Careless*: Most people know what *careless* means. Here again is a word which only sounds like the question word. You would not use GARRULOUS to describe a neglectful person.

(C) *Overly talkative*: There is nothing to indicate that this phrase is not a synonym for GARRULOUS. Do not eliminate it as a possibility.

(D) *Defensive*: You can think of synonyms for this one, like *protective*, *safe-guarding*, and maybe even *fortress* and *garrison*. In general any word that sounds like the question word should be avoided. You would do well to eliminate *defensive* as a possibility.

(E) *Dishonest:* There is not much to indicate that this is not a synonym for GARRULOUS, and none of the synonyms for *dishonest* sounds like the question word. It cannot be eliminated entirely.

The choice is now between (C) and (E); *overly talkative* and *dishonest*. If you have no idea at all regarding the meaning of GARRULOUS, then you must guess. Since three of the choices have already been eliminated, you have a much better chance to guess correctly.

GARRULOUS: The dictionary defines it as: "given to continual and tedious talking," "habitually loquacious," "chattering," "verbose." Therefore, (C) "overly talkative" is the correct answer.

Tests and Answers

The answer key will be found at the end of these practice tests.

Vocabulary Test 1

Directions: For each question in this examination, select the appropriate letter preceding the word which is most nearly the same in meaning as the capitalized word. Mark the answer sheet with the letter of that answer.

Allow 4 minutes for this test.

1. ACCLIMATE
    (A) predict weather
    (B) become accustomed to
    (C) enjoy good climate
    (D) drill thoroughly

2. AFFABLE
    (A) friendly
    (B) silly
    (C) legendary
    (D) dismayed

3. CAPTIOUS
    (A) headstrong
    (B) grasping
    (C) enchanting
    (D) critical

4. CONGENITAL
    (A) harmonious
    (B) sympathetic
    (C) inherent
    (D) fringed

5. CORROBORATE
    (A) connect
    (B) cooperate
    (C) confirm
    (D) rust

6. EDIFY
    (A) proclaim
    (B) revise
    (C) whirl
    (D) enlighten

7. STEALTHY
    (A) disobedient
    (B) slender
    (C) discontented
    (D) sly

8. IMPOTENT
    (A) worthless
    (B) meaningless
    (C) powerless
    (D) fearless

9. OSTENTATIOUS
    (A) protruding
    (B) wealthy
    (C) decorative
    (D) showy

10. REDUNDANT
    (A) concise
    (B) reappearing
    (C) superfluous
    (D) lessened

END OF TEST

Vocabulary Test 2

Allow 4 minutes for this test.

1. ERGONOMICS
   (A) arrangement
   (B) effective work
   (C) utilization
   (D) pleasant

2. MERIT
   (A) goodness
   (B) portion
   (C) works
   (D) occult

3. TENACITY
   (A) fierceness
   (B) boldness
   (C) persistency
   (D) courage

4. SEMANTICS
   (A) branch of military service
   (B) art of disputation
   (C) scientific agriculture
   (D) science of meanings

5. FUNDAMENTAL
   (A) adequate
   (B) essential
   (C) official
   (D) truthful

6. PROCRASTINATION
   (A) putting aside
   (B) excuses
   (C) misunderstanding
   (D) analysis

7. DISORGANIZATION
   (A) expansion
   (B) alien
   (C) privilege
   (D) confusion

8. UNCOUTH
   (A) moronic
   (B) boorish
   (C) despicable
   (D) malicious

9. FOSTER
   (A) obliterate
   (B) improvise
   (C) nurture
   (D) disconcert

10. AUGMENT
   (A) conclude
   (B) suggesting
   (C) increase
   (D) unite

END OF TEST

Vocabulary Test 3

Directions: For each of the following questions, select the appropriate letter preceding the word that is opposite in meaning to the capitalized word. Mark the answer sheet with the letter of that answer.

1. CAUSE
   (A) affect
   (B) result
   (C) question
   (D) matter
   (E) accident

2. PITHY
   (A) wooden
   (B) boring
   (C) inane
   (D) bareheaded
   (E) virtuous

3. PROGRESS
   - (A) halt
   - (B) change
   - (C) invert
   - (D) follow
   - (E) lead

4. RURAL
   - (A) suburban
   - (B) exurban
   - (C) arid
   - (D) urban
   - (E) watery

5. ATTRITION
   - (A) partition
   - (B) subjugation
   - (C) death
   - (D) decision
   - (E) adding on

6. ARCHAIC
   - (A) novel
   - (B) dug up
   - (C) buried
   - (D) pointed
   - (E) satanic

7. ELAN
   - (A) horror
   - (B) fear
   - (C) bravery
   - (D) depth
   - (E) apathy

8. PROFIT
   - (A) ratio
   - (B) gross
   - (C) net
   - (D) loss
   - (E) mark-down

9. REST
   - (A) sleep
   - (B) activity
   - (C) wake
   - (D) speak
   - (E) snore

10. BIRTH
   - (A) life
   - (B) age
   - (C) youth
   - (D) childlessness
   - (E) death

END OF TEST

Vocabulary Test 4

Directions: For each of the following questions, select the appropriate letter proceding the word that is opposite in meaning to the capitalized word. Mark the answer sheet with the letter of that answer.

1. RESCIND
   - (A) provide
   - (B) reinstate
   - (C) cancel
   - (D) mutilate
   - (E) correct

2. AFFABLE
   - (A) unbent
   - (B) untruthful
   - (C) unfriendly
   - (D) unable
   - (E) unreliable

3. CAUSTIC
   - (A) sleepy
   - (B) cleansing
   - (C) unintelligent
   - (D) resultant
   - (E) soothing

4. ADAMANT
   - (A) effeminate
   - (B) prayerful
   - (C) yielding
   - (D) courageous
   - (E) reluctant

5. AFFECTATION
    (A) hatred
    (B) security
    (C) cause
    (D) result
    (E) modesty

6. VULNERABLE
    (A) reverent
    (B) innocent
    (C) unassailable
    (D) inflated
    (E) playful

7. ABATEMENT
    (A) addition
    (B) guarantee
    (C) denial
    (D) danger
    (E) flood

8. PERTURBED
    (A) disrespectful
    (B) penetrable
    (C) tractable
    (D) cheerful
    (E) relaxed

9. AVARICE
    (A) kindness
    (B) detriment
    (C) starvation
    (D) sorrow
    (E) generosity

10. ABHORRENCE
    (A) revelation
    (B) detachment
    (C) engagement
    (D) admiration
    (E) avoidance

END OF TEST

Answer Key for Practice Tests

Vocabulary Test 1

1. B	3. D	5. C	7. D	9. D
2. A	4. C	6. D	8. C	10. C

Vocabulary Test 2

1. B	3. C	5. B	7. D	9. C
2. A	4. D	6. A	8. B	10. C

Vocabulary Test 3

1. **(B) RESULT.** The **RESULT** is the end product of a **CAUSE.** A synonym for **RESULT** is *effect*. Do not confuse *effect* with *affect*, which means influence.

2. **(C)** That which is **INANE** is empty and pointless. That which is **PITHY** has substance and point.

3. **(A) HALT.** To **PROGRESS** is to move forward.

4. **(D) URBAN** means pertaining to a city or town. **RURAL** pertains to the country, especially agricultural areas. *Suburban* and *exurban* fall between the opposites.

5. **(E) ADDING ON. ATTRITION** means the wearing away.

6. **(A) NOVEL,** meaning new. **ARCHAIC** means ancient.

7. **(E) APATHY. ELAN** refers to eagerness for action.

8. **(D) LOSS** is the true opposite of **PROFIT.**

9. **(B) ACTIVITY** is motion. **REST** is freedom from activity.

10. **(E) DEATH. BIRTH** is the beginning of a continuum that ends in **DEATH.**

Vocabulary Test 4

1. **(B) REINSTATE.** To **RESCIND** is to take back, so the *best* antonym is a reversal of the process. **PROVIDE** might serve as an antonym if there were no better choice.

2. **(C) UNFRIENDLY. AFFABLE** means sociable.

3. **(E) SOOTHING. CAUSTIC** means sharp or abrasive.

4. **(C) YIELDING. ADAMANT** means impenetrable and firm.

5. **(E) MODESTY. AFFECTATION** refers to a putting on of airs.

6. **(C) UNASSAILABLE. VULNERABLE** means susceptible to attack or wounds.

7. **(A) ADDITION. ABATEMENT** means diminution.

8. **(E) RELAXED.** One who is **PERTURBED** is agitated.

9. **(E) GENEROSITY. AVARICE** is greed.

10. **(D) ADMIRATION. ABHORRENCE** is loathing or hatred.

Posttest and Answers

Directions: For each of the following questions, select the appropriate letter preceding the word which is most nearly the same in meaning as the capitalized word. Mark the answer sheet with the letter of that answer.

Allow 4 minutes for this posttest.

1. LINGERED
   (A) pulled
   (B) watched
   (C) played
   (D) remained

2. PUNCTUAL
   (A) polite
   (B) cautious
   (C) prepared
   (D) prompt

3. COMPENSATION
   (A) assistance
   (B) payment
   (C) initiative
   (D) understanding

4. OBLITERATED
   (A) restored
   (B) effaced
   (C) marred
   (D) perfected

5. RATIFICATION
   (A) confirmation
   (B) consideration
   (C) adjustment
   (D) disclosure

6. ABHORRENT
   (A) difficult
   (B) repugnant
   (C) uninteresting
   (D) tedious

7. COPYRIGHT
   (A) one who owns property
   (B) business organization
   (C) exclusive right
   (D) abundance of riches

8. INTRASTATE
   (A) between states
   (B) geographical areas
   (C) transports across states
   (D) within the state

9. APATHY
   (A) lean
   (B) emotional
   (C) insensibility
   (D) normal

10. EXCISE
    (A) exchange of articles
    (B) conditioning the body
    (C) prorate
    (D) tax

Directions: For each of the following questions, select the appropriate letter preceding the word that is opposite in meaning to the capitalized word. Mark the answer sheet with the letter of that answer.

11. PERTINENT
    (A) inappropriate
    (B) prudent
    (C) truthful
    (D) applicable
    (E) careful

12. DOGMATIC
    (A) bovine
    (B) canine
    (C) yielding
    (D) unprincipled
    (E) opinionated

13. INTREPID
    (A) feasible
    (B) cowardly
    (C) fanciful
    (D) fearless
    (E) willing

14. TENACITY
    (A) firmness
    (B) sagacity
    (C) temerity
    (D) discouragement
    (E) thinness

15. STERILE
    (A) antique
    (B) unclean
    (C) germ-proof
    (D) austere
    (E) artistic

16. CREDIBLE
    (A) believable
    (B) intelligent
    (C) correct
    (D) suitable
    (E) unbelievable

17. MORTGAGER
    (A) lender
    (B) giver
    (C) receiver
    (D) reckoner
    (E) dictator

18. IGNOMINY
    (A) fame
    (B) ill luck
    (C) disgrace
    (D) despair
    (E) illiteracy

19. PRODIGAL
    (A) wasteful
    (B) marvelous
    (C) ominous
    (D) harmless
    (E) thrifty

20. VOLUBLE
    (A) bulky
    (B) glib
    (C) desirable
    (D) reticent
    (E) fat

END OF POSTTEST

Answer Key for Posttest

1. D	5. A	9. C	13. B	17. C
2. D	6. B	10. D	14. D	18. A
3. B	7. C	11. A	15. B	19. E
4. B	8. D	12. C	16. E	20. D

Verbal Analogies Answer Sheet

Pretest

1 Ⓐ Ⓑ Ⓒ Ⓓ   3 Ⓐ Ⓑ Ⓒ Ⓓ   5 Ⓐ Ⓑ Ⓒ Ⓓ   7 Ⓐ Ⓑ Ⓒ Ⓓ   9 Ⓐ Ⓑ Ⓒ Ⓓ
2 Ⓐ Ⓑ Ⓒ Ⓓ   4 Ⓐ Ⓑ Ⓒ Ⓓ   6 Ⓐ Ⓑ Ⓒ Ⓓ   8 Ⓐ Ⓑ Ⓒ Ⓓ 10 Ⓐ Ⓑ Ⓒ Ⓓ

Verbal Analogies Test 1

1 Ⓐ Ⓑ Ⓒ Ⓓ Ⓔ   3 Ⓐ Ⓑ Ⓒ Ⓓ Ⓔ   5 Ⓐ Ⓑ Ⓒ Ⓓ Ⓔ   7 Ⓐ Ⓑ Ⓒ Ⓓ Ⓔ   9 Ⓐ Ⓑ Ⓒ Ⓓ Ⓔ
2 Ⓐ Ⓑ Ⓒ Ⓓ Ⓔ   4 Ⓐ Ⓑ Ⓒ Ⓓ Ⓔ   6 Ⓐ Ⓑ Ⓒ Ⓓ Ⓔ   8 Ⓐ Ⓑ Ⓒ Ⓓ Ⓔ 10 Ⓐ Ⓑ Ⓒ Ⓓ Ⓔ

Verbal Analogies Test 2

1 Ⓐ Ⓑ Ⓒ Ⓓ Ⓔ   3 Ⓐ Ⓑ Ⓒ Ⓓ Ⓔ   5 Ⓐ Ⓑ Ⓒ Ⓓ Ⓔ   7 Ⓐ Ⓑ Ⓒ Ⓓ Ⓔ   9 Ⓐ Ⓑ Ⓒ Ⓓ Ⓔ
2 Ⓐ Ⓑ Ⓒ Ⓓ Ⓔ   4 Ⓐ Ⓑ Ⓒ Ⓓ Ⓔ   6 Ⓐ Ⓑ Ⓒ Ⓓ Ⓔ   8 Ⓐ Ⓑ Ⓒ Ⓓ Ⓔ 10 Ⓐ Ⓑ Ⓒ Ⓓ Ⓔ

Verbal Analogies Test 3

1 Ⓐ Ⓑ Ⓒ Ⓓ   3 Ⓐ Ⓑ Ⓒ Ⓓ   5 Ⓐ Ⓑ Ⓒ Ⓓ   7 Ⓐ Ⓑ Ⓒ Ⓓ   9 Ⓐ Ⓑ Ⓒ Ⓓ
2 Ⓐ Ⓑ Ⓒ Ⓓ   4 Ⓐ Ⓑ Ⓒ Ⓓ   6 Ⓐ Ⓑ Ⓒ Ⓓ   8 Ⓐ Ⓑ Ⓒ Ⓓ 10 Ⓐ Ⓑ Ⓒ Ⓓ

Verbal Analogies Test 4

1 Ⓐ Ⓑ Ⓒ Ⓓ   3 Ⓐ Ⓑ Ⓒ Ⓓ   5 Ⓐ Ⓑ Ⓒ Ⓓ   7 Ⓐ Ⓑ Ⓒ Ⓓ   9 Ⓐ Ⓑ Ⓒ Ⓓ
2 Ⓐ Ⓑ Ⓒ Ⓓ   4 Ⓐ Ⓑ Ⓒ Ⓓ   6 Ⓐ Ⓑ Ⓒ Ⓓ   8 Ⓐ Ⓑ Ⓒ Ⓓ 10 Ⓐ Ⓑ Ⓒ Ⓓ

Posttest

1 Ⓐ Ⓑ Ⓒ Ⓓ   3 Ⓐ Ⓑ Ⓒ Ⓓ   5 Ⓐ Ⓑ Ⓒ Ⓓ   7 Ⓐ Ⓑ Ⓒ Ⓓ   9 Ⓐ Ⓑ Ⓒ Ⓓ
2 Ⓐ Ⓑ Ⓒ Ⓓ   4 Ⓐ Ⓑ Ⓒ Ⓓ   6 Ⓐ Ⓑ Ⓒ Ⓓ   8 Ⓐ Ⓑ Ⓒ Ⓓ 10 Ⓐ Ⓑ Ⓒ Ⓓ

VERBAL ANALOGIES

Introductory Pretest and Answers

Directions: In these pretest questions, each of the two CAPITALIZED words have a certain relationship to each other. Following the capitalized words are other pairs of words. Select the lettered pair that is related in the same way as the two CAPITALIZED words are related to each other. Mark the answer sheet with the letter of that answer.

Allow 4 minutes for this pretest.

1. JAIL : CRIME
   (A) judge : criminal
   (B) freedom : bird
   (C) prison : thief
   (D) cemetery : death

2. MUMBLE : TALK
   (A) orate : speak
   (B) scrawl : write
   (C) bumble : buzz
   (D) yell : shout

3. FRAGILE : CRACK
   (A) potent : enervate
   (B) irreducible : reduce
   (C) frangible : strengthen
   (D) pliable : bend

4. KEY : DOOR
   (A) combination : safe
   (B) keyhole : porthole
   (C) lock : key
   (D) opening : closing

5. MICROMETER : BURETTE
   (A) microscope : germ
   (B) microbe : thorn
   (C) chemist : biologist
   (D) ruler : dropper

6. FULLBACK : FIELD
   (A) halfback : infield
   (B) baseball : stadium
   (C) boxer : ring
   (D) medal : winner

7. PROTEIN : MEAT
   (A) calories : cream
   (B) energy : sugar
   (C) cyclamates : diet
   (D) starch : potatoes

8. CHARCOAL : WOOD
   (A) peat : carbon
   (B) electricity : gas
   (C) fire : ash
   (D) coke : coal

9. APIARY : BEE
   (A) aquarium : swim
   (B) sky : airplane
   (C) aviary : bird
   (D) zoo : animal

10. PAPER : REAM
    (A) eggs : dozen
    (B) newspaper : stand
    (C) apartment : room
    (D) candy : wrapper

END OF PRETEST

Answer Key for Pretest

1. D	3. D	5. D	7. D	9. C
2. B	4. A	6. C	8. D	10. A

Study Hints

On examinations verbal analogy questions are designed so either one or two words are missing, and you are then given choices from which you must determine the exact relationship between words. Solving an analogy problem involves the ability to detect relationships.

Rules

Two important steps to analogy success:

1. Determine the relationship between the first two words.

2. Find the same relationship among the choices which follow the first two words.

1. Determining the relationship.

Directions: Each question consists of two words which have some relationship to each other. From the five following pairs of words, select the one which is related in the same way as the words of the CAPITALIZED pair:

ARC : CIRCLE
(A) segment : cube
(B) angle : triangle
(C) tangent : circumference
(D) circle : cube
(E) cube : square

An arc is part of a circle, just as an angle is part of a triangle. The other choices do not bear this PART : WHOLE relationship. Therefore, (B) is correct.

With the foregoing line of reasoning, you probably eliminated choice (A) immediately. Choice (B) seemed correct. Did you give it *final* acceptance without considering the remaining choices? In this analogy question, choice (B), as it turned out, was the correct choice. However, let us change the question slightly:

ARC : CIRCLE
(A) segment : cube
(B) angle : triangle
(C) tangent : circumference
(D) circle : cube
(E) line : square

With the change in the (E) choice, (B) is no longer the best answer. An angle is a particular part of a triangle, but a line is any part of the perimeter of a square as is the arc any part of a circle, so (E) is best.

This illustration should caution you not to "jump to conclusions." Consider *all* choices carefully before you reach your conclusion.

2. Use the word that shows the relationship.

The best way of determining the correct answer to an analogy question is to provide the word or phrase which shows the relationship that exists between the first two words. Let us illustrate with the following analogy question:

CLOCK : TIME
(A) hour : latitude
(B) thermometer : temperature
(C) weather : climate
(D) tide : moon

The problem here is to determine which choice has the same relationship that *clock* has to *time*. Let's provide the word or phrase which shows the relationship between *clock* and *time*. The word is *measures*. Choice (B), then is the correct answer since a thermometer *measures* temperature.

You will find many of the choices which you are given have some relationship to the opening pair. You must be sure to select that choice which bears a relationship most closely approximating the relationship between the opening two words.

CLOCK : TIME—THERMOMETER :
- (A) hour
- (B) degrees
- (C) temperature
- (D) climate
- (E) weather

Or the question may be put:

CLOCK : TIME as THERMOMETER is to
- (A) hour
- (B) degrees
- (C) temperature
- (D) climate
- (E) weather

The problem is to determine which of the lettered words has the same relationship to *thermometer* as time has to *clock*.

The best way of determining the correct answer is to provide the word or phrase which shows the relationship between these words. In the example above, the word is *measure*. However, this may not be enough. The analogy must be correct in exact meaning. Climate or weather would not be exact enough. Temperature (C) is the correct answer.

You will find many of the choices you have to select from have some relationship to the third word. You must select the answer with a relationship most closely approximating the relationship between the first two words.

What the Analogy Question Measures

The ability to detect the exact nature of the relationship between words is a function of your intelligence. The analogy question tests your ability to see a relationship between words and to apply this relationship to other words. In a sense, the verbal analogy test is a vocabulary test, but it is also a test of your ability to analyze meanings, to think things out, to see the relationship between ideas and words, and to avoid confusion of ideas.

Three Forms of the Analogy Question

Type 1.

From the four (or five) pairs of words which follow, you are to select the pair which is related in the same way as the words of the CAPITALIZED pair.

Example:

SPELLING : PUNCTUATION
- (A) pajamas : fatigue
- (B) powder : shaving
- (C) bandage : cut
- (D) biology : physics

SPELLING and PUNCTUATION are elements of the mechanics of English; BIOLOGY and PHYSICS are two of the subjects that make up the field of

science. The other choices do not possess this PART : PART relationship. Therefore, (D) is the correct answer.

Type 2.

Another popular form is the type in which two words are followed by a third word. The latter is related to one word in a group of choices in the same way the first two words are related.

Example:

WINTER is to SUMMER as COLD is to
- (A) wet
- (B) future
- (C) warm
- (D) freezing

WINTER and SUMMER bear an opposite relationship. COLD and WARM have the same type of opposite relationship. Therefore, (C) is the correct answer.

Type 3.

Still another analogy form is that in which one of the four relationship elements is not specified. From choices offered, regardless of the position, you are to select the one choice which completes the relationship with the other three items.

Example:

SUBMARINE : FISH as _____ : BIRD
- (A) kite
- (B) limousine
- (C) feather
- (D) chirp

Both a SUBMARINE and a FISH are found in the water; both a KITE and BIRD are customarily seen in the air. Consequently, (A) is the correct answer.

Kinds of Analogies

Following are typical kinds of analogies that appear on examinations. Practice these and check your answers at the end to see which kind you need additional practice in.

1. **PURPOSE**
   GLOVE : BALL
   - (A) hook : fish
   - (B) winter : weather
   - (C) game : pennant
   - (D) stadium : seats

2. **CAUSE AND EFFECT**
   RACE : FATIGUE
   - (A) track : athlete
   - (B) ant : bug
   - (C) fast : hunger
   - (D) walking : running

3. **PART TO WHOLE**
   SNAKE : REPTILE
   - (A) patch : thread
   - (B) removal : snow
   - (C) struggle : wrestle
   - (D) hand : clock

4. **PART TO PART**
   GILL : FIN
   - (A) tube : antenna
   - (B) instrument : violin
   - (C) sea : fish
   - (D) salad : supper

5. **ACTION TO OBJECT**
   KICK : FOOTBALL
   - (A) kill : bomb
   - (B) break : pieces
   - (C) question : team
   - (D) smoke : pipe

6. **OBJECT TO ACTION**
   STEAK : BROIL
   - (A) bread : bake
   - (B) food : sell
   - (C) wine : pour
   - (D) sugar : spill

7. **SYNONYM**
   ENORMOUS : HUGE
   - (A) rogue : rock
   - (B) muddy : unclear
   - (C) purse : kitchen
   - (D) black : white

8. **ANTONYM**
   PURITY : EVIL
   - (A) suavity : bluntness
   - (B) north : climate
   - (C) angel : horns
   - (D) boldness : victory

9. **PLACE**
   MIAMI : FLORIDA
   - (A) Chicago : United States
   - (B) New York : Albany
   - (C) United States : Chicago
   - (D) Albany : New York

10. **DEGREE**
    WARM : HOT
    (A) glue : paste
    (B) climate : weather
    (C) fried egg : boiled egg
    (D) bright : genius

11. **CHARACTERISTIC**
    IGNORANCE : POVERTY
    (A) blood : wound
    (B) money : dollar
    (C) schools : elevators
    (D) education : stupidity

12. **SEQUENCE**
    SPRING : SUMMER
    (A) Thursday : Wednesday
    (B) Wednesday : Monday
    (C) Monday : Sunday
    (D) Wednesday : Thursday

13. **GRAMMATICAL**
    RESTORE : CLIMB
    (A) segregation : seem
    (B) into : nymph
    (C) tearoom : although
    (D) overpower : seethe

14. **NUMERICAL**
    4 : 12
    (A) 10 : 16
    (B) 9 : 27
    (C) 3 : 4
    (D) 12 : 6

15. **ASSOCIATION**
    DEVIL : WRONG
    (A) color : sidewalk
    (B) slipper : state
    (C) ink : liquid
    (D) picture : bed

Answer Key for Sample Questions

1. A	4. A	7. B	10. D	13. D
2. C	5. D	8. A	11. A	14. B
3. D	6. A	9. D	12. D	15. C

Tests and Answers

The answer key will be found at the end of these practice tests.

Verbal Analogies Test 1

Directions: In these test questions, each of the two CAPITALIZED words have a certain relationship to each other. Following the capitalized words are other pairs of words. Select the lettered pair that is related in the same way as the two CAPITALIZED words are related to each other. Mark the answer sheet with the letter of that answer.

Allow 4 minutes for this test.

1. CONDONE : OFFENSE
    (A) punish : criminal
    (B) mitigate : penitence
    (C) overlook : aberration
    (D) mistake : judgment
    (E) ignore : loyalty

2. SPASM : PAIN
    (A) flash : light
    (B) respite : thought
    (C) tender : touch
    (D) pinch : taste
    (E) sound : noise

3. VIBRATION : SOUND
    (A) gravity : pull
    (B) watercolor : paint
    (C) drowning : accident
    (D) worm : reptile
    (E) drought : plague

4. BRASS : COPPER
    (A) zinc : iron
    (B) pewter : tin
    (C) lead : gold
    (D) mercury : antimony
    (E) silicon : carbon

5. OXYGEN : GASEOUS
    (A) feather : light
    (B) mercury : fluid
    (C) iron : heavy
    (D) sand : grainy
    (E) mountain : high

6. AGILE : ACROBAT
    (A) grease : mechanic
    (B) peanuts : vendor
    (C) plant : fruit
    (D) eloquent : orator
    (E) fast : car

7. CAT : MOUSE
    (A) bird : worm
    (B) dog : tail
    (C) trap : cheese
    (D) hide : seed
    (E) light : kerosene

8. POWER : BATTERY
    (A) vitamins : metabolism
    (B) recuperation : well
    (C) exercise : strength
    (D) automobile : engine
    (E) heat : kerosene

9. VANILLA : BEAN
    (A) tabasco : stem
    (B) chili : flower
    (C) mint : fruit
    (D) ginger : root
    (E) sage : berry

10. ENERGY : DISSIPATE
    (A) ring : finger
    (B) atom : split
    (C) food : heat
    (D) money : squander
    (E) gas : generate

END OF TEST

Verbal Analogies Test 2

Allow 4 minutes for this test.

1. NOSE : FACE
    (A) ring : finger
    (B) stem : root
    (C) knob : door
    (D) shoe : foot
    (E) leaf : vine

2. PECK : BUSHEL
    (A) pound : ounce
    (B) quart : gallon
    (C) pint : cup
    (D) minute : second
    (E) rod : yard

3. RIFLE : SOLDIER
    (A) bow : arrow
    (B) sword : knight
    (C) horse : cowboy
    (D) canteen : marine
    (E) lock : robber

4. DEER : VENISON
    (A) pig : hog
    (B) sheep : mutton
    (C) lamb : veal
    (D) duck : roast
    (E) beef : stew

5. DEPRESSION : UNEMPLOYMENT
    (A) legislation : lobbying
    (B) emaciation : unhappiness
    (C) capital : interest
    (D) deterioration : rust
    (E) recession : inefficiency

6. INTEGER : DECIMAL
    (A) 100 : 10
    (B) 1 : 0
    (C) decimal : fraction
    (D) whole number : fraction
    (E) 100 : percent

7. ICING : CAKE
   (A) veneer : table
   (B) frost : lake
   (C) pastry : bakery
   (D) slicing : rake
   (E) paper : page

8. CHALK : CHALKBOARD
   (A) door : handle
   (B) table : chair
   (C) ink : paper
   (D) dog : tail
   (E) type : paint

9. THROW : BALL
   (A) shoot : trigger
   (B) pat : dog
   (C) mew : cat
   (D) boil : shell
   (E) finish : furniture

10. FRUGAL : ECONOMICAL
   (A) fragile : solid
   (B) prosperous : wealthy
   (C) fruitful : sunny
   (D) regal : comical
   (E) spendthrift : miser

END OF TEST

Verbal Analogies Test 3

Allow 4 minutes for this test.

1. WRITE : LETTER
   (A) pen : paper
   (B) drink : glass
   (C) act : part
   (D) rhyme : poem

2. PLANTS : COAL
   (A) water : fish
   (B) air : gas
   (C) animals : oil
   (D) rocks : heat

3. INTIMIDATE : FEAR
   (A) maintain : satisfaction
   (B) astonish : wonder
   (C) soothe : concern
   (D) feed : hunger

4. CELEBRATE : MARRIAGE
   (A) lament : bereavement
   (B) report : injury
   (C) announce : birthday
   (D) face : penalty

5. NEGLIGENT : REQUIREMENT
   (A) careful : position
   (B) cautions : injury
   (C) remiss : duty
   (D) easy : hard

6. GOBBLE : TURKEY
   (A) poison : cobra
   (B) bark : tree
   (C) trunk : elephant
   (D) twitter : bird

7. LAWYER : CLIENT
   (A) student : pupil
   (B) mechanic : automobile
   (C) doctor : patient
   (D) stenographer : letters

8. STOVE : KITCHEN
   (A) sink : bathroom
   (B) window : bedroom
   (C) television : living room
   (D) trunk : attic

9. MARGARINE : BUTTER
   (A) cream : milk
   (B) lace : cotton
   (C) egg : chicken
   (D) nylon : silk

10. GAZELLE : SWIFT
   (A) horse : slow
   (B) wolf : sly
   (C) swan : graceful
   (D) lion : tame

END OF TEST

Verbal Analogies Test 4

Allow 4 minutes for this test.

1. FEATHERS : PLUCK
   - (A) goose : duck
   - (B) garment : weave
   - (C) car : drive
   - (D) wool : shear

2. ORANGE : MARMALADE
   - (A) tomato : ketchup
   - (B) potato : vegetable
   - (C) jelly : jam
   - (D) cake : picnic

3. CIRCLE : SPHERE
   - (A) square : triangle
   - (B) balloon : jet plane
   - (C) heaven : hell
   - (D) wheel : orange

4. ANIMOSITY : HOSTILITY
   - (A) colossal : picayune
   - (B) pique : emotion
   - (C) pandemonium : hullabaloo
   - (D) hyperbole : poetry

5. SPEEDY : GREYHOUND
   - (A) sluggish : sloth
   - (B) clever : fox
   - (C) animate : animal
   - (D) innocent : lamb

6. SATURNINE : MERCURIAL
   - (A) Saturn : Venus
   - (B) redundant : wordy
   - (C) heavenly : starry
   - (D) adagio: allegro

7. BANISH : APOSTATE
   - (A) reward : traitor
   - (B) request : assistance
   - (C) welcome : ally
   - (D) avoid : truce

8. OPEN : SECRETIVE
   - (A) mystery : detective
   - (B) tunnel : toll
   - (C) forthright : snide
   - (D) better : best

9. FIN : FISH
   - (A) engine : auto
   - (B) propeller : airplane
   - (C) five : ten
   - (D) teeth : stomach

10. GOLD : PROSPECTOR
    - (A) medicine : doctor
    - (B) prayer : preacher
    - (C) wood : carpenter
    - (D) clue : detective

END OF TEST

Answer Key for Practice Tests

Verbal Analogy Test 1

1.	C	3.	D	5.	B	7.	A	9.	D
2.	A	4.	B	6.	D	8.	E	10.	D

Verbal Analogy Test 2

1.	C	3.	B	5.	D	7.	A	9.	B
2.	B	4.	B	6.	D	8.	C	10.	B

Verbal Analogy Test 3

1.	C	3.	B	5.	C	7.	C	9.	D
2.	C	4.	A	6.	D	8.	A	10.	C

Verbal Analogy Test 4

1.	D	3.	D	5.	A	7.	C	9.	B
2.	A	4.	C	6.	D	8.	C	10.	D

Posttest and Answers

Directions: In these posttest questions, each of the two CAPITALIZED words have a certain relationship to each other. Following the capitalized words are other pairs of words. Select the lettered pair that is related in the same way as the two CAPITALIZED words are related to each other. Mark the answer sheet with the letter of that answer. Correct answers to this posttest will be found at the end of this test.

Allow 4 minutes for this posttest.

1. GUN : HOLSTER
   (A) shoe : soldier
   (B) sword : warrior
   (C) ink : pen
   (D) books : school bag

2. HYBRID : THOROUGHBRED
   (A) steel : iron
   (B) fruit : tree
   (C) stallion : mare
   (D) highbrow : lowbrow

3. SMILE : AMUSEMENT
   (A) yell : game
   (B) yawn : ennui
   (C) wink : vulgarity
   (D) cry : havoc

4. DEBATE : SOLILOQUY
   (A) crowd : mob
   (B) Hamlet : Macbeth
   (C) Lincoln : Douglas
   (D) group : hermit

5. CUP : DRINK
   (A) plate : supper
   (B) plate : fork
   (C) plate : dine
   (D) plate : silver

6. HYDRO : WATER
   (A) helio : sun
   (B) Reno : divorce
   (C) canto : score
   (D) Hires : root beer

7. PEACH : BEET
   (A) grape : apple
   (B) potato : tomato
   (C) currant : raspberry
   (D) cherry : radish

8. MODESTY : ARROGANCE
   (A) debility : strength
   (B) cause : purpose
   (C) passion : emotion
   (D) finance : Wall Street

9. DEVIL : WRONG
   (A) color : sidewalk
   (B) slipper : state
   (C) ink : writing
   (D) picture : bed

10. FOOD : HUNGER
    (A) sleep : night
    (B) sleep : dream
    (C) sleep : weariness
    (D) sleep : health

END OF POSTTEST

Answer Key for Posttest

1. D	3. B	5. C	7. D	9. C
2. A	4. D	6. A	8. A	10. C

Spelling and Word Usage Answer Sheet

Pretest

1 Ⓐ Ⓑ Ⓒ Ⓓ   6 Ⓐ Ⓑ Ⓒ Ⓓ   11 Ⓐ Ⓑ Ⓒ Ⓓ   16 Ⓐ Ⓑ Ⓒ Ⓓ   21 Ⓐ Ⓑ Ⓒ Ⓓ
2 Ⓐ Ⓑ Ⓒ Ⓓ   7 Ⓐ Ⓑ Ⓒ Ⓓ   12 Ⓐ Ⓑ Ⓒ Ⓓ   17 Ⓐ Ⓑ Ⓒ Ⓓ   22 Ⓐ Ⓑ Ⓒ Ⓓ
3 Ⓐ Ⓑ Ⓒ Ⓓ   8 Ⓐ Ⓑ Ⓒ Ⓓ   13 Ⓐ Ⓑ Ⓒ Ⓓ   18 Ⓐ Ⓑ Ⓒ Ⓓ   23 Ⓐ Ⓑ Ⓒ Ⓓ
4 Ⓐ Ⓑ Ⓒ Ⓓ   9 Ⓐ Ⓑ Ⓒ Ⓓ   14 Ⓐ Ⓑ Ⓒ Ⓓ   19 Ⓐ Ⓑ Ⓒ Ⓓ   24 Ⓐ Ⓑ Ⓒ Ⓓ
5 Ⓐ Ⓑ Ⓒ Ⓓ   10 Ⓐ Ⓑ Ⓒ Ⓓ   15 Ⓐ Ⓑ Ⓒ Ⓓ   20 Ⓐ Ⓑ Ⓒ Ⓓ   25 Ⓐ Ⓑ Ⓒ Ⓓ

Spelling and Word Usage Test 1

1 Ⓐ Ⓑ Ⓒ Ⓓ   3 Ⓐ Ⓑ Ⓒ Ⓓ   5 Ⓐ Ⓑ Ⓒ Ⓓ   7 Ⓐ Ⓑ Ⓒ Ⓓ   9 Ⓐ Ⓑ Ⓒ Ⓓ
2 Ⓐ Ⓑ Ⓒ Ⓓ   4 Ⓐ Ⓑ Ⓒ Ⓓ   6 Ⓐ Ⓑ Ⓒ Ⓓ   8 Ⓐ Ⓑ Ⓒ Ⓓ   10 Ⓐ Ⓑ Ⓒ Ⓓ

Spelling and Word Usage Test 2

1 Ⓐ Ⓑ Ⓒ Ⓓ   3 Ⓐ Ⓑ Ⓒ Ⓓ   5 Ⓐ Ⓑ Ⓒ Ⓓ   7 Ⓐ Ⓑ Ⓒ Ⓓ   9 Ⓐ Ⓑ Ⓒ Ⓓ
2 Ⓐ Ⓑ Ⓒ Ⓓ   4 Ⓐ Ⓑ Ⓒ Ⓓ   6 Ⓐ Ⓑ Ⓒ Ⓓ   8 Ⓐ Ⓑ Ⓒ Ⓓ   10 Ⓐ Ⓑ Ⓒ Ⓓ

Spelling and Word Usage Test 3

1 Ⓐ Ⓑ Ⓒ   3 Ⓐ Ⓑ Ⓒ   5 Ⓐ Ⓑ Ⓒ   7 Ⓐ Ⓑ Ⓒ   9 Ⓐ Ⓑ Ⓒ
2 Ⓐ Ⓑ Ⓒ   4 Ⓐ Ⓑ Ⓒ   6 Ⓐ Ⓑ Ⓒ   8 Ⓐ Ⓑ Ⓒ   10 Ⓐ Ⓑ Ⓒ

Spelling and Word Usage Test 4

1 Ⓐ Ⓑ Ⓒ Ⓓ Ⓔ   3 Ⓐ Ⓑ Ⓒ Ⓓ Ⓔ   5 Ⓐ Ⓑ Ⓒ Ⓓ Ⓔ   7 Ⓐ Ⓑ Ⓒ Ⓓ Ⓔ   9 Ⓐ Ⓑ Ⓒ Ⓓ Ⓔ
2 Ⓐ Ⓑ Ⓒ Ⓓ Ⓔ   4 Ⓐ Ⓑ Ⓒ Ⓓ Ⓔ   6 Ⓐ Ⓑ Ⓒ Ⓓ Ⓔ   8 Ⓐ Ⓑ Ⓒ Ⓓ Ⓔ   10 Ⓐ Ⓑ Ⓒ Ⓓ Ⓔ

Posttest

1 Ⓐ Ⓑ Ⓒ Ⓓ   6 Ⓐ Ⓑ Ⓒ Ⓓ   11 Ⓐ Ⓑ Ⓒ Ⓓ   16 Ⓐ Ⓑ Ⓒ Ⓓ   21 Ⓐ Ⓑ Ⓒ Ⓓ
2 Ⓐ Ⓑ Ⓒ Ⓓ   7 Ⓐ Ⓑ Ⓒ Ⓓ   12 Ⓐ Ⓑ Ⓒ Ⓓ   17 Ⓐ Ⓑ Ⓒ Ⓓ   22 Ⓐ Ⓑ Ⓒ Ⓓ
3 Ⓐ Ⓑ Ⓒ Ⓓ   8 Ⓐ Ⓑ Ⓒ Ⓓ   13 Ⓐ Ⓑ Ⓒ Ⓓ   18 Ⓐ Ⓑ Ⓒ Ⓓ   23 Ⓐ Ⓑ Ⓒ Ⓓ
4 Ⓐ Ⓑ Ⓒ Ⓓ   9 Ⓐ Ⓑ Ⓒ Ⓓ   14 Ⓐ Ⓑ Ⓒ Ⓓ   19 Ⓐ Ⓑ Ⓒ Ⓓ   24 Ⓐ Ⓑ Ⓒ Ⓓ
5 Ⓐ Ⓑ Ⓒ Ⓓ   10 Ⓐ Ⓑ Ⓒ Ⓓ   15 Ⓐ Ⓑ Ⓒ Ⓓ   20 Ⓐ Ⓑ Ⓒ Ⓓ   25 Ⓐ Ⓑ Ⓒ Ⓓ

SPELLING AND WORD USAGE

Introductory Pretest and Answers

Directions: In this pretest all words but one of each group are spelled correctly. Indicate the misspelled word in each group. Mark the answer sheet with the letter of that answer.

Allow 5 minutes for this pretest.

1. (A) throat
   (B) within
   (C) sheets
   (D) twentyfive

2. (A) scarf
   (B) settlement
   (C) sweep
   (D) wondring

3. (A) propertey
   (B) pennies
   (C) gathering
   (D) eastern

4. (A) copper
   (B) ribben
   (C) considered
   (D) further

5. (A) character
   (B) oasis
   (C) governer
   (D) lonely

6. (A) anounce
   (B) local
   (C) grasshopper
   (D) across

7. (A) historical
   (B) dustey
   (C) kindly
   (D) humbug

8. (A) current
   (B) comunity
   (C) cement
   (D) calves

9. (A) changeing
   (B) explained
   (C) diameter
   (D) consent

10. (A) sword
    (B) reckord
    (C) signed
    (D) taste

Directions: This part offers four suggested spellings for each word. Choose the spelling you know to be correct. Mark the answer sheet with the letter of that answer.

11. (A) sufficiantly
    (B) sufisiently
    (C) sufficiently
    (D) suficeintly

12. (A) intelligence
    (B) inteligence
    (C) intellegence
    (D) intelegence

13. (A) abundence
    (B) abundance
    (C) abundants
    (D) abundents

71

14. (A) elemanate
    (B) elimenate
    (C) elliminate
    (D) eliminate

15. (A) resonance
    (B) resonnance
    (C) resonence
    (D) reasonance

Directions: Each of the following four word groups contain only one word that is spelled correctly. Choose the correctly spelled word and mark the answer sheet with the letter of that answer.

16. (A) constrictive
    (B) proposel
    (C) partisipated
    (D) desision

17. (A) comtroller
    (B) inadequasy
    (C) resolusion
    (D) promotion

18. (A) progresive
    (B) dependent
    (C) secsion
    (D) reciepts

19. (A) seperate
    (B) speciallized
    (C) funshions
    (D) publicity

20. (A) instrament
    (B) vicinity
    (C) offical
    (D) journale

Word Usage

Directions: In each of the following groups of sentences, select the one sentence where a word is used *incorrectly*. Mark the answer sheet with the letter of that answer.

21. (A) In order to save valuable time in the meeting, the minutes were abridged.
    (B) Everyone except Amy attended the conference.
    (C) The director was given access to the confidential records.
    (D) It took years of experience to become adapt at public speaking.

22. (A) The newest addition of *Practice for Clerical, Typing, and Stenographic Tests* was written by a new author.
    (B) I have always done my best as a secretary.
    (C) The New Jersey coast is subject to mild winters but heavy fog.
    (D) The procedures and policies were changed for the new governor's benefit.

23. (A) When I got married on February 2, I approached the altar with great joy.
    (B) The prosecutor made inflammable statements to the jury.
    (C) The supervisor and the staff became very upset and quarreled.
    (D) We tried to run the race backward.

24. (A) I have a great deal of capital in reserve for my old age.
    (B) I am by vocation a teacher and a counselor.
    (C) I received many complements on my outstanding typing and shorthand skills and techniques.
    (D) Considering all her past problems, she gave a creditable performance in handling the new word processing center.

25. (A) In spite of his handicap, he went on to be the best typist we had.
    (B) The new receptionist is just as good as the previous one.
    (C) A disinterested supervisor, he was inclined to forget all the good things his subordinates did.
    (D) The word processors complained that the manager's handwriting was illegible.

END OF PRETEST

Answer Key for Pretest

1. D	6. A	11. C	16. A	21. D
2. D	7. B	12. A	17. D	22. A
3. A	8. B	13. B	18. B	23. B
4. B	9. A	14. D	19. D	24. C
5. C	10. B	15. A	20. B	25. C

Study Hints

In most cases the first impression a potential employer receives of you is from your application form and resume. Misspelled words will draw attention away from your application. The employer will lose faith in your skills and ability as a worker.

Spelling is not a simple matter. You have to work to improve your spelling skills. When taking these tests, there are certain things you should and should not do. Here are some tips for you:

1. Know your weak areas and review the rules in those areas. The Pretest will aid you in this determination.

2. Memorize certain spelling words rather than trying to apply a rule. Look at the word, spell the word aloud, write the word down, and attempt to use it in a sentence. Finally keep repeating the spelling until it is memorized.

3. Read a rule slowly, be sure you understand it, read it again. Then spell words that pertain to the rule. Check your answers with the dictionary. Spell the word aloud again.

4. When spelling words, sound words out for the proper pronunciation. Many times you mispronounce a word, thus, you misspell the word. Proper pronunciation is a key to spelling improvement.

5. Learn to use a dictionary, a synonym and homonym book, and other spelling reference sources. However, don't let it become a time waster by looking up every single word.

6. Keep a notebook or card file of words you often misspell. Review the list and use the words daily. You can summarize the steps necessary to improve your spelling by practicing the following:

   • Look at the word.
   • Visualize the word in your mind.
   • Pronounce the word (look in the dictionary if you are not sure of its pronunciation).
   • Listen to your pronunciation.
   • Know the definition of the word.
   • Spell the word several times to yourself and also aloud.
   • Write a sentence using the word.
   • Check the word with the dictionary.
   • Practice using the word.

7. Learn to spell words that are technical or pertain specifically to your field.

8. Underline or circle the parts of words which trip you up. Focus your attention on those areas of the word.

9. As you read pay close attention to the spelling of words.

10. Know the pitfalls of:

    a. One-word versus two-word usage.

    b. One-word, two-word, or hyphenated-word usage.

11. Watch for changes in pronunciation without changes in spelling. Also watch for changes in both spelling and pronunciation.

Rules

The importance of spelling cannot be overestimated. Bad spelling is a principal cause of failure among candidates.

We offer here a brief set of rules based on our study of many tests. After working through the same examination questions with these rules in mind, start your list of any words which you have misspelled.

1. *EI or IE Rule*

   I before *e* (Examples: friend, belief, niece, grieve) except after *c* (Examples: deceit, ceiling, conceive, receipt) or when sounded like *a* (Examples: vein, neighbor, feign, heinous, or weigh).

   Exceptions: either, neither, height, foreign, sovereign, forfeit, seize, counterfeit, financier, leisure, weird

   Note: This rule also does not apply when the *ie* combination is pronounced *eh* even when it immediately follows the letter *c*. (Examples: ancient, conscience, deficient, efficient, proficient)

2. *S or ES Rule*

   a. Add *es* to words ending is *s, sh, x,* or *z*. (Examples: rush, rushes; success, successes; bench, benches; fox, foxes)

   b. Add *es* to words ending in *y* after a consonant, but first change *y* to *i*. (Examples: try, tries, tried; lady, ladies)

   c. However, if the word ends in *y* preceded by a vowel, keep the *y* when adding a suffix. (Examples: day, days; attorney, attorneys; spray, sprayer)

   d. Add *s* alone to any other word where *s* is needed. (Examples: boy, boys; chair, chairs; friend, friends; want, wants; decide, decides)

3. *L or LL Rule*

   a. Final *l* is doubled following a single vowel in words of one syllable. (Examples: fall, bell, sill, doll, hull)

   b. Final *l* is doubled following a single vowel in words of more than one syllable, when the stress falls on the last syllable. (Examples: recall, fortell, distill)

   c. Final *l* is single following more than one vowel in words of one syllable. (Examples: bail, real, soul, feel)

   d. Final *l* is single following more than one vowel in words of more than one syllable when the stress falls on the last syllable. (Examples: conceal, ideal, detail)

   e. Final *l* is single following a single vowel in words of more than one syllable, when the stress falls before the last syllable. (Examples: marginal, alcohol, dismal)

4. *Suffixes*

   a. Suffixes are syllables that are added to a base word to make a new word. Some common suffixes are: *-able, -ed, -er, -ful, -ing, -less, -ly, -ment, -ness, -ous*. You can add suffixes to many base words without changing the spelling of either the base word or the suffix. However, some base words must be changed slightly before you can add the suffix. Here are some rules for these changes.

   b. In words ending in silent *e*, drop the *e* when the suffix begins with a vowel. (Examples: dine + ing = dining; locate + ion = location; use + able = usable; like, likeable; love, loved; trace, tracer)

   Exceptions: Words ending in *ce* and *ge* retain *e* before *-able* and *-ous* in order to retain the soft sounds of *c* and *g*. (Examples: peace + able = peaceable; courage + ous = courageous)

   c. Drop the *e* in words ending in *dge*. (Examples: judge, judgment; acknowledge, acknowledging)

   d. Silent *e* is usually kept before a suffix beginning with a consonant. (Examples: care + less = careless; late + ly = lately; one + ness = oneness; game + ster = gamester)

   Exceptions: truly, duly, awful, argument, wholly, ninth, mileage, dyeing, acreage, canoeing, judgment)

   e. In words ending in *y*, change *y* to *i* after a consonant in words of more than one syllable. (Examples: lovely, lovelier; accompany, accompaniment; tardy, tardiness; levy, levied)

   f. In words ending in *y* keep the *y* when you add *ing*. (Examples: rally, rallying; fry, frying; reply, replying; destroy, destroying)

   g. In words ending in *y* keep the *y* when you add *ly* or *ness* to words of one syllable. (Examples: sly, slyly, slyness; shy, shyly, shyness; dry, dryly, dryness)

Exceptions: day, daily; lay, laid; say, said; slay, slain; pay, paid

h. In words ending in a consonant, double the final consonant if it follows a single vowel in words of one syllable, and if the suffix begins with a vowel. (Examples: fat, fatter; hop, hopping; wed, wedding)

i. In words ending in a consonant, double the final consonant if it follows a single vowel in words of more than one syllable and the stress remains on the same syllable. (Examples: refer, referred; control, controlled)

1. A word ending in *er* or *ury* doubles the *r* in the past tense if the word is accented on the last syllable. (Examples: occur, occurred; prefer, preferred; transfer, transferred)

2. A word ending in *er* does not double the *r* in the past tense if the accent falls on other than the last syllable. (Examples: answer, answered; offer, offered; differ, differed)

3. When *-full* is added to the end of a noun to form an adjective, the final *l* is dropped. (Examples: cheerful, cupful, hopeful)

5. *Prefixes*
Prefixes are syllables that go in front of a base word to make a new word. Some common prefixes are: *ab-, ac-, ad-, bi-, com-, con-, de-, dis-, en-, for-, fore-, il-, im-, in-, ir-, mal-, mis-, over-, per-, pro-, re-, under-*. You can add any prefix to a base word without changing the spelling of either the prefix or the base word.

a. All words beginning with *over-* are one word. (Examples: overcast, overcharge, overhear)

b. All words with the prefix *self-* are hyphenated. (Examples: self-control, self-defense, self-evident)

6. *Possessives*

a. Contractions should not be confused with possessive pronouns. (Examples: *it's* means *it is*; *you're* means *you are*)

b. Don't use apostrophes with possessive or relative pronouns. (Examples: their, your, whose)

c. If singular or plural noun does not end in *s*, add apostrophe and *s*. (Examples: lawyer, laywer's)

d. If singular or plural noun does end in *s*, add apostrophe. (Examples: Jesus' workers)

7. *Other Rules*

a. *-cede, -ceed, -sede* (Except for supersede, exceed, proceed, and succeed, all words having this sound end in *-cede*.)

b. Numbers from twenty-one to ninety-nine are hyphenated.

c. *Percent* is never hyphenated.

d. Words ending in *c* add *k* before an ending beginning with *e*, *i*, or *y*. (Example: colic, colicky)

e. The letter *q* is always followed by *u*. (Examples: *qu*iz, bou*qu*et, ac*qu*ire)

Tests and Answers

The answer key will be found at the end of these practice tests.

After you have finished each test, check your answers against the correct answers at the end of this section. Make a list of words you missed and plan to study those words by writing them over again until you have no difficulty with them.

Spelling and Word Usage Test 1

Directions: In this test all words but one of each group are spelled correctly. Indicate the misspelled word in each group. Mark the answer sheet with the letter of that answer.

Allow 3 minutes for this test.

1. (A) executive
   (B) rainbow
   (C) irigation
   (D) multiply

2. (A) acquarium
   (B) aerial
   (C) liver
   (D) delivered

3. (A) final
   (B) deoderant
   (C) foundation
   (D) hardships

4. (A) salary
   (B) weekley
   (C) swallow
   (D) wilderness

5. (A) seashore
   (B) chopping
   (C) recieving
   (D) lipstick

6. (A) inkwell
   (B) boxing
   (C) hickery
   (D) major

7. (A) quantities
   (B) toilet
   (C) spinach
   (D) servent

8. (A) ragged
   (B) subtract
   (C) pajammas
   (D) paragraph

9. (A) unhappy
   (B) zebra
   (C) sheperd
   (D) percent

10. (A) sucessful
    (B) tuberculosis
    (C) splash
    (D) playground

END OF TEST

Spelling and Word Usage Test 2

Directions: This test gives four suggested spellings for each word listed. Choose the spelling you know to be correct. Mark the answer sheet with the letter of that answer.

Allow 3 minutes for this test.

1. (A) transeint
   (B) transient
   (C) trancient
   (D) transent

2. (A) heratage
   (B) heritage
   (C) heiritage
   (D) heretage

3. (A) exibition
   (B) exhibition
   (C) exabition
   (D) exhebition

4. (A) iniatiative
   (B) enitiative
   (C) initative
   (D) initiative

5. (A) similiar
   (B) simmilar
   (C) similar
   (D) simuler

6. (A) anticipate
   (B) antisipate
   (C) anticapate
   (D) antisapate

7. (A) conscious
   (B) consious
   (C) conscius
   (D) conseous

8. (A) referance
   (B) refference
   (C) referese
   (D) reference

9. (A) paralell
   (B) parellel
   (C) parellell
   (D) parallel

10. (A) auxillary
    (B) auxilliary
    (C) auxilary
    (D) auxiliary

END OF TEST

Spelling and Word Usage Test 3

Directions: Write the letter of the word in parentheses that correctly completes each of the following sentences. Mark the answer sheet with the letter of that answer.

Allow 3 minutes for this test.

1. The new director decided to pay a (A) personal, (B) personnel visit.

2. John finally (A) passed, (B) past the clerk-typist examination.

3. The stenographer Grade 1 (A) precedes, (B) proceeds the stenographer Grade 2 title.

4. The (A) principal, (B) principle of the thing is that everyone must perform satisfactorily.

5. Everyone was there (A) accept, (B) expect, (C) except him.

6. A full (A) complement, (B) compliment of staff attended the speaker's session.

7. Everyone needs a (A) recipe, (B) receipt for success.

8. The (A) cite, (B) sight, (C) site for our new office building is located on Route 18.

9. In case (A) their, (B) there, (C) they're going, please make sure they have reservations.

10. The clerical supervisor will schedule a (A) biannual, (B) biennial meeting in July and in January.

END OF TEST

Spelling and Word Usage Test 4

Directions: Each question consists of four words, any or all of which may be spelled incorrectly. On your answer sheet mark:

(A) if ONLY ONE word is misspelled.
(B) if TWO WORDS are misspelled.
(C) if THREE WORDS are misspelled.
(D) if ALL FOUR WORDS are misspelled.
(E) if NO WORDS are misspelled.

1. professor
   weight
   realize
   warrent

2. sabbatical
   accomplish
   occasionally
   publicity

3. associate
   bookeeping
   carefully
   bureau

4. dictater
   beforhand
   deceit
   yacht

5. accidently
    supervisor
    efficiently
    regrettable

6. bureau
    manifest
    scheduling
    medieval

7. auxilary
    machinary
    distorsion
    blamable

8. synthesis
    harrassment
    exemplify
    nevertheless

9. receiveable
    bankrupcy
    chronological
    marital

10. facsimile
    requisition
    liability
    hearth

END OF TEST

Answer Key for Practice Tests

Spelling and Word Usage Test 1

1.	C	3.	B	5.	C	7.	D	9.	C
2.	A	4.	B	6.	C	8.	C	10.	A

Spelling and Word Usage Test 2

1.	B	3.	B	5.	C	7.	A	9.	D
2.	B	4.	D	6.	A	8.	D	10.	D

Spelling and Word Usage Test 3

1.	A	3.	A	5.	C	7.	A	9.	C
2.	A	4.	B	6.	A	8.	C	10.	A

Spelling and Word Usage Test 4

1.	A	3.	B	5.	A	7.	C	9.	B
2.	E	4.	B	6.	E	8.	A	10.	E

Posttest and Answers

Spelling

Directions: In this posttest all words but one of each group are spelled correctly. Indicate the misspelled word in each group. Mark the answer sheet with the letter of that answer.

Allow 5 minutes for this posttest.

1. (A) capitol
   (B) imminent
   (C) esctasy
   (D) patient

2. (A) panicy
   (B) feudal
   (C) yacht
   (D) bureau

3. (A) arouse
   (B) embarass
   (C) journal
   (D) lucrative

4. (A) actually
   (B) chauffer
   (C) emphasis
   (D) proletarian

5. (A) marital
   (B) symmetrical
   (C) scissors
   (D) apologetice

6. (A) description
   (B) heinous
   (C) plagiarism
   (D) bookeeping

7. (A) existence
   (B) ingenuous
   (C) publisity
   (D) regrettable

8. (A) sophamore
   (B) colossal
   (C) correlation
   (D) medallion

9. (A) beatitude
   (B) proceeding
   (C) equiped
   (D) concede

10. (A) accessible
    (B) complacency
    (C) forfeit
    (D) mischevious

Directions: This part offers four suggested spellings for each word. Choose the spelling you know to be correct. Mark the answer sheet with the letter of that answer.

11. (A) accumalation
    (B) accumulation
    (C) acumulation
    (D) accumullation

12. (A) consumation
    (B) consummation
    (C) consumeation
    (D) consomation

13. (A) disapearance
    (B) disappearance
    (C) disappearense
    (D) disappearence

14. (A) interuption
    (B) interruption
    (C) interrupsion
    (D) interrupcion

15. (A) acquiesence
    (B) acquiescence
    (C) aquiescense
    (D) acquiesance

Directions: Each of the following four word groups contain only one word that is spelled correctly. Choose the correctly spelled word and mark the answer sheet with the letter of that answer.

16. (A) authority
    (B) simlar
    (C) refering
    (D) preferebly

17. (A) suficient
    (B) wheather
    (C) actueally
    (D) minimum

18. (A) volentary
    (B) syllabus
    (C) embodiing
    (D) pertanent

19. (A) simplified
    (B) comunity
    (C) enfasis
    (D) advant

20. (A) approppriate
    (B) expedient
    (C) adopshun
    (D) satisfactarily

Word Usage

Directions: In each of the following groups of sentences, select the one sentence where a word is used *incorrectly*. Mark the answer sheet with the letter of that answer.

21. (A) Tomorrow, each of my staff will be responsible for coordinating a portion of the training conference.
    (B) The summers in Pittsburgh produced very loud lightening bolts.
    (C) Regardless of the weather, we are going to the annual meeting.
    (D) This is the least desirable of the alternatives.

22. (A) The secretary who fell over the typewriter cord is lying down.
    (B) The director told us that this is the latest procedures manual.
    (C) Plan 2 will supersede plan 3.
    (D) She used illness as an alibi for her lateness.

23. (A) The Attorney General is persecuting the individuals who violated the rules and regulations.
    (B) The card dealer swindled the gamblers out of their money.
    (C) If you're ready, you can leave the job now.
    (D) Employees who lose their speed will be transferred out of the center.

24. (A) Get in touch with me in a few days.
    (B) The homeowner is anxious to sell the house as soon as possible.
    (C) The receptionist opposed the new policy as a matter of principle.
    (D) I shall try to do better the next time I take shorthand.

25. (A) For the sake of office safety, we divided the work among the ten individuals.
    (B) Rose made fewer errors than the other principal clerks.
    (C) The child aggravates me with his constant questions.
    (D) When the high school cooperative student graduates from high school, she will work full time.

END OF POSTTEST

Answer Key For Posttest

1. C	6. D	11. B	16. A	21. B
2. A	7. C	12. B	17. D	22. D
3. B	8. A	13. B	18. B	23. A
4. B	9. C	14. B	19. A	24. B
5. D	10. D	15. B	20. B	25. C

English Grammar Answer Sheet

Pretest

1 Ⓐ Ⓑ Ⓒ Ⓓ	5 Ⓐ Ⓑ Ⓒ Ⓓ	9 Ⓐ Ⓑ Ⓒ Ⓓ	13 Ⓐ Ⓑ Ⓒ Ⓓ	17 Ⓐ Ⓑ Ⓒ Ⓓ
2 Ⓐ Ⓑ Ⓒ Ⓓ	6 Ⓐ Ⓑ Ⓒ Ⓓ	10 Ⓐ Ⓑ Ⓒ Ⓓ	14 Ⓐ Ⓑ Ⓒ Ⓓ	18 Ⓐ Ⓑ Ⓒ Ⓓ
3 Ⓐ Ⓑ Ⓒ Ⓓ	7 Ⓐ Ⓑ Ⓒ Ⓓ	11 Ⓐ Ⓑ Ⓒ Ⓓ	15 Ⓐ Ⓑ Ⓒ Ⓓ	19 Ⓐ Ⓑ Ⓒ Ⓓ
4 Ⓐ Ⓑ Ⓒ Ⓓ	8 Ⓐ Ⓑ Ⓒ Ⓓ	12 Ⓐ Ⓑ Ⓒ Ⓓ	16 Ⓐ Ⓑ Ⓒ Ⓓ	20 Ⓐ Ⓑ Ⓒ Ⓓ

English Grammar Test 1

1 Ⓐ Ⓑ Ⓒ Ⓓ	3 Ⓐ Ⓑ Ⓒ Ⓓ	5 Ⓐ Ⓑ Ⓒ Ⓓ	7 Ⓐ Ⓑ Ⓒ Ⓓ	9 Ⓐ Ⓑ Ⓒ Ⓓ
2 Ⓐ Ⓑ Ⓒ Ⓓ	4 Ⓐ Ⓑ Ⓒ Ⓓ	6 Ⓐ Ⓑ Ⓒ Ⓓ	8 Ⓐ Ⓑ Ⓒ Ⓓ	10 Ⓐ Ⓑ Ⓒ Ⓓ

English Grammar Test 2

1 Ⓐ Ⓑ Ⓒ Ⓓ	3 Ⓐ Ⓑ Ⓒ Ⓓ	5 Ⓐ Ⓑ Ⓒ Ⓓ	7 Ⓐ Ⓑ Ⓒ Ⓓ	9 Ⓐ Ⓑ Ⓒ Ⓓ
2 Ⓐ Ⓑ Ⓒ Ⓓ	4 Ⓐ Ⓑ Ⓒ Ⓓ	6 Ⓐ Ⓑ Ⓒ Ⓓ	8 Ⓐ Ⓑ Ⓒ Ⓓ	10 Ⓐ Ⓑ Ⓒ Ⓓ

English Grammar Test 3

1 Ⓐ Ⓑ Ⓒ Ⓓ	3 Ⓐ Ⓑ Ⓒ Ⓓ	5 Ⓐ Ⓑ Ⓒ Ⓓ	7 Ⓐ Ⓑ Ⓒ Ⓓ	9 Ⓐ Ⓑ Ⓒ Ⓓ
2 Ⓐ Ⓑ Ⓒ Ⓓ	4 Ⓐ Ⓑ Ⓒ Ⓓ	6 Ⓐ Ⓑ Ⓒ Ⓓ	8 Ⓐ Ⓑ Ⓒ Ⓓ	10 Ⓐ Ⓑ Ⓒ Ⓓ

English Grammar Test 4

1 Ⓐ Ⓑ Ⓒ Ⓓ	3 Ⓐ Ⓑ Ⓒ Ⓓ	5 Ⓐ Ⓑ Ⓒ Ⓓ	7 Ⓐ Ⓑ Ⓒ Ⓓ	9 Ⓐ Ⓑ Ⓒ Ⓓ
2 Ⓐ Ⓑ Ⓒ Ⓓ	4 Ⓐ Ⓑ Ⓒ Ⓓ	6 Ⓐ Ⓑ Ⓒ Ⓓ	8 Ⓐ Ⓑ Ⓒ Ⓓ	10 Ⓐ Ⓑ Ⓒ Ⓓ

Posttest

1 Ⓐ Ⓑ Ⓒ Ⓓ	5 Ⓐ Ⓑ Ⓒ Ⓓ	9 Ⓐ Ⓑ Ⓒ Ⓓ	13 Ⓐ Ⓑ Ⓒ Ⓓ	17 Ⓐ Ⓑ Ⓒ Ⓓ
2 Ⓐ Ⓑ Ⓒ Ⓓ	6 Ⓐ Ⓑ Ⓒ Ⓓ	10 Ⓐ Ⓑ Ⓒ Ⓓ	14 Ⓐ Ⓑ Ⓒ Ⓓ	18 Ⓐ Ⓑ Ⓒ Ⓓ
3 Ⓐ Ⓑ Ⓒ Ⓓ	7 Ⓐ Ⓑ Ⓒ Ⓓ	11 Ⓐ Ⓑ Ⓒ Ⓓ	15 Ⓐ Ⓑ Ⓒ Ⓓ	19 Ⓐ Ⓑ Ⓒ Ⓓ
4 Ⓐ Ⓑ Ⓒ Ⓓ	8 Ⓐ Ⓑ Ⓒ Ⓓ	12 Ⓐ Ⓑ Ⓒ Ⓓ	16 Ⓐ Ⓑ Ⓒ Ⓓ	20 Ⓐ Ⓑ Ⓒ Ⓓ

ENGLISH GRAMMAR

Introductory Pretest and Answers

Directions: In each of the following pretest groups of sentences, select the one sentence that is grammatically *incorrect*. Mark the answer sheet with the letter of that sentence. Correct answers to this pretest will be found at the end of this examination.

Allow 8 minutes for this pretest.

1. (A) The information was extremely difficult to obtain.
   (B) It was him who made the supper.
   (C) The reservation for Mark and her was made too late.
   (D) There are a lot of movies listed in the paper.

2. (A) Mother said that neither Father nor Uncle Jack is going.
   (B) The bush, as well as the tree, is covered with snow.
   (C) Who did John ask to go to the store?
   (D) The Board of Education is meeting on Friday morning.

3. (A) Both Mary and Carol received her assignments from the clerical supervisor.
   (B) Text editors are used on most word processors.
   (C) The invitation asked for John and me to attend the dinner.
   (D) The supervisor as well as the employees took a lunch break.

4. (A) The pineapple upside down cake was freshly baked.
   (B) Jenny ran in the local marathon at Mercer County Park.
   (C) The buses and cars has been parked at the special casino parking garage.
   (D) Mark Spitz won seven gold medals in the Olympics.

5. (A) The law prescribed when and to whom the tax should be paid.
   (B) Each monitor must have his or her room prepared for the trainees by 8 a.m.
   (C) Finally management and labor has agreed to postpone the strike.
   (D) The new employees eagerly reported for work.

6. (A) The manager recommended that we purchase new data processing equipment.
   (B) My favorite training classes are typing, shorthand, and English grammar.
   (C) The pots and pans have been wrapped for moving.
   (D) One of the secretaries left their attache case on the receptionist's desk.

7. (A) Each of the contestants have a chance to win the Miss America contest which is held in Atlantic City, New Jersey.
   (B) A dependent clause never stands alone.
   (C) A limerick is a short poem with a catchy rhyme.
   (D) In the directions, the same idea is expressed four different ways.

8. (A) "Which" is a pronoun that causes reference problems.
   (B) I gave $5 to the file clerk whom I think will repay me next week.
   (C) Adverbs should be placed near the words they modify.
   (D) Select the lettered pair that is related to the noun.

9. (A) Clauses should be placed near the word they modify.
   (B) Many years ago I had seen Wilson in the opera.
   (C) The subject of a verb is in the nominative case.
   (D) A subject consisting of two or more nouns joined by a coordinating conjunction takes a plural verb.

10. (A) James is one of those stenographers who is always late to work.
    (B) Adjectives are classified according to the work they do.
    (C) When she graduates college she will be twenty-one.
    (D) He invited Marlene and me to dinner.

11. (A) They are as old as we.
    (B) She is older than he.
    (C) Whom do you suppose paid us a call?
    (D) Punish whoever is the guilty party.

12. (A) It is I.
    (B) Can it be they?
    (C) Can it be he?
    (D) It would be impossible for you and I.

13. (A) This is the death wish for we individualists.
    (B) She had a great deal of trouble with the supervisor of the store.
    (C) I, who am older, know better than you.
    (D) The man's hair is blond.

14. (A) Is there any criticism of Michael's going?
    (B) Everybody tried their hardest.
    (C) He has but one aim, to succeed.
    (D) Everything would have turned out right if she had only waited.

15. (A) She doesn't like to involve herself in such activity.
    (B) The use of liquor is dangerous.
    (C) The attorney general, as well as many of his aides, has been involved in the investigation.

    (D) Either the fifth or the seventh of the courses they have laid open are to be accepted.

16. (A) The fighting and wrestling of the two men is excellent.
    (B) The worst feature of the play was the abominable actors.
    (C) There are, at present, a child and two dogs.
    (D) The subject of a verb is in the nominative case, even when the verb is remote, or understood.

17. (A) Guard against the improper attraction of *who* into the objective case by intervening expressions.
    (B) When he saw me he says his prayers.
    (C) It is usually awkward and slightly illogical to attribute possession to inanimate objects.
    (D) Do not use *don't* in the third person singular.

18. (A) Mounting the curb, the empty car crossed the sidewalk and came to rest against a building.
    (B) Memorize the principal parts of the most common irregular verbs.
    (C) He spoke slow and careful.
    (D) The generic term *business owner* should be used in place of businessman.

19. (A) She looks beautiful.
    (B) The man gave the wrong reply.
    (C) The boy answered incorrectly.
    (D) He always has and will do it.

20. (A) We hoped you would have come to the party that we had last Saturday night.
    (B) I intended to go.
    (C) In the parlor my cousin kept a collection of animals which he had shot.
    (D) He said that Earth is a planet.

END OF PRETEST

Answer Key for Pretest

1.	B	5.	C	9.	B	13.	A	17.	B
2.	C	6.	D	10.	C	14.	B	18.	C
3.	A	7.	A	11.	C	15.	D	19.	D
4.	C	8.	B	12.	D	16.	A	20.	A

Study Hints

The most important skill a clerk, typist, or stenographer must have is a good command of the English language. You must be able to understand, interpret, and use good English both in the office and at home. It is important that you master both the written and oral forms of communication. Many office employees are promoted because of their ability to use correct grammar. Employees must use the correct usage in letters, memos, reports, forms, conferences, staff meetings, training classes, on the telephone, and in basic communications with subordinates, peers, and superiors.

Be sure to practice and pay attention to both the spoken and written language. Read books, magazines, and newspapers, and notice correct English usage. Listen to commentators, public speakers, television, and radio personalities.

When you read, attempt to proofread the material carefully. When you read the newspaper, advertisements, etc., mark errors, look up rules, and practice saying sentences correctly.

Rules

Here are a few major rules. Check with an English grammar book for additional ones.

1. A verb should agree in number with the subject, not with the predicate noun or pronoun. A singular subject needs a singular verb; a plural subject needs a plural verb.

2. A subject consisting of two or more nouns joined by *and* takes a plural verb.

3. A subject consisting of two or more nouns joined by *or* or *nor* takes a singular verb.

4. When the conjunctions *either/or* and *neither/nor* are used, the number of the verb agrees with the number of the last subject.

5. Nouns that are collective units usually take a singular verb if they are understood as one; if they are understood as individuals within the group, use a plural verb.

6. A pronoun agrees with its antecedent in person, number, gender, and case.

7. *Each, either, neither, anyone, anybody, somebody, someone, every, everyone, one, no one,* and *nobody* are singular. Each of these words takes a singular verb.

8. The words *who* and *whoever* take the nominative (the subject of the verb) case; and the words *whom* and *whomever* take the objective (the object of the verb) case.

9. Nouns or pronouns connected by a form of the verb *to be* should always be in the nominative case. However, a pronoun that is the object of a preposition or of a transitive verb must be in the objective case.

Sample Question and Explanation

Example: The most acceptable of the following sentences is:

- (A) It is us you meant.
- (B) It is us whom you meant.
- (C) It is us who you meant.
- (D) It is we you meant.

Since *us* is in the objective case, the only correct choice is (D). The nominative or subject case follows the verb "to be." Nominative pronouns are: *I, we, she, he, they, it,* and *who.*

Tests and Answers

The answer key will be found at the end of these practice tests.

English Grammar Test 1

Directions: In each of the following groups of sentences, select the one sentence that is grammatically *incorrect.* Mark the answer sheet with the letter of that sentence.

Allow 4 minutes for this test.

1. (A) He would not accept of my hospitality.
   (B) He is a pleasant person until challenged.
   (C) We still do not know to whom to turn.
   (D) Try to locate the revised financial report.

2. (A) Why should he mind your having taken the stapler?
   (B) If you are really interested in a clerical career, pursue it.
   (C) While May was on vacation, Mrs. Smith was the supervisor.
   (D) All staff members declined except she.

3. (A) Nothing is to be gained by further discussion.
   (B) No applicant has received a second chance.
   (C) The arrangement of the desks and chairs give the department a neat appearance.
   (D) No employee considered to be indispensable will be assigned to the new office.

4. (A) Be sure your staff fully understands these principles and rules.
   (B) The employer found that each of the applicants were qualified to perform the duties of assistant sales manager.
   (C) The key for my desk has been hidden.
   (D) Not one of my employees has chosen to take a vacation in July.

5. (A) You look well today, after this illness.
   (B) In our office in the morning, things really begin to happen.
   (C) The stenographic notes must have fallen behind the secretary's desk.
   (D) The office manager invited you to set down for a minute.

Directions: In each of the following groups of sentences select the sentence that is most acceptable. Mark the answer sheet with the letter of that sentence.

6. (A) This is entirely between you and he.
   (B) This is completely between you and he.
   (C) This is between you and him.
   (D) This is between he and you.

7. (A) As I said, neither of them are guilty.
   (B) As I said neither of them are guilty.
   (C) As I said neither of them is guilty.
   (D) As I said, neither of them is guilty.

8. (A) What kind of a substance is insulin?
   (B) What kind of substance is insulin?
   (C) What kind a substance is insulin?
   (D) Of what kind of substance is insulin?

9. (A) Your pen is different from mine.
   (B) Your pen is different to mine.
   (C) Your pen is different than mine.
   (D) Your pen is different then mine.

10. (A) The lawyer's client sat besides him.
    (B) The client sat beside his lawyer.
    (C) The client sat besides his lawyer.
    (D) His client sat besides him.

END OF TEST

English Grammar Test 2

Allow 4 minutes for this test.

1. (A) Regardless of the weather, work will be held tomorrow.
   (B) We tried to quickly finish the work.
   (C) People get used to prosperity easily.
   (D) This is Miss Moore, the manager I was telling you about.

2. (A) The informal discussions that took place during lunch was fun.
   (B) The invoice shows $14.79 for merchandise purchased in June.
   (C) Amiable persons make amicable adjustments.
   (D) Being unable to hear the speaker, we fell asleep.

3. (A) Every member of our staff has derived much pleasure from it.
   (B) Swimming is more enjoyable than dancing.
   (C) Neither one of the employees are eligible for the promotion to senior clerk typist.
   (D) The scouts walked a mile farther than they had intended.

4. (A) These mistakes have been brought to the supervisor's attention.
   (B) No folder has been took out of the file room.
   (C) A letter to the Commissioner should have been mailed yesterday.
   (D) The personnel director will sign the papers later.

5. (A) Whom did you see first, Mrs. Smith or Miss White?
   (B) She is a good secretary who I believe will be an asset to you.
   (C) This is the section whom the supervisor said would complete the final report.
   (D) I have been talking to the new accountant whom you hired yesterday.

6. (A) Give us correspondence secretaries credit for preparing an office reference manual.
   (B) Dan and he work for the Director of Administration.
   (C) We word processing operators were asked to work overtime.
   (D) It might be her who is arriving late each morning and leaving early each day.

7. (A) The original, as well as the copies, are to be dated with the new stamper.
   (B) In the reception area there is an oak desk, as well as other attractive pieces.
   (C) Neither one of the new employees is applying herself.
   (D) Which employee is farther down the promotion line?

8. (A) Office clerks have other duties besides filing.
   (B) The new employee is different from the retired one.
   (C) Our new location has not only been painted but also newly decorated.
   (D) When you finish the report, please see that the memoranda is signed and sent.

9. (A) The new salary scale is retroactive to October 1.
    (B) The supervisor can easily find the mistakes.
    (C) Are the new automated typewriter ribbons different than those formerly purchased?
    (D) Mary did not receive her pay check this month.

10. (A) There are in the back of the office two doors for emergency exits.
    (B) Can you give me a list of the employees who is retiring this year?
    (C) There are a limited number of reference books available.
    (D) To whom did you award the promotion?

END OF TEST

English Grammar Test 3

Allow 4 minutes for this test.

1. (A) Tell the secretary what she wants to know.
    (B) The accident damaged the typewriters, but no one was hurt.
    (C) The clerical supervisor informed the employees of what their responsibilities are and to whom they should report.
    (D) At the staff meeting, against who were objections raised?

2. (A) The typists are seated in the large office, and the stenographers is in the small one.
    (B) Each supervisor is very well qualified to take over.
    (C) Our new typist promised that she will arrive early tomorrow.
    (D) Only one person in our department of hundreds is to be honored.

3. (A) The director could not help reveal the nature of the information.
    (B) The new clerical supervisor grew impatient with the subordinates.
    (C) It seemed strange that the assistant didn't have no messages.
    (D) The result of the clerk typist examination is between them and me.

4. (A) We persuaded both him and his assistant.
    (B) One of the highlights of the new training program was his discussing the power of advertising.
    (C) We expected her to be correct in her stenographic work.
    (D) The selected clerk typist or stenographer are going to the new training program with the head of personnel.

5. (A) The monitor or the printer need adjustment.
    (B) These reports have been word processed by our new employees.
    (C) Neither this memorandum nor that one justifies more input.
    (D) Disks, computers, and auxiliary equipment were ordered for us.

6. (A) A typist and stenographer is needed as a new employee.
    (B) The only time the supervisor admonished the employee was when he made a serious error.
    (C) The annual report remains incomplete.
    (D) A few days' delay could hurt our profits.

7. (A) The popularity of magazines directed to business and government has increased tremendously.
    (B) No one except you and me believe these magazines are worth reading.
    (C) The Lotus 1 2 3 project is on the desk in the outer office.
    (D) Miss Vansant is the secretary whom we hired.

8. (A) Miss Wilson is the kind of typist every supervisor needs.
    (B) Whom did you say we should hire—the person who takes dictation or the person with the college degree?
    (C) People should be hired on the basis of their personalities instead of their education.
    (D) If you were me, would you accept these letters with errors?

9. (A) People's efficiency on the job are seriously affected by illness and worry.
    (B) When people are seriously ill for a prolonged period, their jobs are usually affected.
    (C) I could hardly believe that people's jobs are so influenced by psychological factors.
    (D) There is a feeling that he and Mr. Smith, our director, have met secretly.

10. (A) Almost everyone gets to the office earlier than she.
    (B) The committees' reports has always followed the report from the treasury.
    (C) The treasurer is the most intelligent person we have in our organization.
    (D) If it weren't for the treasurer's report, the meeting would have been over by five o'clock.

END OF TEST

English Grammar Test 4

Allow 4 minutes for this test.

1. (A) Our office planned its budget for next year.
    (B) I'll never agree to John changing his job.
    (C) Either of the methods is OK with us.
    (D) There are a number of points we must evaluate.

2. (A) By January 1, she shall have chosen a new supervisor.
    (B) The number of typewritten errors is not a shock to the supervisor.
    (C) She is the only one of the word processors who agrees with the manager.
    (D) Neither Laurie nor Monica will begin her vacation the last week of August.

3. (A) Mrs. Elder is one of those individuals whom you can count on.
    (B) I proposed that Maria be elected president of the club.
    (C) That was a great bunch of people.
    (D) Neither Mrs. Crider nor her clerk typists have any time to work overtime.

4. (A) Special training is needed by us data-entry workers.
    (B) It should make no difference either to them or to us if you attend the seminar on Saturday.
    (C) A supervisor who is fair and equal to all employees is respected.
    (D) Can you prove to your supervisor that Jim is as considerate as him?

5. (A) To what satellite office were the two ac-
        countants, Tim and Joyce, transferred?
    (B) The two outstanding employees have
        been Jeffrey and she.
    (C) The clerk typists, Sundai and her, typed
        all handwritten correspondence.
    (D) I have been meeting with the new em-
        ployee whom personnel hired last week.

6. (A) To whom should the memo be ad-
        dressed?
    (B) Miss Chalmers asked, ''Who did you in-
        vite to the staff meeting?''
    (C) Mr. Hrees is the one who decided to call
        the meeting to order.
    (D) You are one of twenty individuals whom
        we have nominated for a promotion.

7. (A) A number of our offices has partitions.
    (B) Both Betty and Milo are eligible to re-
        ceive promotional recommendations.
    (C) Neither the typist nor the stenographer
        knows what happened to the edict.
    (D) The director and assistant director of our
        department are in the office today.

8. (A) The manager doesn't hire new em-
        ployees, personnel does.
    (B) Each of the letters and envelopes have
        been sent.
    (C) Would you object to my leaving the of-
        fice early?
    (D) Rose and I are inputting all correspon-
        dence on the electronic typewriter.

9. (A) There are a number of proposals we must
        consider before we make our decision.
    (B) A ream of bond paper was shipped to us
        last week.
    (C) Every one of the accountants attend col-
        lege.
    (D) The memo was carefully written and its
        meaning is clear, concise, and correct.

10. (A) I like this new kind of computer.
    (B) The paper lies on the floor.
    (C) Neither they nor the supervisor feels the
        decision was fair.
    (D) Which do you think is best, a word
        processor or a computer?

END OF TEST

Answer Key for Practice Tests

English Grammar Test 1

1.	A	3.	C	5.	D	7.	D	9.	A
2.	D	4.	B	6.	C	8.	B	10.	B

English Grammar Test 2

1.	B	3.	C	5.	C	7.	A	9.	C
2.	A	4.	B	6.	D	8.	D	10.	B

English Grammar Test 3

1.	D	3.	C	5.	A	7.	B	9.	A
2.	A	4.	D	6.	A	8.	D	10.	B

English Grammar Test 4

1.	B	3.	C	5.	C	7.	A	9.	C
2.	A	4.	D	6.	B	8.	B	10.	D

Posttest and Answers

Directions: In each of the following groups of sentences, select the one sentence that is grammatically INCORRECT. Mark the answer sheet with the letter of that sentence. Correct answers to this posttest will be found at the end of this test.

Allow 8 minutes for this posttest.

1. (A) The employees were all ready to see it.
    (B) The supervisor began to realize how much she had done.
    (C) Mary expect to leave the office at once for a new job.
    (D) He, not I, is the one to decide.

2. (A) Since Mary, with her two assistants, is to be with us, it might be better to rent a cab.
    (B) He asked you and I to attend the spring semester.
    (C) When you answer the telephone, simply say, "This is she speaking."
    (D) We were not entirely dissatisfied with the office conditions.

3. (A) If it had been her, she would have accepted the position.
    (B) I can but do my best in the office.
    (C) I cannot help comparing him with his predecessor, John.
    (D) Neither Tom nor Harry was present for the meeting.

4. (A) It was superior in every way to the book previously used.
    (B) His testimony today is different from that of yesterday.
    (C) I like this kind of paper better than any other.
    (D) They wrote to her and I about six months ago about the lost letter.

5. (A) Who did they say won the basketball game?
    (B) All three of us—you, him, and she—will attend the conference in Dallas.
    (C) The question of who should be supervisor arose.
    (D) As long as you are ready, you may as well start promptly.

6. (A) A new set of rules and regulations has been made.
    (B) Reports that the union strike has been settled were circulated yesterday.
    (C) Neither the stenographer nor the clerk typist has returned from lunch.
    (D) We, Sandra and myself, are in charge of the filing section.

7. (A) The reason the new supervisor was unsuccessful was that he had fewer responsibilities.
    (B) New York is larger than any other city in New York State.
    (C) The department consists of three distinct sections, of which the personnel one is by far the larger.
    (D) We would rather die than surrender.

8. (A) Honor as well as profit are to be gained by these studies.
    (B) It has been functioning as a graduate school ever since.
    (C) Neither Miss Ondo nor Miss Macari was present for the training session.
    (D) The supervisor regarded whomever the manager honored with disdain.

9. (A) Neither his words nor his action was justifiable.
    (B) We all prefer those other kinds of candy.
    (C) We read each other's letters.
    (D) There was often disagreement as to whom was the better Shakespearean actor, Evans or Gielgud.

10. (A) The door opens, and in walk Jane and Lena.
    (B) The supervisor and myself were the only ones at the gathering.
    (C) Never before have I seen anyone who has the skill Marlene has when she types.
    (D) Can it be said that the better of the two automatic typewriters is less expensive?

11. (A) They was once together in the same group.
    (B) Microfilm is a method of copying records in miniature.
    (C) Because of increasing need for information, many organizations are using microfilm as a solution to some of their information problems.
    (D) Since microfilm cannot be viewed by the naked eye, the micro images are magnified by a reader or reader printer.

12. (A) Each year there are more and more time-saving machines designed and manufactured to lighten the work load.
    (B) Some are simply improved versions of standard equipment such as the typewriter; others are recent additions to the modern office such as miniature electronic calculators.
    (C) Before selecting a new piece of equipment, careful consideration should have been given to various important factors.
    (D) Some of these factors are nature of the work, economy, speed, quality of output, operator training time, and service maintenance cost.

13. (A) Some collators will count, line up, and staple pages, in addition to arranging them in order.
    (B) Collators come in all sizes and some are high-speed, fully-automated models.
    (C) If an office staff sends out large amounts of mail to the same people, an addressing machine will eliminate the need to type labels on envelopes.
    (D) Folding machines folds paper for mailing; they are used for bulk mailings.

14. (A) Inserting machines carry the mailing operation further by gathering the folded letters or papers and inserting them into envelopes.
    (B) Some machines will even have collect letters, fold and insert them, seal the envelopes, and stamp and address them.
    (C) If there is a need to get a lot of correspondence out, it is possible to rent a postage meter.

    (D) A postage meter automatically seals envelopes and stamps them.

15. (A) A duplex envelope is an envelope composed of two sections securely fastened together so they become one mailing piece.
    (B) This type of envelope makes it possible for a first-class letter to be delivered simultaneously with third- or fourth-class matter and yet not requires payment of the much higher first-class postage rate on the entire mailing.
    (C) Neither of his employees is more knowledgeable than he.
    (D) Neither Mr. Wayne nor Mr. Waynes was sure he had the right bill.

16. (A) The proofreading of material typed from copy is performed more accurately and more speedily when two persons perform this work as a team.
    (B) The person who did not do the typing should read aloud the original copy while the person who did the typing should check the reading against the typed copy.
    (C) The reader should speak slow and distinct.
    (D) When reading figures, the reader should speak very slowly and repeat the figures, using a different grouping of numbers when repeating the figures.

17. (A) Work measurement concerns accomplishment or productivity.
    (B) It has to do with results; it does not deal with the amount of energy used up, although in many cases this may be in direct proportion to the work output.
    (C) Work measurement not only helps a manager to distribute work loads fairly, but it also enables him/her to define work success in actual units, evaluate employee performance, and determine where corrective help is needed.
    (D) Work measurement are accomplished by measuring the amount produced, measuring the time spent to produce it, and relating the two.

18. (A) Anne is the woman whom I think is best suited for the clerical supervisory position.
    (B) I hope this is the end of the snow season.
    (C) First-class postage is paid only on the letter which goes in the small compartment, third- or fourth-class postage being paid on the contents of the larger compartment.
    (D) The larger compartment generally has an ungummed flap or clasp for sealing.

19. (A) My whole staff, including the security guard, think you should represent us at the conference.
    (B) I am willing to accept any excuse my secretary gave for being late this morning.
    (C) Everyone expects her to score the highest on the examination.
    (D) The monthly report lay where the file clerk left it.

20. (A) One of the products our company manufactures is computer paper.
    (B) This is a major problem every word processing supervisor faces with their staff.
    (C) I feel very bad about what happened in the Department of Health and Education.
    (D) Who do you think will become the next President of the United States?

END OF POSTTEST

Answer Key for Posttest

1.	C	5.	B	9.	D	13.	D	17.	D
2.	B	6.	D	10.	B	14.	B	18.	A
3.	A	7.	C	11.	A	15.	B	19.	A
4.	D	8.	A	12.	C	16.	C	20.	B

Reading Comprehension Answer Sheet

Pretest

1 Ⓐ Ⓑ Ⓒ Ⓓ Ⓔ   4 Ⓐ Ⓑ Ⓒ Ⓓ Ⓔ   7 Ⓐ Ⓑ Ⓒ Ⓓ Ⓔ   9 Ⓐ Ⓑ Ⓒ Ⓓ Ⓔ   11 Ⓐ Ⓑ Ⓒ Ⓓ Ⓔ
2 Ⓐ Ⓑ Ⓒ Ⓓ Ⓔ   5 Ⓐ Ⓑ Ⓒ Ⓓ Ⓔ   8 Ⓐ Ⓑ Ⓒ Ⓓ Ⓔ   10 Ⓐ Ⓑ Ⓒ Ⓓ Ⓔ   12 Ⓐ Ⓑ Ⓒ Ⓓ Ⓔ
3 Ⓐ Ⓑ Ⓒ Ⓓ Ⓔ   6 Ⓐ Ⓑ Ⓒ Ⓓ Ⓔ

Reading Comprehension Test 1

1 Ⓐ Ⓑ Ⓒ Ⓓ Ⓔ   3 Ⓐ Ⓑ Ⓒ Ⓓ Ⓔ   5 Ⓐ Ⓑ Ⓒ Ⓓ Ⓔ   7 Ⓐ Ⓑ Ⓒ Ⓓ Ⓔ   9 Ⓐ Ⓑ Ⓒ Ⓓ Ⓔ
2 Ⓐ Ⓑ Ⓒ Ⓓ Ⓔ   4 Ⓐ Ⓑ Ⓒ Ⓓ Ⓔ   6 Ⓐ Ⓑ Ⓒ Ⓓ Ⓔ   8 Ⓐ Ⓑ Ⓒ Ⓓ Ⓔ   10 Ⓐ Ⓑ Ⓒ Ⓓ Ⓔ

Reading Comprehension Test 2

1 Ⓐ Ⓑ Ⓒ Ⓓ Ⓔ   5 Ⓐ Ⓑ Ⓒ Ⓓ Ⓔ   9 Ⓐ Ⓑ Ⓒ Ⓓ Ⓔ   13 Ⓐ Ⓑ Ⓒ Ⓓ Ⓔ   17 Ⓐ Ⓑ Ⓒ Ⓓ Ⓔ
2 Ⓐ Ⓑ Ⓒ Ⓓ Ⓔ   6 Ⓐ Ⓑ Ⓒ Ⓓ Ⓔ   10 Ⓐ Ⓑ Ⓒ Ⓓ Ⓔ   14 Ⓐ Ⓑ Ⓒ Ⓓ Ⓔ   18 Ⓐ Ⓑ Ⓒ Ⓓ Ⓔ
3 Ⓐ Ⓑ Ⓒ Ⓓ Ⓔ   7 Ⓐ Ⓑ Ⓒ Ⓓ Ⓔ   11 Ⓐ Ⓑ Ⓒ Ⓓ Ⓔ   15 Ⓐ Ⓑ Ⓒ Ⓓ Ⓔ   19 Ⓐ Ⓑ Ⓒ Ⓓ Ⓔ
4 Ⓐ Ⓑ Ⓒ Ⓓ Ⓔ   8 Ⓐ Ⓑ Ⓒ Ⓓ Ⓔ   12 Ⓐ Ⓑ Ⓒ Ⓓ Ⓔ   16 Ⓐ Ⓑ Ⓒ Ⓓ Ⓔ   20 Ⓐ Ⓑ Ⓒ Ⓓ Ⓔ

Reading Comprehension Test 3

1 Ⓐ Ⓑ Ⓒ Ⓓ Ⓔ   4 Ⓐ Ⓑ Ⓒ Ⓓ Ⓔ   7 Ⓐ Ⓑ Ⓒ Ⓓ Ⓔ   10 Ⓐ Ⓑ Ⓒ Ⓓ Ⓔ   13 Ⓐ Ⓑ Ⓒ Ⓓ Ⓔ
2 Ⓐ Ⓑ Ⓒ Ⓓ Ⓔ   5 Ⓐ Ⓑ Ⓒ Ⓓ Ⓔ   8 Ⓐ Ⓑ Ⓒ Ⓓ Ⓔ   11 Ⓐ Ⓑ Ⓒ Ⓓ Ⓔ   14 Ⓐ Ⓑ Ⓒ Ⓓ Ⓔ
3 Ⓐ Ⓑ Ⓒ Ⓓ Ⓔ   6 Ⓐ Ⓑ Ⓒ Ⓓ Ⓔ   9 Ⓐ Ⓑ Ⓒ Ⓓ Ⓔ   12 Ⓐ Ⓑ Ⓒ Ⓓ Ⓔ   15 Ⓐ Ⓑ Ⓒ Ⓓ Ⓔ

Reading Comprehension Test 4

1 Ⓐ Ⓑ Ⓒ Ⓓ Ⓔ   5 Ⓐ Ⓑ Ⓒ Ⓓ Ⓔ   9 Ⓐ Ⓑ Ⓒ Ⓓ Ⓔ   13 Ⓐ Ⓑ Ⓒ Ⓓ Ⓔ   16 Ⓐ Ⓑ Ⓒ Ⓓ Ⓔ
2 Ⓐ Ⓑ Ⓒ Ⓓ Ⓔ   6 Ⓐ Ⓑ Ⓒ Ⓓ Ⓔ   10 Ⓐ Ⓑ Ⓒ Ⓓ Ⓔ   14 Ⓐ Ⓑ Ⓒ Ⓓ Ⓔ   17 Ⓐ Ⓑ Ⓒ Ⓓ Ⓔ
3 Ⓐ Ⓑ Ⓒ Ⓓ Ⓔ   7 Ⓐ Ⓑ Ⓒ Ⓓ Ⓔ   11 Ⓐ Ⓑ Ⓒ Ⓓ Ⓔ   15 Ⓐ Ⓑ Ⓒ Ⓓ Ⓔ   18 Ⓐ Ⓑ Ⓒ Ⓓ Ⓔ
4 Ⓐ Ⓑ Ⓒ Ⓓ Ⓔ   8 Ⓐ Ⓑ Ⓒ Ⓓ Ⓔ   12 Ⓐ Ⓑ Ⓒ Ⓓ Ⓔ

Posttest

1 Ⓐ Ⓑ Ⓒ Ⓓ Ⓔ   5 Ⓐ Ⓑ Ⓒ Ⓓ Ⓔ   9 Ⓐ Ⓑ Ⓒ Ⓓ Ⓔ   13 Ⓐ Ⓑ Ⓒ Ⓓ Ⓔ   17 Ⓐ Ⓑ Ⓒ Ⓓ Ⓔ
2 Ⓐ Ⓑ Ⓒ Ⓓ Ⓔ   6 Ⓐ Ⓑ Ⓒ Ⓓ Ⓔ   10 Ⓐ Ⓑ Ⓒ Ⓓ Ⓔ   14 Ⓐ Ⓑ Ⓒ Ⓓ Ⓔ   18 Ⓐ Ⓑ Ⓒ Ⓓ Ⓔ
3 Ⓐ Ⓑ Ⓒ Ⓓ Ⓔ   7 Ⓐ Ⓑ Ⓒ Ⓓ Ⓔ   11 Ⓐ Ⓑ Ⓒ Ⓓ Ⓔ   15 Ⓐ Ⓑ Ⓒ Ⓓ Ⓔ   19 Ⓐ Ⓑ Ⓒ Ⓓ Ⓔ
4 Ⓐ Ⓑ Ⓒ Ⓓ Ⓔ   8 Ⓐ Ⓑ Ⓒ Ⓓ Ⓔ   12 Ⓐ Ⓑ Ⓒ Ⓓ Ⓔ   16 Ⓐ Ⓑ Ⓒ Ⓓ Ⓔ   20 Ⓐ Ⓑ Ⓒ Ⓓ Ⓔ

READING COMPREHENSION

Introductory Pretest and Answers

Directions: The reading passages given below are followed by questions based on their content. After reading the passages, choose the best answer to each question. The questions are to be answered on the basis of what is stated or implied in the passages. Mark the answer sheet with the letter of that answer.

Allow 10 minutes for this test.

Reading Passage 1

What gave this country the isolation it enjoyed in the nineteenth century was the statesmanship of Jefferson, Adams, Madison, and Monroe on this side of the Atlantic and men like Canning on the other side. American independence of the European system did not exist in the two centuries before the Monroe Doctrine of 1832, and it has not existed in the century which began in 1914.

1. According to the above passage
   (A) America enjoyed greater isolation from European affairs from 1832 to 1914 than before or after.
   (B) The isolation of this country from European affairs was, prior to 1914, the result of our geographic position.
   (C) Canning was a statesman living in the twentieth century.
   (D) America is less isolated today than it has ever been.
   (E) The statesmanship of Washington helped to keep America free from foreign entanglements.

Reading Passage 2

It may be said that the problem in adult education seems to be not the piling up of facts but practice in thinking.

2. According to the above passage
   (A) educational methods for adults and young people should differ.
   (B) adults do not seem to retain new facts.
   (C) adults seem to think more than young people.
   (D) a well-educated adult is one who thinks but does not have a store of information.
   (E) adult education should stress ability to think.

Reading Passage 3

The secretarial profession is a very old one and has increased in importance with the passage of time. In today's automated times, the vast expansion of health and social service industries has greatly increased the need and opportunities for secretaries; and for the first time in history their number has become large.

3. The passage best supports the statement that the secretarial profession
   (A) is older than the health and social service industries.
   (B) did not exist in ancient times.
   (C) has greatly increased in size.
   (D) demands higher training than it did formerly.

Reading Passage 4

The likelihood of America's exhausting her natural resources seems to be growing less. All kinds of waste products are being reworked and new uses are constantly being found for almost everything. We are getting more use out of our goods and are making many new by-products out of what was formerly thrown away.

97

4. The passage best supports the statement that we seem to be in less danger of exhausting our resources because
   - (A) economy is found to lie in the use of substitutes.
   - (B) more service is obtained from a given amount of material.
   - (C) we are allowing time for nature to restore them.
   - (D) supply and demand are better controlled.

Reading Passage 5

Telegrams should be clear, complete, concise, and brief. Omit all unnecessary words. The parts of speech most often used in telegrams are nouns, verbs, adjectives, and adverbs. If possible, do without pronouns, prepositions, articles, and copulative verbs. Use simple sentences rather than complex or compound ones.

5. The passage best supports the statement that in writing telegrams one should always use
   - (A) common and simple words.
   - (B) only nouns, verbs, adjectives, and adverbs.
   - (C) incomplete sentences.
   - (D) only the words essential to the meaning.

Reading Passage 6

The prevention of accidents makes it necessary not only that safety devices be used to guard exposed machinery but also that mechanics be instructed in safety rules which they must follow for their own protection, and that lighting in the plant be adequate.

6. The passage best supports the statement that industrial accidents
   - (A) may be due to ignorance.
   - (B) are always avoidable.
   - (C) usually result from inadequate machinery.
   - (D) cannot be entirely overcome.

Reading Passage 7

Work measurement concerns accomplishment or productivity. It has to do with results; it does not deal with the energy used up, although in many cases this may be in direct proportion to the work output. Work measurement not only helps a manager to distribute work loads fairly, but also to define work success in actual units, to evaluate employee performance, and to determine where corrective help is needed. Work measurement is accomplished by measuring the amount produced, measuring the time spent to produce it, and relating the two. To illustrate, it is common to speak of so many letters processed within a given time. The number of letters processed become meaningful when related to the time taken.

Much of the work in an office can be measured accurately and inexpensively. The extent of work measurement possible in any given case will depend upon the particular type of office tasks performed. Usually from two-thirds to three-fourths of all work in an office can be measured. It is true that difficulty in work measurement is met, for example, when the office work is irregular and not repeated often or when the work is primarily mental rather than manual. These are problems, but they are used as excuses for doing no work measurement far more frequently than is justified.

7. According to the above passage, which of the following best illustrates the type of information obtained as a result of work measurement?
   - (A) A file clerk takes one hour to file 150 folders.
   - (B) A correspondence secretary types five letters.
   - (C) A stenographer works harder typing from shorthand notes than from handwritten rough draft notes.
   - (D) A clerk keeps track of employees' time by computing sick leave, annual leave, and overtime leave.

8. The above passage does *not* say that work measurement can be used to help a supervisor to determine
   - (A) why an employee is performing poorly on the job.
   - (B) who are the fast and slow workers in the unit.
   - (C) how the work should be distributed among the employees in the unit.
   - (D) how long it should take to perform a certain task.

9. According to the above passage, the kind of work that would be most difficult to measure would be such work as
   (A) sorting mail.
   (B) designing a form for a new procedure.
   (C) photocopying various materials.
   (D) answering inquiries with form letters.

10. The excuses mentioned in the above passage for failure to perform work measurement can be best summarized as the
   (A) repetitive nature of the work.
   (B) costs involved in carrying out accurate work measurement.
   (C) inability to use properly the obtained results from work measurement.
   (D) difficulty involved in measuring certain types of work.

Reading Passage 8

The leader of an industrial enterprise has two principal functions. He or she must manufacture and distribute a product at a profit, and he or she must keep individuals and groups of individuals working effectively together.

11. The paragraph best supports the statement that an industrial leader should be able to
   (A) increase the distribution of his or her plant's products.
   (B) introduce large-scale production methods.
   (C) coordinate the activities of employees.
   (D) profit by the experience of other leaders.

Reading Passage 9

Numerous benefits to the employer as well as to the worker have resulted from physical examinations of employees. Such examinations are intended primarily as a means of increasing efficiency and production, and they have been found to accomplish these ends.

12. The paragraph best supports the statement that physical examinations
   (A) may serve to increase output.
   (B) are a source of greater gain to employers than to employees.
   (C) are required in some plants.
   (D) often reveal serious defects previously unknown.
   (E) always are worth more than they cost.

END OF PRETEST

Answer Key for Pretest

1. A	4. B	7. A	10. D
2. E	5. D	8. A	11. C
3. C	6. A	9. B	12. A

Study Hints

In our modern society, reading is basic to survival. Beyond the functional literacy necessary for daily living, fluent literacy is now necessary for advancement on the competitive job scene. It is not sufficient for a worker to be able to follow step-by-step directions. You must read through the material, pick out important details, and interpret the meaning of a paragraph or document.

You have been developing reading skills and habits, for most of your life. You have probably had some experience with answering questions based upon your reading. Fortunately both reading itself, and, even more so, answering questions based upon that reading are skills which you can improve with training and practice. You can upgrade your reading ability; but you must have a *plan*, a *procedure*, and a *method*.

First, understand that there are two aspects of success in reading interpretation: reading speed, and reading understanding. There are many individuals who read with excellent comprehension, but who read too slowly. Remember, there is a time limit on your examination. On the other hand, there are those who read rapidly but do not thoroughly understand what they are reading. These test-takers will answer few of the comprehension test questions correctly.

Many people read very slowly and with little comprehension, yet are completely unaware of just how badly they do read. You were probably taught to read letter by letter; gradually, as you matured, you learned to read word by word. As an adult, however, you should be able to read a complete phrase as quickly as you once read one letter. If you cannot do this or have trouble in understanding what you read, you should practice reading intensively, attend an adult evening school, or find some other means of assistance available through your local school district. Most people, with a little effort, can increase the speed of their reading significantly.

Your ability to comprehend what you read will keep pace with your increase in speed. You will absorb as many ideas per page as before and get many more ideas per unit of reading time.

It has been demonstrated that those who read best also read quickly. Heavier concentration is required for rapid reading, and concentration is what enables a reader to grasp important ideas contained in the reading material.

A good paragraph has one central thought—that is, a topic sentence. Your main task is to locate and absorb that thought while reading the paragraph. The correct interpretation of the paragraph is based upon that thought and not upon your opinions, prejudices, or preferences. If a selection consists of two or more paragraphs, the correct interpretation is based on the central idea of the entire passage. The ability to grasp the central idea of a passage can be gained by practice, (which will also increase the speed with which you read).

An important rule to follow in seeking to improve your reading ability is to force yourself to increase your speed. Just as you once stopped reading letter by letter, now learn to stop reading word by word. Force yourself to read by whole *phrases* and *sentences*. Move your eyes rapidly across the line of type, skimming it. Don't permit your eyes to stop for individual words, but try to reconstruct the whole idea even if a word has been missed. Proceed quickly through the paragraph in this skimming fashion, without rereading or backtracking to a missed word.

If you find yourself failing to comprehend what you read, read it over several times rapidly, until you do understand. Do not slow down on rereading. At first, you may find yourself missing some of the ideas. Practice, however, increase both your reading speed and your ability to comprehend what you read.

Certain physical factors affect your reading. You should always read sitting in a comfortable position, erect, with head slightly inclined. The light should be excellent, with both an indirect and a direct source available. Direct light should come from behind you and slightly above your shoulder, in such a way that the type is evenly illuminated. Hold the reading matter at your own best reading distance and at a convenient height, so you don't stoop or squint. It goes without saying that, if you need glasses, you should certainly use them when reading.

An important aspect of your reading is vocabulary building. You must know the meaning of every word in a passage in order to understand the passage thoroughly. The sentence context will sometimes help you to arrive at the meaning of a word, but the context method is not to be depended upon. The most effective reader has a rich, extensive vocabulary. As you read, make a list of unfamiliar words. Include in your list words you understand within the context of the article, but you cannot really define. You should also mark words you do not understand at all. Then go to your dictionary and look up *every* new and unfamiliar word. Write the word and its definition in a special notebook.

(Note: See the sections on vocabulary and spelling on pp. 47 and 71 for further review.)

These varied reading passages question you in several ways. Can you quickly grasp the main idea? Can you remember and associate specific details? Can you judge the truth or falsity of what you read? Can you make reasonable inferences from your reading?

Success with reading questions depends on more than reading comprehension. You must also know how to draw the answers from the reading selection and be able to distinguish the *best* one.

It is a good idea to approach reading comprehension questions by reading the questions—not the answer choices—before you read the selection. The questions will alert you to look for certain details, ideas, and points of view. Underscore key words in the questions. These will help you direct your attention as you read.

Next skim the selection very rapidly to get an idea of its subject matter and its organization. If key words or ideas pop out at you, underline them, but do not consciously search out details in the preliminary skimming.

Next read the selection very carefully with comprehension in mind. Underscore the important words as you have been doing in your practice readings.

Finally, return to the question. Read each question carefully. Misreading of questions is a major cause of error on reading comprehension tests. Read all the answer choices. Eliminate the obviously incorrect answers. You may be left with only one possible answer. If you find yourself with more than one possible answer, reread the question. Then skim the passage once more, focusing on the underlined segments. By now you should be able to conclude which answer is *best*.

Many examination points are lost because you ignore the author's hints as to what he or she thinks is most important. Watch for such phrases as: "Note that . . ." "Of importance is . . ." These give clues to what the writer is stressing as do topic sentences. Beware of negatives and all-inclusive statements. Watch particularly words like *always, ever, all, only, every, absolutely, complete, none, entirely,* etc., as previously mentioned.

Between now and the examination day, you must work to improve your reading concentration and comprehension. Here are some hints and a quick review of all the above mentioned points:

1. Your daily newspaper provides excellent material to improve your reading. Read the editorial pages of various newspapers.

2. Book reviews (also drama and movie reviews) are an excellent source.

3. Magazine articles provide a variety of vocabulary words.

4. Make a point of reading all the way through any article that you begin.

5. Do not be satisfied with reading the first paragraph or two.

6. Read with a pencil in hand. Underscore details and ideas that seem to be crucial to the meaning of the article.

7. Look for points of view, arguments, and supporting information.

8. After reading the article, summarize it yourself. Answer these questions:
   * Do you know the purpose of the article?
   * The main idea presented?
   * The attitude of the author?
   * The points over which there is controversy?
   * Did you find certain information lacking?
   * Did you look up the meanings of words you do not know or you aren't sure of?

9. Using the above points, refer to your underlines:

   * Did you focus on important words and ideas?
   * Did you read with comprehension?

Sample Questions and Explanations

Let us now demonstrate with an actual examination-type reading question how to apply all the above points.

Sample Reading Selection

Vacations were once the prerogative of the privileged few, even as late as the nineteenth century. Now they are considered the right of all, except for such unfortunate masses as, for example, the bulk of China's and India's population, for whom life, save for sleep and brief periods of rest, is uninterrupted toil.

Vacations are more necessary now than once because the average life is less well-rounded and has become increasingly departmentalized. I suppose the idea of vacations, as we conceive it, would be incomprehensible to primitive peoples. Rest of some kind has, of course, always been a part of the rhythm of human life, but earlier ages did not find it necessary to organize it in the way that modern day people have done. Holidays and feast days were sufficient.

With modern man's increasing tensions, with the stultifying quality of so much of his/her work, this break in the year's routine became steadily more necessary. Vacations became mandatory for the purpose of renewal and repair, better known as "R & R." And so it came about that in the United States, the most self-indulgent of nations, the tensest, and the most departmentalized, vacations have come to take a predominant place in domestic conversation.

Example 1. The title below that best expresses the ideas of this passage is
   (A) Vacation Preferences.
   (B) Vacations: The Topics of Conversation.
   (C) Vacations in Perspective.
   (D) The Well-Organized Vacation.
   (E) Renewal, Refreshment, and Repair.

Example 2. We need vacations now more than ever before because we have

(A) a more carefree nature.
(B) much more free time.
(C) little diversity in our work.
(D) less emotional stability.
(E) a higher standard of living.

Example 3. It is implied in the passage that the lives of Americans are very
(A) habitual.
(B) ennobling.
(C) patriotic.
(D) varied.
(E) independent.

Example 4. As used in the passage, the word "prerogative" (line 1) most nearly means
(A) habit.
(B) privilege.
(C) request.
(D) demand.
(E) hope.

After applying the reading steps we have previously discussed look at Question 1. Eliminate (D) immediately because it is irrelevant. The selection refers in no way to organization of a vacation. Eliminate (B). . . . vacations are often a topic of conversation but that is not the point of this passage. Since (A), (C), and (E) remain as possible correct choices, check them. Since (C) is an all-inclusive title and (A) and (E) are not all-inclusive, (C) is the correct choice as the best title for the passage. In arriving at the correct answer, we have considered only the facts given or definitely understood. We were on the alert for trick expressions and "catch words." There were none in Question 1.

Now proceed in the same manner in answering the other example questions 2, 3, and 4 to come up with the correct answers of:

1. (C)   2. (C)   3. (A)   4. (B)

Tests and Answers

Reading Comprehension Test 1

Reading Passage 1

Arsonists are persons who set fires deliberately. They don't look like criminals, but they cost the nation millions of dollars in property loss and sometimes, loss of life. Arsonists set fires for many different reasons. Sometimes a shopkeeper sees no way out of losing his business, and sets fire to it so he can collect the insurance. Another type of arsonist wants revenge, and sets fire to the home or shop of someone he feels has treated him unfairly. Some arsonists just like the excitement of seeing the fire burn and watching the firefighters at work; arsonists of this type have even been known to help fight the fire.

1. The writer of this passage feels that arsonists
   (A) usually return to the scene of the crime.
   (B) work at night.
   (C) don't look like criminals.
   (D) never leave their fingerprints.

2. An arsonist is a person who
   (A) intentionally sets a fire.
   (B) enjoys watching fires.
   (C) wants revenge.
   (D) needs money.

3. Arsonists have been known to help fight fires because they
   (A) felt guilty.
   (B) enjoyed the excitement.
   (C) wanted to earn money.
   (D) didn't want anyone hurt.

4. Shopkeepers sometimes become arsonists in order to
   (A) commit suicide.
   (B) collect insurance money.
   (C) hide a crime.
   (D) raise their prices.

5. The point of this passage is that arsonists
   (A) would make good firefighters.
   (B) are not criminals.
   (C) are mentally ill.
   (D) are not all alike.

Reading Passage 2

A painter being instructed in his duties was told by his foreman, "Experience is the best teacher."

6. Of the following, the one which most nearly expresses the meaning of this quotation is:
   (A) A good teacher will make a hard job look easy.

(B) Bad experience does more harm than good.
(C) Lack of experience will make an easy job hard.
(D) The best way to learn to do a thing is by doing it.

Reading Passage 3

Fruits, vegetables, grains and nuts shall be sold at retail by avoirdupois weight or numerical count.

7. Of the following, the one which does *not* satisfy the requirements of the above statement is a sale of
(A) eight ounces of peanuts.
(B) one dozen tomatoes.
(C) one pound of hominy grits.
(D) two quarts of cherries.

Reading Passage 4

Even minor cuts should be properly cared for so that there will be no chance for infection to set in. Amputations and even death have resulted from small neglected wounds.

8. According to this statement,
(A) a small wound is more likely to become infected than a large one.
(B) minor cuts should not be neglected.
(C) more people die from small wounds than from large ones.
(D) small wounds are always worse than they look.

Reading Passage 5

A foreman who made an error in his report was told by his superior, "To stumble twice against the same stone is disgraceful."

9. Of the following, the statement that most nearly expresses the meaning of this quotation is:
(A) Always guard against errors.
(B) A person who makes errors should feel ashamed.
(C) Every person makes an error now and then.
(D) Repeated errors deserve criticism.

Reading Passage 6

In dispatching elevators, the first consideration shall be handling the traffic, and the second, maintaining short, even intervals between cars.

10. According to this statement, when there is heavy traffic the starter should
(A) assign an equal number of runs to each operator.
(B) handle a car himself to speed up the movement of traffic.
(C) keep short, even intervals between cars.
(D) load cars quickly and dispatch immediately.

END OF TEST

Reading Comprehension Test 2

Directions: Answer the following questions by using the information contained in the passages below. Each question consists of a statement. Decide whether the statement is true or false. Mark the answer sheet with (A) for *true*, or (B) for *false*.

Allow 8 minutes for this test.

Reading Passage 1

The elimination of sewage from the waters around New York constitutes a problem that for generations has challenged the best engineering minds in the national, state, and city governments. This perplexing problem had been and continues to be the subject of countless conferences participated in by the authorities of the states of New Jersey, Connecticut, and New York and the United States Government. New York City took the first forward step to correct the great evil of emptying raw sewage into the waters surrounding this city. Progress was made toward a sewage disposal system and complete plans were presented, showing a comprehensive system embracing the five boroughs.

1. The problem of eliminating sewage from the waters around New York had challenged the best engineering minds of the national, state, and city governments.

2. St. Louis took the first forward step toward solving the problem mentioned in question 1.

3. Countless conferences had been held on the problem of eliminating sewage from the waters surrounding New York.

4. Only New York authorities had participated in these conferences.

5. No progress has been made toward a sewage disposal system.

6. Complete plans were presented.

7. All five boroughs were included in the comprehensive system of sewage disposal.

8. The passage characterizes the practice of emptying raw sewage into the waters surrounding this city as perplexing.

9. The elimination of sewage from the waters surrounding New York City had been a challenge to the best engineering minds for exactly five years.

10. The chief characteristic of the sewage disposal system presented was not mentioned.

Reading Passage 2

Litter baskets were used in many cities but the size and design, the number employed, and the service given them varied considerably. Observations indicated that the baskets should be very numerous in some places. They should be looked upon as a definite part of the city's cleaning equipment and as such should be kept in good condition and repair. The baskets should not be too cheap looking nor too ornamental, but they should be designed with due regard to the service which they are to perform and the lesson which their presence conveys.

11. Litter baskets were used in more than one city.

12. All the cities use the same style of litter baskets.

13. All cities employ their litter baskets in the same way.

14. Litter baskets should be distributed equally throughout a city.

15. Litter baskets should be looked upon as a definite part of the city's cleaning equipment.

16. The litter basket should convey a lesson.

17. The litter baskets should be the most economical the city can find.

18. The litter baskets should be designed for ornamental purposes only.

19. Observation indicated that the baskets should be very numerous in some places.

20. The litter baskets should be cheap looking.

END OF TEST

Reading Comprehension Test 3

Directions: Carefully read each passage and the questions that follow it. Then answer the questions on the basis of the information given in the passage. Mark the answer sheet with the letter of that answer.

Allow 20 minutes for this test.

Reading Passage 1

Whether or not the nerve impulses in various nerve fibers differ in kind is a question of great interest in physiology. The usually accepted view is that they are identical in character in all fibers and vary only in intensity.

1. Judging from the information contained in the above passage it could be most correctly assumed that
   (A) nerve fibers are the product of neural impulses.
   (B) nerve fibers are usually accepted as differing in kind.
   (C) the nature of neural impulses is still questionable.
   (D) the student of physiology accepts the view that nerve impulses sometimes differ in intensity.
   (E) the character of nerve fibers is accepted as being constant.

Reading Passage 2

In a lightning-like military advance, similar to that used by the Germans, the use of persistent chemicals is unnecessary. It might even be a considerable detriment to a force advancing over a broad front.

2. According to the above passage,
    (A) chemicals should not be used by a defending army.
    (B) the Germans advanced in a narrow area.
    (C) an advancing army may harm itself through the use of chemicals.
    (D) chemicals are unnecessary if warfare is well-organized.
    (E) chemical warfare is only effective if used by an advancing army.

Reading Passage 3

The X-ray has gone into business. Developed primarily to aid in diagnosing human ills, the machine now works in packing plants, in foundries, in service stations, and in dozens of ways contributes to precision and accuracy in industry.

3. According to the above passage, the X-ray
    (A) was first developed to aid business.
    (B) is more of a help to business than to medicine.
    (C) is being used to improve the functioning of industry.
    (D) is more accurate for packing plants than for foundries.
    (E) increases the output of such industries as service stations.

Reading Passage 4

For the United States, Canada has become the most important country in the world. Yet, there are few countries about which Americans know less. Canada is the third largest country in the world; only Russia and China are larger. The area of Canada is more than a quarter of the whole British Empire.

4. According to the above passage,
    (A) the British Empire is smaller than Russia or China.
    (B) the territory of China is greater than that of Canada.

(C) Americans know more about Canada than about China or Russia.
(D) the United States is the most important nation in the world as far as Canada is concerned.
(E) the Canadian population is more than one quarter the population of the British Empire.

Reading Passage 5

When a classification of facts results in a simple principle describing the relationship and sequences of any group, that principle usually leads to the discovery of a wider range of phenomena in the same or related fields.

5. Which phrase most adequately describes the preceding passage?
    (A) Relationship between group classifications.
    (B) Establishment of principles derived from group relationships and sequences.
    (C) Association of phenomena in a wide range of varied fields.
    (D) Establishment of general laws in undiscovered fields.
    (E) Discovery of not regarded phenomena in their relationships and sequences to varied groups.

Reading Passage 6

In humid climates a thick growth of vegetation with a mattress of interlacing roots usually protects the moist soil from wind. However, in arid regions, vegetation is either wholly lacking, or scant growths are found huddled in detached clumps leaving patches of unprotected ground. Since there is little or no moisture present to make the soil particles cohere, they are readily lifted and scattered by the wind.

6. According to the passage,
    (A) vegetation is always present in humid climates.
    (B) lack of moisture decreases cohesion.
    (C) moisture is an important element in soil and rock erosion.

(D) wind is the chief agent in the dispersal of topsoil.

(E) tree roots are closely associated with the thick growth of vegetation in moist climates.

Reading Passage 7

It is not necessary to travel great distances to other lands to find interesting, valuable scientific results. Here in the U.S. there are treasures to be found which may be gone in a few years. Although the frontier has disappeared, there are still vast areas along the Atlantic seaboard and in the Mississippi Valley that are practically unexplored. Museums and universities sponsor expeditions for photographs of native wild birds and recordings of their voices. They are particularly interested in species endangered by encroaching civilization.

7. The writer points out that the Atlantic states provide
    (A) a rich field for scientific investigation.
    (B) a high level of civilization.
    (C) opportunities for travel.
    (D) great museums and universities.
    (E) vast areas.

8. The author mentions museum expeditions sent out to
    (A) create bird sanctuaries.
    (B) domesticate wild birds.
    (C) kill and retrieve birds for exhibits.
    (D) take pictures of birds.
    (E) capture native birds.

9. The kind of treasure this passage refers to is
    (A) buried gold.
    (B) new territory.
    (C) museum collections.
    (D) exact knowledge of a wildlife.
    (E) natural beauty.

Reading Passage 8

Next morning I saw for the first time an animal that is rarely encountered face to face. It was a wolverine. Though relatively small and rarely weighing more than 40 pounds, he is, above all animals, the one most hated by the Indians and trappers. He is a fine tree climber and a relentless destroyer. Deer, reindeer, and even moose succumb to his attacks. We sat on a rock and watched him come, a bobbing blackish-brown rascal. Since the male wolverine occupies a very large hunting area and fights to the death any other male that intrudes on his domain, wolverines are always scarce. So in order to avoid extinction wolverines need all the protection that man can give. As a trapper, Henry wanted me to shoot him, but I refused. This is the most fascinating and little known of all our wonderful predators. His hunchback gait was awkward and ungainly, lopsided yet tireless.

10. Wolverines are very scarce because
    (A) they suffer in the survival of the fittest.
    (B) they are afraid of all humankind.
    (C) they are seldom protected by man.
    (D) trappers take their toll of them.
    (E) their food supply is limited.

11. Henry is
    (A the author
    (B) the author's dog
    (C) a hunchback
    (D) a gamewarden
    (E) the author's companion

12. The author of this selection is most probably
    (A) a conscientious naturalist.
    (B) an experienced hunter.
    (C) an inexperienced trapper.
    (D) a young Indian.
    (E) a farmer.

Reading Passage 9

Using new tools and techniques, scientists, almost unnoticed, are remaking the world of plants. They have already remodeled 65 varieties of flowers, fruits, vegetables, and trees. Among other things they gave us tobacco that resists disease, cantaloupes that are immune to the blight, and lettuce with crisper leaves. The chief new tool they are using is colchicine, a poisonous drug, which has astounding effects upon growth and upon heredity. It creates new varieties with astonishing frequency, where such mutations occur but rarely in nature. Colchicine has thrown new light on the fascinating jobs of the plant hunters. The Department of Agriculture sends people all over the world to find plants already here. Scientists have crossed these foreign plants with those at home, thereby adding many desirable characteristics to our farm crops. The colchicine technique has enormously facilitated their work because hybrids so often can be made fertile. It also takes so few generations of plants now to build a new variety with the qualities desired.

13. The title below that best expresses the idea of this passage is
    (A) Plant Growth and Heredity.
    (B) New Plants for Old.
    (C) Remodeling Plant Life.
    (D) A More Abundant World.
    (E) The Fascination of Plant Hunting.

14. Mutation in plant life results in
    (A) diseased plants.
    (B) hybrids.
    (C) new varieties.
    (D) fertility.
    (E) larger and stronger plants.

15. Colchicine speeds the improvement of plant species because it
    (A) makes possible the use of foreign plants.
    (B) makes use of natural mutations.
    (C) makes hybrid plants fertile.
    (D) can be used with 65 different vegetables, fruits, and flowers.
    (E) makes plants immune to disease and blight.

END OF TEST

Reading Comprehension Test 4

Allow 20 minutes for this test.

Reading Passage 1

The mental attitude of employees toward safety is exceedingly important in preventing accidents. All efforts designed to keep safety on the employees' mind and to keep accident prevention a live subject in the office will help substantially in a safety program. Although it may seem strange, it is common for people to be careless. Therefore, safety education is a continuous process.

Explain all safety rules, and give all employees the reasons for their rigid enforcement. Telling employees to be careful or giving similar general safety warnings and slogans is probably of little value. Inform employees of basic safety fundamentals. Do this through staff meetings, informal suggestions to employees, movies, and safety instruction cards. Safety instruction cards provide the employees with specific suggestions about safety and serve as a series of timely reminders helping to keep safety on the minds of employees. Pictures, posters, and cartoon sketches on bulletin boards located in areas continually used by employees arouse the employees' interest in safety. It is usually good to supplement this type of safety promotion with intensive individual follow-up.

1. The above passage implies that the *least* effective of the following safety measures is
   (A) rigid enforcement of safety rules.
   (B) getting employees to think of safety.
   (C) elimination of unsafe conditions in the office.
   (D) telling employees to stay alert always.

2. The reason given by the passage for maintaining ongoing safety education is that
   (A) people are often careless.
   (B) office tasks are often dangerous.
   (C) the value of safety slogans increases with repetition.
   (D) safety rules change frequently.

3. Which one of the following safety aids is most likely to be preferred by the author of this passage
   (A) A cartoon of a man tripping over a carton and yelling "Keep aisles clear!"
   (B) A poster with a large number "one" and a caption saying "Safety First."
   (C) A photograph of a very neatly arranged office.
   (D) A large sign with the word "THINK" in capital letters.

4. Of the following, the best title for the above passage is
   - (A) "Basic Safety Fundamentals."
   - (B) "Enforcing Safety Among Careless Employees."
   - (C) "Attitudes Toward Safety."
   - (D) "Making Employees Aware of Safety."

Reading Passage 2

The discussion of the art of stowing goods in a storeroom may seem to be devoting too much attention to the elementary common sense matters. Yet, system and method in stowing is the foundation of orderliness and care in the handling of things and, therefore, the beginning of system and control in the storeroom. If methods are reduced to standards and standard methods of stowing each class of goods are insisted upon and reduced to rules, the result will be such neatness and uniformity that inspection and accounting will be greatly facilitated. The exceptions to good stowing, by their very conspicuousness, will then be easily noticed and corrected.

5. The best way to insure methodical stowing is to
   - (A) inspect all merchandise on receipt.
   - (B) establish proper accounting methods.
   - (C) make a daily count of commodities in the storehouse.
   - (D) set up procedures for stowing every commodity.
   - (E) lecture employees on the importance of good stowing.

6. Of a system of stowing it is least true to say that once adopted it
   - (A) improves the appearance of the storeroom.
   - (B) reduces the work of the stock assistants.
   - (C) requires no supervision.
   - (D) reduces loss.
   - (E) helps in inventory.

Reading Passage 3

Capital in the form of money or securities is very carefully guarded. Those in charge must render an accounting for every penny. Capital in the form of material or merchandise, equipment, and supplies is not so carefully guarded, and in fact, is frequently unprotected. Accounting of stores in many cases is inefficient, with little or no idea as to when stores are used or for what purpose they are used. The work of the storekeeping department should be to safeguard, account for, and keep always available the stores of a concern.

7. The purpose of knowing "when stores are used" is chiefly
   - (A) to determine how long the supply of a stock must fall before ordering additional stock.
   - (B) to determine the proper time for physical inventory.
   - (C) to determine the form of stock records.
   - (D) to set up proper material specifications.
   - (E) to have enough requisition forms available at all times.

8. Which of the following is *not* a task of a storekeeping department?
   - (A) Filling orders.
   - (B) Computing values.
   - (C) Recording quantities.
   - (D) Comparing records.
   - (E) Producing new materials.

Reading Passage 4

Whenever a government agency has need for supplies, materials, or equipment that are stock items, it prepares and forwards a requisition slip to the proper warehouse. These requisitions must be signed by a duly authorized employee of the requesting department whose signature is already on file at the warehouse to which the requisition is forwarded or presented. When the warehouse receives a requisition, it is immediately registered and given an identification number which serves to identify the transaction in all future dealings with the requisitioning agency. From this point it is progressed to the editing clerk at the warehouse for the deletion of those items which are not stocked. At the same time, the editing clerk ascertains if sufficient funds are available by reference to the warehouse copy of the budgetary code pamphlet, published and kept current by the Bureau of Accounting, Department of Purchase. From this point the requisition is then forwarded to the respective section within the warehouse that will fill the requisition.

9. If a requisition is referred to in a letter, it is best to do so by
   (A) signature.
   (B) number.
   (C) subject matter.
   (D) item.
   (E) issuing clerk.

10. Aside from the Budgetary Code pamphlet, the material an editing clerk would find most useful in performing the duties listed in the passage above is
    (A) a blank requisition form.
    (B) a back order requisition.
    (C) a copy of the government budget.
    (D) a perpetual inventory.
    (E) a floor plan of the warehouse.

11. The number of points at which the requisition is examined in the warehouse is
    (A) one.
    (B) two.
    (C) three.
    (D) four.
    (E) five.

Reading Passage 5

The first consideration in shooting a revolver is how to stand in a steady position. You may almost face the target in assuming a comfortable shooting stance, or you may face away from the target as much as 90 degrees and still find it possible to stand easily and quietly. The principle point to observe is to spread the feet apart at least 8 inches. This varies with the individual according to the length of his/her legs. Stand firmly on both feet. Do not bend either leg at the knee and be careful to develop a stance which does not allow the body to lean backward or forward. Ease and naturalness in posture with body muscles relaxed is the secret of good shooting form. The shooting arm should be straight, with the weight of the pistol supported, not so much by the arm, as by the muscles of the shoulder. Do not tense any muscle of the arm or hand while holding the revolver; especially avoid locking the elbow. The grip of the gun should be seated in the hand so an imaginary line drawn along the forearm would pass through the bore of the gun. The heel of the hand should reach around the stock far enough to go past the center line of the gun. The thumb can be either alongside the hammer, on top of the frame, or it can be pointed downward toward the

tip of the trigger finger. The high position is preferable, because when you are shooting rapid fire, the thumb will have a shorter distance to move to reach the hammer spur.

12. One of the subjects discussed in the above passage is the proper method of
    (A) leading a moving target.
    (B) squeezing the trigger.
    (C) gripping the revolver.
    (D) using revolver sights.

13. According to the above passage, the secret of good shooting form is
    (A) proper sighting of the target.
    (B) a relaxed and natural position.
    (C) firing slowly and carefully.
    (D) keeping the thumb alongside the hammer.

14. For proper shooting stance, it is recommended that the weight of the pistol be supported by
    (A) the muscles of the shoulder.
    (B) locking the elbow.
    (C) the muscles of the forearm.
    (D) tensing the wrist muscles.

15. The chief advantage of employing a high thumb position in firing a revolver is to
    (A) maintain a more uniform grip.
    (B) achieve greater accuracy.
    (C) achieve better recoil control.
    (D) facilitate more rapid shooting.

16. When firing a revolver at a target, the angle at which the officers should face the target
    (A) is 45 degrees.
    (B) is 90 degrees.
    (C) is greater for taller persons.
    (D) varies naturally from person to person.

17. According to the above passage, the revolver should be held in such a manner that the
    (A) bore of the revolver is slightly below the heel of the hand.
    (B) revolver, horizontally, is level with the shoulder.
    (C) center line of the revolver is a continuation of the forearm.
    (D) revolver is at a 45-degree angle with the target.

18. Of the following, the most accurate statement concerning proper shooting position is that the
    (A) left knee should be bent slightly.
    (B) feet should be spread at least 8 inches apart.
    (C) officer should lean slightly forward as s/he fires each shot.
    (D) weight of the body should be on the right foot.

END OF TEST

Answer Key for Practice Tests

Reading Comprehension Test 1

1. C	3. B	5. D	7. D	9. D
2. A	4. B	6. D	8. B	10. C

Reading Comprehension Test 2

1. A	5. B	9. B	13. B	17. B
2. B	6. A	10. A	14. B	18. B
3. A	7. A	11. A	15. A	19. A
4. B	8. A	12. B	16. A	20. B

Reading Comprehension Test 3

1. C	4. B	7. A	10. A	13. C
2. C	5. B	8. D	11. E	14. C
3. C	6. B	9. D	12. A	15. C

Reading Comprehension Test 4

1. D	5. D	9. B	13. B	16. D
2. A	6. C	10. D	14. A	17. C
3. A	7. A	11. C	15. D	18. B
4. D	8. E	12. C		

Posttest and Answers

Directions: The reading passages given below are followed by questions based on their content. After reading the passages, choose the best answer to each question. The questions are to be answered on the basis of what is stated or implied in the passages. Mark the answer sheet with the letter of that answer.

Allow 25 minutes for this test.

Reading Passage 1

Basic to every office is the need for proper lighting. Inadequate lighting is a familiar cause of fatigue and serves to create a somewhat dismal atmosphere in the office. One requirement of proper lighting is that it be of an appropriate intensity. Intensity is measured in foot-candles. According to the Illuminating Engineering Society of New York, for casual seeing tasks such as in reception rooms, inactive file rooms, and other service areas, the light should be 30 foot-candles. For ordinary seeing tasks such as reading, working in active file rooms and mail rooms, the lighting should be 100 foot-candles. For very difficult seeing tasks such as accounting, transcribing, and business machine use, the light should be 150 foot-candles.

Lighting intensity is only one requirement. Avoid shadows and glare. For example, the larger the proportion of a ceiling filled with lighting units, the more glare-free and comfortable the lighting will be. Natural lighting from windows is not too dependable because on dark, wintry days, windows yield little usable light. On sunny, summer afternoons, the glare from windows may be very distracting. Desks should not face windows. Finally, the main lighting source should be overhead and to the left of the user.

1. According to the above passage, insufficient light in the office may cause
    (A) glare.
    (B) shadows.
    (C) tiredness.
    (D) distraction.

2. Based on the above passage, which of the following must be considered when planning lighting arrangements?
    (A) The natural light present.
    (B) The work to be done.

    (C) The level of difficulty of work to be done.
    (D) The type of activity to be carried out.

3. It can be inferred from the above passage that a well-coordinated lighting scheme is likely to result in
    (A) greater employee productivity.
    (B) elimination of light reflection.
    (C) lower lighting cost.
    (D) more use of natural light.

4. Of the following, the best title for the above passage is
    (A) Characteristics of Light.
    (B) Light Measurement Devices.
    (C) Factors to Consider When Planning Lighting Systems.
    (D) Comfort vs. Cost When Devising Lighting Arrangement.

5. According to the above passage, a foot-candle is a measurement of the
    (A) number of bulbs used.
    (B) strength of the light.
    (C) contrast between glare and shadow.
    (D) proportion of the ceiling filled with lighting units.

6. According to the above passage, the number of foot-candles of light that would be needed to copy figures onto a payroll is
    (A) less than 30 foot-candles.
    (B) 30 foot-candles.
    (C) 100 foot-candles.
    (D) 150 foot-candles.

Reading Passage 2

Television has just about reached in 20 years the goal toward which print has been working for 500; to extend its audience to include the entire population. In 1993 in the United States, nine out of ten families will watch 65 million sets playing an average of five hours a day.

7. According to the above passage
   (A) the entire nation has TV sets.
   (B) nine out of ten individuals watch an average of five hours a day.
   (C) the TV viewing public grew much more rapidly than did the reading public.
   (D) there are more TV sets in the United States than in other countries.
   (E) the total possible TV audience is larger than the reading public.

Reading Passage 3

Just as the procedure of a collection department must be clear-cut and definite, the steps being taken with the sureness of a skilled chess player, so the various paragraphs of a collection letter must show clear organization, giving evidence of a mind that, from the beginning, has had a specific end in view.

8. The selection best supports the statement that a collection letter should always
   (A) show a spirit of sportsmanship.
   (B) be divided into several paragraphs.
   (C) express confidence in the debtor.
   (D) be brief, but courteous.
   (E) be carefully planned.

Reading Passage 4

Approximately 19,000 fatal accidents in 1982 were sustained in industry. There were approximately 130 nonfatal injuries to each fatal injury.

9. According to the above passage, the number of nonfatal accidents during 1982 was approximately
   (A) 146,000
   (B) 190,000
   (C) 1,150,000
   (D) 2,500,000
   (E) 3,200,000

Reading Passage 5

The capacity of banks to grant loans depends mainly on the amount of money deposited with them by the public. However, it is a fact that banks not only can, but do lend more than is deposited with them. If such lending is carried to excess, it leads to inflation.

10. On the basis of the preceding passage it is most reasonable to conclude that
    (A) banks often indulge in the vicious practice of lending more than is deposited with them.
    (B) in the long run, a sound banking policy operates for the mutual advantage of the bankers and the public.
    (C) inflation is usually the result of excess lending by the banks.
    (D) bank lending is always in direct ratio with bank deposits.

Reading Passage 6

Neither the revolution in manufacturing nor in agriculture could have proceeded without those brilliant inventions in transportation and communication which have bound country to city, nation to nation, and continent to continent.

11. Judging from the contents of the preceding passage it can most precisely be indicated that
    (A) nations have been brought together more closely by transportation than by manufacturing and agriculture.
    (B) progress in communication and transportation has been essential to progress in manufacturing and agriculture.
    (C) changes in manufacturing and agriculture are characterized by a revolutionary process.
    (D) industrial changes must be preceded by brilliant inventions in communications.
    (E) both industry and transportation serve to bind country to city, nation to nation, and continent to continent.

Reading Passage 7

Flu travels exactly as fast as man. In oxcart days its progress was slow. In 1918 people could girdle the globe in 8 weeks, and that is exactly the time it took the flu to complete its encirclement of the earth. Today, by jets and air transport, man moves at higher speed. This modern speed makes the advent of the flu unpredictable from day to day. It all means that our control over this disease must be commensurately swift.

12. The title below that best expresses the idea of this passage is
    (A) Flu Around the World.
    (B) The World Epidemic of Flu in 1918.
    (C) How Jets Spread the Flu.
    (D) Unpredictability of the Flu.
    (E) The Effect of Speed Upon the Spread of the Flu.

13. The author states that more adequate control of the flu is necessary nowadays because
    (A) it may occur during any season.
    (B) it may occur anywhere on earth.
    (C) the germs can travel as fast as an airplane.
    (D) man can not travel fast enough to escape it.

Reading Passage 8

Why people choose varying ways to solve their problems is not known. Yet, what an individual does when she/he is thwarted remains a reasonably good key to understanding his/her personality. If his/her responses to thwartings are emotional explosions and irrational excuses, she/he is tending to live in an unreal world. She/he may need help to regain the world of reality, the cause-and-effect world recognized by generations of thinkers and scientists. Perhaps she/he needs encouragement to redouble his/her efforts. Perhaps on the other hand, she/he is striving for the impossible and needs to substitute a worthwhile activity within the range of his/her abilities. It is wise to learn the nature of the world and of oneself in relation to it, and to meet each situation as intelligently and as adequately as one can.

14. The title below that best expresses the idea of this passage is
    (A) Adjusting to Life.
    (B) Escape From Reality.
    (C) Understanding Personality.
    (D) Emotional Control.
    (E) The Nature of the World.

15. The writer argues that all should
    (A) substitute new activities for old.
    (B) analyze their relation to the world.
    (C) seek encouragement from others.
    (D) redouble their efforts.
    (E) avoid thwartings.

Reading Passage 9

Each year there are more and more time-saving machines designed and manufactured to lighten the work load. Some are simply improved versions of standard equipment such as the typewriter; others are more recent additions to the modern office such as miniature electronic calculators. Before selecting a new piece of equipment, careful consideration should be given to various important factors: nature of the work, economy, speed, quality of output, operator training time, and service maintenance cost.

For example, assembling and preparing letters, reports, brochures, etc., for mass mailing can be a slow and tiresome process if done by hand. Machines for collating, folding and inserting, addressing, and mailing can save considerable time and cost and reduce fatigue.

Collators gather papers together into sets. Some collators will count, line up, and staple pages, in addition to arranging them in order. Collators come in all sizes and some are high-speed, fully-automated models.

If an office staff sends out large amounts of mail to the same people, an addressing machine will eliminate the need to type labels on envelopes. Folding machines fold papers for mailing. They are used for bulk mailings.

Inserting machines carry the mailing operation further by gathering the folded letters or papers and inserting them into envelopes. Some machines will even collect letters, fold and insert them, seal the envelopes, and stamp and address them.

If there is a need to get a lot of correspondence out, it is possible to rent a postage meter. A postage meter automatically seals envelopes and stamps them. It can get the mail out in about a quarter of the time it would otherwise take. The postage meter is taken to the post office periodically and set for the amount of postage purchased.

16. According to the information in the passage above, one recent addition to the office that is used to save time is the
    (A) microprocessor.
    (B) word processor.
    (C) miniature calculator.
    (D) computer terminal.

17. According to the information in the passage above, which one of the following is *not* indicated as an advantage of using a postage meter?
    (A) Time can be saved in getting out correspondence.
    (B) Letters will be inserted in mailing envelopes.
    (C) Mailing envelopes will be sealed.
    (D) Mailing envelopes will be stamped.

18. According to the information in the passage above, one function of a collator is to
    (A) fold envelopes.
    (B) multiply and divide.
    (C) insert letters.
    (D) staple pages together.

19. According to the information in the passage above, which one of the following is *not* mentioned or indicated as an important advantage in using a variety of modern office machines?
    (A) Work is easier.
    (B) Time is saved.
    (C) Office workers are eliminated.
    (D) Quality is improved.

20. In the preceding passage, which one of the following is not indicated as an important consideration in selecting new office equipment?
    (A) Cost savings.
    (B) Time savings.
    (C) Training difficulty.
    (D) Office morale.

END OF POSTTEST

Answer Key for Posttest

1. C	5. B	9. D	13. E	17. B
2. D	6. D	10. C	14. A	18. D
3. A	7. C	11. B	15. B	19. C
4. C	8. E	12. E	16. C	20. D

Filing/Records Management Answer Sheet

Pretest

1 Ⓐ Ⓑ Ⓒ Ⓓ Ⓔ	5 Ⓐ Ⓑ Ⓒ Ⓓ Ⓔ	9 Ⓐ Ⓑ Ⓒ Ⓓ Ⓔ	13 Ⓐ Ⓑ Ⓒ Ⓓ Ⓔ	17 Ⓐ Ⓑ Ⓒ Ⓓ
2 Ⓐ Ⓑ Ⓒ Ⓓ Ⓔ	6 Ⓐ Ⓑ Ⓒ Ⓓ Ⓔ	10 Ⓐ Ⓑ Ⓒ Ⓓ Ⓔ	14 Ⓐ Ⓑ Ⓒ Ⓓ Ⓔ	18 Ⓐ Ⓑ Ⓒ Ⓓ
3 Ⓐ Ⓑ Ⓒ Ⓓ Ⓔ	7 Ⓐ Ⓑ Ⓒ Ⓓ Ⓔ	11 Ⓐ Ⓑ Ⓒ Ⓓ Ⓔ	15 Ⓐ Ⓑ Ⓒ Ⓓ Ⓔ	19 Ⓐ Ⓑ Ⓒ Ⓓ
4 Ⓐ Ⓑ Ⓒ Ⓓ Ⓔ	8 Ⓐ Ⓑ Ⓒ Ⓓ Ⓔ	12 Ⓐ Ⓑ Ⓒ Ⓓ Ⓔ	16 Ⓐ Ⓑ Ⓒ Ⓓ	20 Ⓐ Ⓑ Ⓒ Ⓓ

Alphabetic Test 1

| 1 Ⓐ Ⓑ Ⓒ Ⓓ Ⓔ | 3 Ⓐ Ⓑ Ⓒ Ⓓ Ⓔ | 5 Ⓐ Ⓑ Ⓒ Ⓓ Ⓔ | 7 Ⓐ Ⓑ Ⓒ Ⓓ Ⓔ | 9 Ⓐ Ⓑ Ⓒ Ⓓ Ⓔ |
| 2 Ⓐ Ⓑ Ⓒ Ⓓ Ⓔ | 4 Ⓐ Ⓑ Ⓒ Ⓓ Ⓔ | 6 Ⓐ Ⓑ Ⓒ Ⓓ Ⓔ | 8 Ⓐ Ⓑ Ⓒ Ⓓ Ⓔ | 10 Ⓐ Ⓑ Ⓒ Ⓓ Ⓔ |

Alphabetic Test 2

| 1 Ⓐ Ⓑ Ⓒ Ⓓ | 3 Ⓐ Ⓑ Ⓒ Ⓓ | 5 Ⓐ Ⓑ Ⓒ Ⓓ | 7 Ⓐ Ⓑ Ⓒ Ⓓ | 9 Ⓐ Ⓑ Ⓒ Ⓓ |
| 2 Ⓐ Ⓑ Ⓒ Ⓓ | 4 Ⓐ Ⓑ Ⓒ Ⓓ | 6 Ⓐ Ⓑ Ⓒ Ⓓ | 8 Ⓐ Ⓑ Ⓒ Ⓓ | 10 Ⓐ Ⓑ Ⓒ Ⓓ |

Numeric Test

| 1 Ⓐ Ⓑ Ⓒ Ⓓ Ⓔ | 3 Ⓐ Ⓑ Ⓒ Ⓓ Ⓔ | 5 Ⓐ Ⓑ Ⓒ Ⓓ Ⓔ | 7 Ⓐ Ⓑ Ⓒ Ⓓ Ⓔ | 9 Ⓐ Ⓑ Ⓒ Ⓓ Ⓔ |
| 2 Ⓐ Ⓑ Ⓒ Ⓓ Ⓔ | 4 Ⓐ Ⓑ Ⓒ Ⓓ Ⓔ | 6 Ⓐ Ⓑ Ⓒ Ⓓ Ⓔ | 8 Ⓐ Ⓑ Ⓒ Ⓓ Ⓔ | 10 Ⓐ Ⓑ Ⓒ Ⓓ Ⓔ |

Geographic Test

1 Ⓐ Ⓑ Ⓒ Ⓓ Ⓔ	6 Ⓐ Ⓑ Ⓒ Ⓓ Ⓔ	11 Ⓐ Ⓑ Ⓒ Ⓓ Ⓔ	15 Ⓐ Ⓑ Ⓒ Ⓓ Ⓔ	19 Ⓐ Ⓑ Ⓒ Ⓓ Ⓔ
2 Ⓐ Ⓑ Ⓒ Ⓓ Ⓔ	7 Ⓐ Ⓑ Ⓒ Ⓓ Ⓔ	12 Ⓐ Ⓑ Ⓒ Ⓓ Ⓔ	16 Ⓐ Ⓑ Ⓒ Ⓓ Ⓔ	20 Ⓐ Ⓑ Ⓒ Ⓓ Ⓔ
3 Ⓐ Ⓑ Ⓒ Ⓓ Ⓔ	8 Ⓐ Ⓑ Ⓒ Ⓓ Ⓔ	13 Ⓐ Ⓑ Ⓒ Ⓓ Ⓔ	17 Ⓐ Ⓑ Ⓒ Ⓓ Ⓔ	21 Ⓐ Ⓑ Ⓒ Ⓓ Ⓔ
4 Ⓐ Ⓑ Ⓒ Ⓓ Ⓔ	9 Ⓐ Ⓑ Ⓒ Ⓓ Ⓔ	14 Ⓐ Ⓑ Ⓒ Ⓓ Ⓔ	18 Ⓐ Ⓑ Ⓒ Ⓓ Ⓔ	22 Ⓐ Ⓑ Ⓒ Ⓓ Ⓔ
5 Ⓐ Ⓑ Ⓒ Ⓓ Ⓔ	10 Ⓐ Ⓑ Ⓒ Ⓓ Ⓔ			

Subject Test 1

1 Ⓐ Ⓑ Ⓒ Ⓓ Ⓔ	4 Ⓐ Ⓑ Ⓒ Ⓓ Ⓔ	7 Ⓐ Ⓑ Ⓒ Ⓓ Ⓔ	10 Ⓐ Ⓑ Ⓒ Ⓓ Ⓔ	13 Ⓐ Ⓑ Ⓒ Ⓓ Ⓔ
2 Ⓐ Ⓑ Ⓒ Ⓓ Ⓔ	5 Ⓐ Ⓑ Ⓒ Ⓓ Ⓔ	8 Ⓐ Ⓑ Ⓒ Ⓓ Ⓔ	11 Ⓐ Ⓑ Ⓒ Ⓓ Ⓔ	14 Ⓐ Ⓑ Ⓒ Ⓓ Ⓔ
3 Ⓐ Ⓑ Ⓒ Ⓓ Ⓔ	6 Ⓐ Ⓑ Ⓒ Ⓓ Ⓔ	9 Ⓐ Ⓑ Ⓒ Ⓓ Ⓔ	12 Ⓐ Ⓑ Ⓒ Ⓓ Ⓔ	15 Ⓐ Ⓑ Ⓒ Ⓓ Ⓔ

Subject Test 2

1 Ⓐ Ⓑ Ⓒ Ⓓ Ⓔ	4 Ⓐ Ⓑ Ⓒ Ⓓ Ⓔ	7 Ⓐ Ⓑ Ⓒ Ⓓ Ⓔ	10 Ⓐ Ⓑ Ⓒ Ⓓ Ⓔ	13 Ⓐ Ⓑ Ⓒ Ⓓ Ⓔ
2 Ⓐ Ⓑ Ⓒ Ⓓ Ⓔ	5 Ⓐ Ⓑ Ⓒ Ⓓ Ⓔ	8 Ⓐ Ⓑ Ⓒ Ⓓ Ⓔ	11 Ⓐ Ⓑ Ⓒ Ⓓ Ⓔ	14 Ⓐ Ⓑ Ⓒ Ⓓ Ⓔ
3 Ⓐ Ⓑ Ⓒ Ⓓ Ⓔ	6 Ⓐ Ⓑ Ⓒ Ⓓ Ⓔ	9 Ⓐ Ⓑ Ⓒ Ⓓ Ⓔ	12 Ⓐ Ⓑ Ⓒ Ⓓ Ⓔ	15 Ⓐ Ⓑ Ⓒ Ⓓ Ⓔ

Information and Procedures Test

| 1 Ⓐ Ⓑ Ⓒ Ⓓ | 3 Ⓐ Ⓑ Ⓒ Ⓓ | 5 Ⓐ Ⓑ Ⓒ Ⓓ | 7 Ⓐ Ⓑ Ⓒ Ⓓ | 9 Ⓐ Ⓑ Ⓒ Ⓓ |
| 2 Ⓐ Ⓑ Ⓒ Ⓓ | 4 Ⓐ Ⓑ Ⓒ Ⓓ | 6 Ⓐ Ⓑ Ⓒ Ⓓ | 8 Ⓐ Ⓑ Ⓒ Ⓓ | 10 Ⓐ Ⓑ Ⓒ Ⓓ |

Posttest

1 Ⓐ Ⓑ Ⓒ Ⓓ Ⓔ	6 Ⓐ Ⓑ Ⓒ Ⓓ Ⓔ	10 Ⓐ Ⓑ Ⓒ Ⓓ Ⓔ	14 Ⓐ Ⓑ Ⓒ Ⓓ Ⓔ	18 Ⓐ Ⓑ Ⓒ Ⓓ
2 Ⓐ Ⓑ Ⓒ Ⓓ Ⓔ	7 Ⓐ Ⓑ Ⓒ Ⓓ Ⓔ	11 Ⓐ Ⓑ Ⓒ Ⓓ Ⓔ	15 Ⓐ Ⓑ Ⓒ Ⓓ Ⓔ	19 Ⓐ Ⓑ Ⓒ Ⓓ
3 Ⓐ Ⓑ Ⓒ Ⓓ Ⓔ	8 Ⓐ Ⓑ Ⓒ Ⓓ Ⓔ	12 Ⓐ Ⓑ Ⓒ Ⓓ Ⓔ	16 Ⓐ Ⓑ Ⓒ Ⓓ Ⓔ	20 Ⓐ Ⓑ Ⓒ Ⓓ
4 Ⓐ Ⓑ Ⓒ Ⓓ Ⓔ	9 Ⓐ Ⓑ Ⓒ Ⓓ Ⓔ	13 Ⓐ Ⓑ Ⓒ Ⓓ Ⓔ	17 Ⓐ Ⓑ Ⓒ Ⓓ	
5 Ⓐ Ⓑ Ⓒ Ⓓ Ⓔ				

FILING/RECORDS MANAGEMENT

Introductory Pretest and Answers

Directions: Consider each group as a unit. In each of the following groups, there is one underlined selection and a series of four other selections in proper order. The spaces between are lettered (A), (B), (C), (D), and (E). Decide where the underlined selection belongs in the series and choose the letter identifying that space as the answer. Mark the answer sheet with the letter of that answer.

Allow 4 minutes for this pretest.

Alphabetic

1. <u>DeMattia, Jessica</u>
   (A)--
       DeLong, Jesse
   (B)--
       DeMatteo, Jessie
   (C)--
       Derby, Jessie S.
   (D)--
       DeShazo, L. M.
   (E)--

2. <u>SanMiguel, Carlos</u>
   (A)--
       SanLuis, Juana
   (B)--
       Santilli, Laura
   (C)--
       Stinnett, Nellie
   (D)--
       Stoddard, Victor
   (E)--

3. <u>Theriault, Louis</u>
   (A)--
       Therien, Annette
   (B)--
       Therien, Elaine
   (C)--
       Thibeault, Gerald
   (D)--
       Thiebeault, Pierre
   (E)--

Numeric

4. <u>374859664</u>
   (A)--
       373849583
   (B)--
       374328472
   (C)--
       374859666
   (D)--
       374859668
   (E)--

5. <u>023859278</u>
   (A)--
       012030485
   (B)--
       013948576
   (C)--
       023582987
   (D)--
       023850118
   (E)--

6. 2002 4637 9485

    (A)--

        2002 4637 9235

    (B)--

        2002 4637 9385

    (C)--

        2002 4637 9463

    (D)--

        2002 4637 9575

    (E)--

Geographic

7. Professional Secretaries
2440 Pershing Road
Kansas City, MO 64108

    (A)--

        Professional Sales
        5345 Wilson Avenue
        Carson City, MO 58465

    (B)--

        Professional Services
        48567 Curshin Lane
        Kainesville, MO 48937

    (C)--

        Professional Scenes
        93 Western Avenue
        Kansas City, MO 64108

    (D)--

        Public Relations
        893 Consensus Avenue
        St. Louis, MO 38533

    (E)--

8. 3M Office Corp.
3M Building
St. Paul, MN 55144

    (A)--

        TS Enterprises
        One Madison Avenue
        St. Paul, CA 48567

    (B)--

        IBM Corporation
        One Culver Road
        Dayton, IL 84757

    (C)--

        NBI Incorporated
        Box 9001
        St. Paul, MN 55144

    (D)--

        Travelers Calculators
        223 East 30th Street
        St. Paul, MN 55144

    (E)--

9. Huron Office Systems
83 Port Huron Lane
Leitchfield, KY 48687

    (A)--

        Keith Carl Inc.
        One Okaun Blvd.
        Honolulu, HI 38444

    (B)--

        The Leitchfield Press
        8 Wake Street
        Lansing, KY 38444

    (C)--

        Personal Reporters
        Box 7374
        Leechfield, KY 48484

    (D)--

        The Free Press
        300 Survey Avenue
        Litchfield, KY 48687

    (E)--

Subject

Directions: One of the five classes of employment, lettered (A) to (E), may be applied to each of the individuals listed below. Choose as your answer the letter of the class in which that name may best be placed. Mark the answer sheet with the letter of that answer.

Class Of Work

    (A) CLERICAL
    (B) EDUCATIONAL
    (C) INVESTIGATIONAL
    (D) MECHANICAL
    (E) ARTISTIC

10. Jacquiline Chalmers   Librarian
11. Stanley Anderson   Computer Programmer
12. Donna Pundt   Graphic Trainee

Directions: One of the five headings, lettered (A) to (E), may be applied to each of the subdivisions listed below. Choose as your answer the letter of the heading in which that subdivision may best be placed. Mark the answer sheet with the letter of that answer.

Headings

    (A) ACCOUNTING
    (B) PERSONNEL
    (C) ADMINISTRATION

(D) PRODUCTION
(E) SALES

13. Special Client
    Orders
14. Job Classifications
15. Director of Training

Information and Procedures

Directions: For each of the following questions, select the choice which best answers the question or completes the statement. Mark the answer sheet with the letter of that answer.

16. How many monthly primary guides are in a card tickler file?
    (A) 30
    (B) 24
    (C) 12
    (D) 28

17. How often should you check a chronologic file?
    (A) Once a week.
    (B) Once a month.
    (C) Once a day.
    (D) Twice a week.

18. Of the following, the best definition of chronologic is
    (A) arrangement of documents in order of time.
    (B) arrangement of documents in alphabetic order.
    (C) arrangement of documents in alpha-numeric order.
    (D) arrangement of documents in numeric order.

19. End guides are used for two purposes: one is to mark the close of a section and the second is
    (A) to mark the resumption of alphabetically filed cards.
    (B) to mark where the new color guides should begin.
    (C) to show a new listing.
    (D) to show that the month begins there.

20. Another name for horizontal card files is
    (A) visual files.
    (B) visible files.
    (C) vertical files.
    (D) valuable files.

END OF PRETEST

Answer Key for Pretest

1. C	5. E	9. D	13. E	17. C
2. B	6. D	10. B	14. B	18. A
3. A	7. D	11. B	15. C	19. A
4. C	8. D	12. E	16. C	20. B

Study Hints

An office needs to file nearly all records, temporarily at least, so they may be quickly found for future reference. Were this not so, it would not be necessary to file them at all—they could be destroyed. Reference to records requires that they be found as soon as possible, which is dependent on how and where they are filed.

Filing may be classified briefly into two types: (1) correspondence filing; and (2) card filing. Over 90 percent of all filing is alphabetic. Because of this, alphabetic filing systems have been given more thought than other filing systems. Folders are merely containers for such correspondence matter. Likewise in card filing, the card is the record to be filed. In both cases proper and speedy filing is dependent upon and controlled by guide cards.

To be efficient, any filing or indexing systems must be simple and logical to operate so anyone can quickly file or find a paper or card. The system must be highly flexible for the following reasons:

1. No two lists of names are exactly alike; that is, no two lists contain the same names.

2. The names in any active file change constantly. Old names are dropped and new names are added.

3. Nearly every file grows over time and this growth must be provided for.

4. The system must be capable of handling from one to thousands of papers or cards for the same name, keeping them all in a definite order so they can be found quickly.

Methods of Filing

Alphabetic

This method is by far the most important and the most frequently used. It is fundamental to the proper operation of all the other filing methods. When alphabetic filing is employed, papers are sorted according to the letters of the alphabet, one letter at a time. Another name for alphabetic filing is name filing. The following are the most important rules governing alphabetic filing:

1. Consider the surname or last name first, then the given or first name or initial, and finally the middle name or initial. Ignore titles (Pres., Secretary, etc.), degrees or honors (Dr., Prof., Ph.D.), titles of respect (Miss, Mr., etc.), and terms of seniority with full names (Sr., Jr., II, 2d, etc.).

   If the surnames or last names are the same, then the one with the initial comes before the one with the name written out. When the first and last names are the same, a name without a middle initial comes before one with a middle initial. When the first and last names are the same, a name with a middle initial comes before one with a middle name beginning with the same initial. All material must be arranged alphabetically down to the last letter of the item.

   > Bonomo, Henry J.
   > Bonomo, Leo
   > Caudwell, Fred
   > Caudwell, Fred J.
   > Caudwell, Fred John
   > Charters, John D. (Dr.)

   a. Many names are pronounced exactly alike but are spelled differently. They must be filed exactly as spelled.

   > Brown, Sandra
   > Browne, Sally Ann

   b. In filing a group of names, all of which have the same surname, three principles must be kept in mind: (1) Nothing comes before something; (2) Initials come before names beginning with the same letter; (3) Spell out abbreviated names in full or nicknames such as Chas. for Charles or Thos. for Thomas.

   > King
   > King, D.
   > King, Dorothy
   > King, Dorothy L.
   > King, Thos. (Thomas)

   c. Mac and Mc are filed exactly as they are spelled—Mac comes before Mc.

   > MacNamara, John
   > McNamara, Jane

   d. Married women's names are filed using their given or first name, middle name or initial, then last name.

   > Mrs. Sean (Marlene) Moran
   > Moran, Marlene

   e. It is recommended that foreign names be filed as written.

   > Poo Yen Coo
   > Quincy, James L.

2. Foreign language articles (such as d', D', Da, de, de la, De La, Del, Des, Di, Du, Fitz, La, Le, M', Mac, Mc, O', San, Santa, St., Te, Ten, Van, vander, Vander, Von, Von der, Zu) are considered part of the name. Ignore the spacing and marks of punctuation.

   > Da Costa, Carl
   > D'Agnota, Ugo
   > De La Gotta, Jesus
   > Des Verney, Elizabeth
   > De Takacs, Maria

3. When the same names appear with different addresses, arrange them alphabetically by town or city, considering state only where there is a duplication of town or city names.

| American Tobacco Co. | Norfolk, VA |
| American Tobacco Co. | Osceola, FL |

4. Names of firms, banks, organizations, corporations, associations, services, and institutions are indexed as written, except where they include the full names of individuals in which case the surnames are considered first, the first name next, the middle name or initial next, and then the remainder of the title. Ignore conjunctions, articles, prepositions (and, the, of, on), and also apostrophes. If the word college or university appears at the beginning of the name, consider the major part of the name.

Rice, A.
Rice, B., & Co.
Rice, Bernard
Rice and Co.
Rice, Edward and Bros.
Rice, Henry and Son
Rice's Big Boys Bakery

Franklin, Benjamin, Hotel
Hopkins, Johns, University
University of New Mexico
Roosevelt, Theodore, High School
Sage, Russell, College

5. Hyphenated surnames are indexed as though the hyphen joined the two parts making one.

Lytton-Strachey, John
Lyttonte, Amadeus

6. Hyphenated firm names are treated as one word.

Oilimatic Heating Company
Oil-O-Matic Heating Company

7. Abbreviations are alphabetized as though they were spelled out in full. Parts of names which are included in filing are: Ltd., Inc., Co., Son, Bros., Mfg., and Corp.

Indus. Bros. of America
Indus. and Loan Assoc.

8. Words which may be spelled either as one or two words are treated as one word.

North Pole Expedition
North East Grocery Corporation

9. Names that begin with numbers should be indexed as if spelled out. The numeral is treated as one word.

8th Avenue Bookshop (eighth)
Fifth Street Church
4th National Bank (fourth)
7th Avenue Restaurant (seventh)

10. Compound geographic names are always treated as separate words.

New Jersey Lighting
New York News Co.
West Chester
West Milton
Westinghouse

11. Government names are filed first under the government (U.S. Government, etc.) then by the largest segment on down. For example:

Kingdom of Sweden, Minister of Trades
U.S. Dept. of Treasury, IRS Division
Dept. of Education, New Jersey State

are filed

New Jersey State Education Department
Sweden, Kingdom Trades Minister
United States Government Treasury Department, Internal Revenue Service Division

12. Parts which are omitted in indexing and filing are the following:

a. The articles (the, a, an) unless it occurs in a foreign name.

b. Conjunctions (And, &,).

c. Prepositions (for, in, of, on, by).

Geographic

When geographic filing is used, the primary matter to be filed is grouped by region or location. The main divisions are first indexed according to state; then by counties, cities, towns, and possibly sales territories;

and last, according to alphabetic arrangement of names of correspondents. This method of filing is used when there is a need to keep material from particular localities in one place. To facilitate the use of a geographic file, an alphabetic card file is kept so letters from a particular correspondent may be located even if the correspondent's address has been forgotten.

Numeric

This method is easy to use and gaining in popularity. Its greatest use is in courts, savings and loan companies, banks, IRS, charge account stores, mail order houses, life insurance companies, and professional offices. This system is desirable if you have to have a quick indication of information or you must maintain confidential records. Numbers are assigned as they come in; thus, a later arrival will receive a higher number. An extensive cross-reference alphabetic card index is kept and by looking up the name one obtains the number. Card indexes are filed in numeric order so it is a simple matter to find one if the number is not known.

If letters are to be filed numerically, a number is assigned to each correspondent with whom the firm does business. Any letter that comes in is placed in the folder assigned to the correspondent. As the firm acquires new correspondents, new numbers are assigned. File clerks consult the card index, register, or an accession book each time they want to file or find a letter. This system is useful where two or three items may be filed under the same name. Variations of numeric filing are terminal digit and middle digit filing.

Numeric filing is used in personal checks, drivers' licenses, insurance policies, social security cards, and credit cards.

Subject

This method is used in cases where there is much correspondence on many subjects between a small number of people. It is used in the Yellow Pages, libraries, supply outlets, research companies, schools, etc. The main difficulty with this method lies in building up a logical, inclusive, and consistent subject classification and adhering to it strictly. Supervision over the subject of filing is usually placed in the hands of a responsible person who reads each letter and writes on it the subject under which it is to be filed.

Tests and Answers

The answer key will be found at the end of these practice tests.

Alphabetic

Sample Question and Explanation

Directions: Consider each group as a unit. In each of the following groups, there is one underlined selection and a series of four other selections in proper order. The spaces between are lettered (A), (B), (C), (D), and (E). Decide where the underlined selection belongs in the series and choose the letter identifying that space as the answer. Mark the answer sheet with the letter of that answer.

O'Bannon, M. J.
  (A)--
      O'Beirne, B. B.
  (B)--
      Oberlin, E. L.
  (C)--
      Oberneir, L. P.
  (D)--
      O'Brian, S. F.
  (E)--

The correct answer is (A), so you would mark the answer sheet with the letter (A). In alphabetical order OBA comes before OBE, thus (A) is the only answer possible.

Alphabetic Test 1

Directions: Consider each group as a unit. In each of the following groups, there is one underlined selection and a series of four other selections in proper order. The spaces between are lettered (A), (B), (C), (D), and (E). Decide where the underlined selection belongs in the series and choose the letter identifying that space as the answer. Mark the answer sheet with the letter of that answer.

Allow 4 minutes for this test.

1. Rensch, Adeline
    (A)--
        Ramsay, Amos
    (B)--
        Remschel, Augusta
    (C)--
        Renshaw, Austin
    (D)--
        Rentzel, Becky
    (E)--

2. Schnyder, Maurice
    (A)--
        Schneider, Martin
    (B)--
        Schneider, Mertens
    (C)--
        Schnyder, Newman
    (D)--
        Schreibner, Norman
    (E)--

3. Freedenburg, C. Erma
    (A)--
        Freedenberg, Emerson
    (B)--
        Freedenberg, Erma
    (C)--
        Freedenberg, Erma E.
    (D)--
        Freedinberg, Erma F.
    (E)--

4. Entsminger, Jacob
    (A)--
        Ensminger, J.
    (B)--
        Entsminger, J. A.
    (C)--
        Entsminger, Jack
    (D)--
        Entsminger, James
    (E)--

5. Iacone, Pete R.
    (A)--
        Iacone, Pedro
    (B)--
        Iacone, Pedro M.
    (C)--
        Iacone, Peter F.
    (D)--
        Iascone, Peter W.
    (E)--

6. Sheppard, Gladys
    (A)--
        Shepard, Dwight
    (B)--
        Shepard, F. H.
    (C)--
        Shephard, Louise
    (D)--
        Shepperd, Stella
    (E)--

7. Thackton, Melvin T.
    (A)--
        Thackston, Milton G.
    (B)--
        Thackston, Milton W.
    (C)--
        Thackston, Theodore
    (D)--
        Thackston, Thomas G.
    (E)--

8. Dunlavey, M. Hilary
   (A)--
   > Dunleavy, Hilary G.

   (B)--
   > Dunleavy, Hilary K.

   (C)--
   > Dunleavy, Hilary S.

   (D)--
   > Dunleavy, Hilery W.

   (E)--

10. Prouty, Martha
    (A)--
    > Proutey, Margaret

    (B)--
    > Proutey, Maude

    (C)--
    > Prouty, Myra

    (D)--
    > Prouty, Naomi

    (E)--

9. Yarbrough, Maria
   (A)--
   > Yabroudy, Margie

   (B)--
   > Yarboro, Marie

   (C)--
   > Yarborough, Marina

   (D)--
   > Yarborough, Mary

   (E)--

END OF TEST

Alphabetic Test 2

Directions: Questions 1 to 5 below each show in Column I names written on four file cards lettered (W), (X), (Y), and (Z) which have to be filed. You are to choose the correct answer lettered (A), (B), (C), or (D) in Column II which represents the proper order of filing according to the rules listed in the Study Hints section. Mark the answer sheet with the letter of that answer. Review the sample first to be sure you understand the correct instructions.

COLUMN I	*COLUMN II*

Example:

(W) Jane Earl	(A) w, y, z, x
(X) James A. Earle	(B) y, w, z, x
(Y) James Earl	(C) x, y, w, z
(Z) J. Earle	(D) x, w, y, z

The correct filing order is shown by the letters, Y, W, Z, X (in that sequence). In Column II, (B) appears in front of the letters Y, W, Z, X (in that sequence), (B) is the correct answer to the sample question. The correct way to file the cards is:

(Y) James Earl
(W) Jane Earl
(Z) J. Earle
(X) James A. Earle

Allow 5 minutes for this test.

<table>
<tr><th colspan="2">COLUMN I</th><th colspan="2">COLUMN II</th></tr>
<tr>
<td>1.</td>
<td>(W) James Rothschild
(X) Julius B. Rothchild
(Y) B. Rothstein
(Z) Brian Joel Rothenstein</td>
<td>(A) x, z, w, y
(B) x, w, z, y
(C) z, y, w, x
(D) z, w, x, y</td>
<td></td>
</tr>
<tr>
<td>2.</td>
<td>(W) George S. Wise
(X) S. G. Wise
(Y) Geo. Stuart Wise
(Z) Prof. Diana Wise</td>
<td>(A) w, y, z, x
(B) x, w, y, z
(C) y, x, w, z
(D) z, w, y, x</td>
<td></td>
</tr>
<tr>
<td>3.</td>
<td>(W) 10th Street Bus Terminal
(X) Buckingham Travel Agency
(Y) The Buckingham Theater
(Z) Burt Tompkins Studio</td>
<td>(A) x, z, w, y
(B) y, x, w, z
(C) w, z, y, x
(D) x, w, y, z</td>
<td></td>
</tr>
<tr>
<td>4.</td>
<td>(W) National Council of American Importers
(X) National Chain Co. of Providence
(Y) National Council on Alcoholism
(Z) National Chain Co.</td>
<td>(A) w, y, x, z
(B) x, z, w, y
(C) z, x, w, y
(D) z, x, y, w</td>
<td></td>
</tr>
<tr>
<td>5.</td>
<td>(W) Dr. Herbert Alvary
(X) Mr. Victor Alvarado
(Y) Alvar Industries
(Z) V. Alvarado</td>
<td>(A) w, y, x, z
(B) z, w, x, y
(C) y, z, x, w
(D) w, z, x, y</td>
<td></td>
</tr>
</table>

Directions: Each of the following exercises consist of a capitalized word which is to be filed correctly *before* one of the words listed after it. Indicate the word before which the key word should be filed by writing the letter preceding the correct answer. Mark the answer sheet with the letter of that answer.

Example: HARMONY
    (A) growth
    (B) hegemony
    (C) holdout
    (D) indicator

The correct answer is (B) (har before heg).

6. BIOGRAPHY
    (A) Bible
    (B) Bibliography
    (C) Bilge
    (D) Biology

7. INQUISITION
    (A) Industry
    (B) Insurance
    (C) International
    (D) Intern

8. OCEANIC
    (A) Occult
    (B) Ohio
    (C) Oklahoma
    (D) Optics

9. IRRIGATION
    (A) Ireland
    (B) Irish
    (C) Iron
    (D) Irving

10. PALEONTOLOGY
    (A) Pacific
    (B) Painting
    (C) Palestine
    (D) Paltry

END OF TEST

Numeric

Numeric Test

Directions: Consider each group as a unit. In each of the following groups, there is one underlined selection and a series of four other selections in proper order. The spaces between are lettered (A), (B), (C), (D), and (E). Decide where the underlined selection belongs in the series and choose the letter identifying that space as the answer. Mark the answer sheet with the letter of that answer.

Example: 38-49-38
(A)--
     37-59-37
(B)--
     38-47-38
(C)--
     38-48-38
(D)--
     38-49-39
(E)--

First look at 38, then go to the second digits 49, then go on to the third digits 38 comes before 39. So the answer has to be (D).

Allow 5 minutes for this test.

1. 9483 8484 3999
    (A)--
         9383 8475 2828
    (B)--
         9482 3747 2999
    (C)--
         9483 8448 3948
    (D)--
         9483 8484 3989
    (E)--

2. 033 44 495 44402 2
    (A)--
         033 33 394 28492 1
    (B)--
         033 34 849 29481 3
    (C)--
         033 44 294 47194 1
    (D)--
         033 44 495 44420 2
    (E)--

3. 49242940272948
    (A)--
         39483049302946
    (B)--
         49242940272984
    (C)--
         49427482094721
    (D)--
         49429474937629
    (E)--

4. 84 93 27 40 77
    (A)--
         83 92 47 29 22
    (B)--
         83 92 48 29 11
    (C)--
         83 93 27 41 67
    (D)--
         83 94 82 67 11
    (E)--

5. 848 395 483 773 384
    (A)--
         848 222 948 109 482
    (B)--
         848 299 472 882 000
    (C)--
         848 395 483 774 382
    (D)--
         848 395 492 839 111
    (E)--

Directions: For each question in this part, read the question carefully and the four lettered choices that follow. Select the choice which best answers the question or completes the statement. Mark the answer sheet with the letter of that answer.

6. Which of the following should be filed first?
    (A)   38 39 58 293
    (B)   38 58 48 299
    (C)   38 59 27 490
    (D)   38 29 87 779
    (E)   38 59 38 386

7. Which of the following should be filed second?
   - (A) 393 293 383 493
   - (B) 384 384 358 329
   - (C) 385 848 391 100
   - (D) 385 386 397 189
   - (E) 386 386 387 388

8. Which of the following should be filed third?
   - (A) 8957 8365 8458 3888
   - (B) 3857 2847 2865 2910
   - (C) 8364 3874 3567 1930
   - (D) 3846 3954 3675 2972
   - (E) 8383 3483 3967 3999

9. Which of the following should be filed fourth?
   - (A) 38492 38483 29298
   - (B) 38492 38473 29472
   - (C) 38495 38574 39483
   - (D) 38473 39573 38483
   - (E) 38477 38592 18882

10. Which of the following should be filed last?
    - (A) 938474 459583
    - (B) 943374 357832
    - (C) 938475 385633
    - (D) 394856 384739
    - (E) 934827 847289

END OF TEST

Geographic

Allow 5 minutes for this test.

Geographic Test

Directions: For each question in this part, read the question carefully and the four lettered choices that follow. Select the choice which best answers the question or completes the statement. Mark the answer sheet with the letter of that answer.

Sample Question and Explanation

Example: Which of the following should be filed first?
- (A) Buffalo, NY
- (B) Charleston, NJ
- (C) Raleigh, NC
- (D) Chester, NY
- (E) Newark, NJ

First look at the states spelled out in full. Alphabetically the first unit New comes before North, then New Jersey comes before New York, so you go to the cities, Charleston comes before Newark alphabetically. The correct answer is (B).

1. Which of the following should be filed first?
   - (A) Al Young's Club
     Levittown, PA
   - (B) Alvin Young
     Levittown, PA
   - (C) Alvin R. Younger
     Levittown, NY
   - (D) Author R. Young
     Levittown, NY
   - (E) A. B. Youngs
     Levittown, NY

2. Which of the following should be filed second?
   - (A) Annie Miller
     Atlantic City, NJ
   - (B) Anne Miller
     Albany, NY
   - (C) Annie Miller's Realty
     Atlantic City, NJ
   - (D) Anne Millers' Agency
     Albany, NY
   - (E) A. Miller Regency Co.
     Atlantic City, NJ

3. Which of the following should be filed third?
    - (A) ZYX Company
      Chester, Delaware
    - (B) XYZ Meat Market
      Chester, Pennsylvania
    - (C) First National Bank
      Pittsburgh, Pennsylvania
    - (D) South West Motor Company
      Chester, Delaware
    - (E) Swiss Bakery
      Chester, Pennsylvania

4. Which of the following should be filed fourth?
    - (A) SouthSide Stationery Corp.
      South Side, Pennsylvania
    - (B) 16 Park Place Hotel
      Sheffield, Alabama
    - (C) Maria's Market
      Sheffield, Alabama
    - (D) St. Paul Department Store
      South Side, Alabama
    - (E) American National Bank
      South Side, Pennsylvania

5. Which of the following should be filed last?
    - (A) Katie Motor Lines
      Turnersville, Pennsylvania
    - (B) Katie Motor Lines
      Tyler, Oklahoma
    - (C) Katie Motor Lines
      Tulsa, Oklahoma
    - (D) Katie Motor Lines
      Twin Rivers, New Jersey
    - (E) Katie Motor Lines
      Turnerville, Pennsylvania

6. Which of the following should be filed first?
    - (A) B & B Mason
      Asheville, NC
    - (B) White Bunny Maternity Shop
      Charlotte, NC
    - (C) Delux Moving Company
      Durham, NC
    - (D) National Vans
      Winston-Salem, NC
    - (E) BKE Kitchen Stoves
      Asheville, NC

7. Which of the following should be filed second?
    - (A) Central Dental Care
      Norfolk, VA
    - (B) Immanuel Baptist Church
      Charleston, WV
    - (C) Campbell Supply House
      Warsaw, VA
    - (D) Home Inspector
      Charleston, WV
    - (E) Armstrong Builders
      Norfolk, VA

Directions: Questions 8 to 22 refer to the chart below. The illustration represents the front of five 3-drawer filing cabinets. The alphabet on the front of each drawer represents the range of letters found in each drawer in that cabinet. Mark the answer sheet with the letter of the cabinet in which that record should be filed geographically. Work quickly and accurately.

Cabinet:	A	B	C	D	E
Drawers:	AA to AM	AN to CA	CB to DE	DF to GD	GE to HA
	HB to IN	IO to LO	LP to MA	MB to NA	NB to NN
	NO to OJ	OK to PA	PB to SA	SB to UA	UB to ZZ

Sample Question and Explanation

NAME	CABINET
Royal Typewriter Company Greenville, PA	A B C D E

Since geographic filing rules say items are to be filed first by the full name of the state, PA (Pennsylvania) would be filed in Cabinet (C).

Allow 5 minutes for this test.

8. Ny-Way Laundry
   Lancaster, PA

9. North Side Speed Way
   Johnstown, NY

10. Maritime News
    St. Petersburg, FL

11. Compack Cars
    Helena, MT

12. R & R Railroad
    Washington, DC

13. Crescent Donuts
    Huber, GA

14. Fairfull Museum
    Honolulu, HI

15. Wiggs Wigs
    Topeka, KS

16. Freeland Raceway
    Butte, MT

17. Simon Says Press
    Prentiss, MS

18. Worth Electric
    St. Paul, MN

19. Marvel Processors
    Raleigh, NC

20. Larry The Barber
    Hartford, CT

21. Etna Insurance
    Fairbanks, AK

22. C & J Construction Co.
    Providence, RI

END OF TEST

Subject Test

Allow 4 minutes for this test.

Subject Test 1

Directions: One of the five classes of employment, lettered (A) to (E), may be applied to each of the individuals listed below. Choose as your answer the letter of the class in which that name may best be placed. Mark the answer sheet with the letter of that answer.

Class Of Work

(A) CLERICAL
(B) EDUCATIONAL
(C) INVESTIGATIONAL
(D) MECHANICAL
(E) ART

Sample Question and Explanation

Example: Lee Ann Crider   Word processor

Since a word processor performs clerical functions, the answer would be (A).

1.	Harry B. Allen	Typewriter Repairman
2.	M. C. Walton	Elevator Operator
3.	Lewis E. Reigner	Typist
4.	John G. Cook	Electrician
5.	H. B. Allen	Reporter
6.	Walter E. Jenkins	Physiotherapist
7.	Clifford H. Wrenn	Telephone Operator
8.	H. A. Schwartz	Plumber
9.	Harry Gruber	Locksmith
10.	Ely Fairbanks	Sculptor
11.	Abraham Hohing	Radio Repairman
12.	Samuel Tapft	Laundry Driver
13.	William M. Murray	Advertising Layout
14.	Herman E. Oral	Motion Picture Operator
15.	L. A. Kurtz	Director of a Nursery School

END OF TEST

Subject Test 2

Allow 4 minutes for this test.

1. H. B. Enderton	Word Processing Operator	9. Danial Larr	Instructor in Hair Styling
2. Robert F. Hallock	Proofreader	10. Oliver M. Barton	Band Leader
3. Joseph L. Hardin	Detective	11. E. Oliver Parmly	Copyholder
4. E. B. Gems	Social Worker Instructor	12. C. Parul Summerall	Silversmith
5. Carter B. Magruder	Blacksmith	13. Louis Friedersdorff	Chemical Research Worker
6. Wilber R. Pierce	Flutist	14. Daniel E. Healy	Dir. of Worker's Education
7. Russell G. Smith	Carpenter	15. Howard Kessinger	Tympani Player
8. Wilber S. Nye	Singer		

END OF TEST

Information and Procedures

Directions: For each question in this part, read the question carefully and the four lettered choices that follow. Select the choice which best answers the question or completes the statement. Mark the answer sheet with the letter of that answer.

Information and Procedures Test

Allow 8 minutes for this test.

1. What type of filing equipment is one in which guides and folders are kept in drawers that are either shelf-like or pull-out types?
   (A) Vertical.
   (B) Lateral.
   (C) Rotary.
   (D) Hanging.

2. What is the name of the process that means very tiny pictures of documents are taken?
   (A) Photocopying.
   (B) Video.
   (C) Planting.
   (D) Microfilming.

3. What is the name of the process that has many small images photographed on transparent film?
   (A) Electrofile.
   (B) Reader-Viewer.
   (C) Microfiche.
   (D) Integrator.

4. Which of the following is not necessary to know when planning an efficient filing system?
   (A) How many people will have access to the files?
   (B) Which systems do you want to use?
   (C) How are the records to be handled?
   (D) Whether to use four- or five-drawer files?

5. Which of the following is *not* a qualification for a file operator?
   (A) College degree.
   (B) Confidentiality.
   (C) Accuracy.
   (D) Dexterity.

6. Which of the following would *not* require cross-referencing?
   (A) Paul-Hoffmann Inc.
   (B) NBC.
   (C) Mary Smithe Limited.
   (D) Proctor and Gamble.

7. The term given to a series of tabs arranged alphabetically is
   (A) folders.
   (B) guides.
   (C) positions.
   (D) expansions.

8. When you have only a few pieces of correspondence, which of the following folders would you use?
   (A) Guide.
   (B) Tab.
   (C) Miscellaneous.
   (D) Alphabetic.

9. Which of the following is <u>not</u> a normal folder cut?
   (A) Full.
   (B) One-half.
   (C) One-third.
   (D) One-eighth.

10. Of the following, the system of filing most generally used is
    (A) alphabetic.
    (B) geographic.
    (C) numeric.
    (D) Dewey decimal.

END OF TEST

Answer Key for Practice Tests

Alphabetic Test 1

1. C	3. D	5. C	7. E	9. E
2. C	4. D	6. D	8. A	10. C

Alphabetic Test 2

1. A	3. B	5. C	7. B	9. D
2. D	4. D	6. D	8. B	10. C

Numeric Test

1. E	3. B	5. C	7. D	9. A
2. D	4. E	6. D	8. C	10. B

Geographic Test

1. D	6. A	11. D	16. D	21. B
2. A	7. A	12. D	17. D	22. C
3. E	8. C	13. E	18. D	
4. E	9. E	14. E	19. A	
5. E	10. D	15. B	20. C	

Subject Test 1

1. D	3. A	5. C	7. A	9. D
2. D	4. D	6. B	8. D	10. E

11.	D	12.	E	13.	E	14.	D	15.	B

Subject Test 2

1.	A	4.	B	7.	D	10.	E	13.	C
2.	A	5.	D	8.	E	11.	A	14.	B
3.	C	6.	E	9.	B	12.	D	15.	E

Information and Procedures Test

1.	B	3.	C	5.	A	7.	B	9.	D
2.	D	4.	D	6.	C	8.	C	10.	A

Posttest and Answers

Directions: Consider each group as a unit. In each of the following groups, there is one underlined selection and a series of four other selections in proper order. The spaces between are lettered (A), (B), (C), (D), and (E). Decide where the underlined selection belongs in the series and choose the letter identifying that space as the answer. Mark the answer sheet with the letter of that answer.

Allow 4 minutes for this posttest.

Alphabetic

1. DeLaTour, Hall F.
    (A)--
    Delargy, Harold
    (B)--
    DeLathouder, Hilda
    (C)--
    Lathrop, Hillary
    (D)--
    LaTour, Hulbert E.
    (E)--

2. Johnston, Edward
    (A)--
    Johnston, Edgar R.
    (B)--
    Johnston, Edmond
    (C)--
    Johnston, Edmund
    (D)--
    Johnstone, Edmund A.
    (E)--

3. Gaston, M. Hubert
    (A)--
    Gaston, Dorothy, M.
    (B)--
    Gaston, Henry N.
    (C)--
    Gaston, Isabel
    (D)--
    Gaston, M. Melvin
    (E)--

Numeric

4. 56 78 4999 203030
    (A)--
    55 78 4999 203845
    (B)--
    56 78 2488 374634
    (C)--
    56 78 5999 384756
    (D)--
    56 78 6847 293478
    (E)--

5. 202-33-4943

(A)--

    202-32-4594

(B)--

    202-32-5558

(C)--

    202-33-4934

(D)--

    202-33-4939

(E)--

6. 08406-1924

(A)--

    08403-1925

(B)--

    08405-1923

(C)--

    08406-1328

(D)--

    08406-1926

(E)--

Geographic

7. Air Carriers International
845 Phoenix Lane
Columbus, OH

(A)--

    Air Couriers Inter.
    One Cedar Lane
    Columbus, OH

(B)--

    American Carriers
    American Building
    Columbus, OH

(C)--

    First Baptist Church
    81 Stoney Lane
    Columbus, OH

(D)--

    Columbus Food Market
    18 Fitch Plaza
    Columbus, OH

(E)--

8. Nurse on Duty
83 Harper Valley Road
Freehold, NJ 07728

(A)--

    Freehold Area Hospital
    689 W. Main St.
    Freehold, NJ 07728

(B)--

    Grove Valley Care Center
    832 Grove Road
    Freehold, NJ 07728

(C)--

    Medi-Quick Nursing Home
    389 River Road
    Freehold, NJ 07728

(D)--

    Mt. Pleasant Home
    Freehold Avenue
    Freehold, NY 89348

(E)--

9. Aigner Business
384 Chambers Street
Chicago, IL 58674

(A)--

    Administrative Data
    83 Office Lane
    Cake, IL 58458

(B)--

    Order of Eagles
    84 Clinton Avenue
    Cane, IL 48656

(C)--

    The Office
    81 Journal Gazette
    Chicago, IL 58674

(D)--

    Rotary Club
    University Boulevard
    Chicago, IL 48573

(E)--

Subject

Directions: One of the five classes of employment, lettered (A) to (E), may be applied to each of the individuals listed below. Choose as your answer the letter of the class in which that name may best be placed. Mark the answer sheet with the letter of that answer.

Class of Work

(A) CLERICAL
(B) EDUCATIONAL
(C) INVESTIGATIONAL
(D) MECHANICAL
(E) ART

10.	Roger Emmory	Police Lt.
11.	Sally Miller	Auditor
12.	Constance Wilson	R.N.

Directions: One of the five headings, lettered (A) to (E), may be applied to each of the subdivisions listed below. Choose as your answer the letter of the heading in which that subdivision may best be placed. Mark the answer sheet with the letter of that answer.

Headings

(A) ACCOUNTING
(B) PERSONNEL
(C) ADMINISTRATION
(D) PRODUCTION
(E) SALES

13. Ledgers
14. Number of assembly belts made
15. How many direct-mail orders were received

Information and Procedures

16. Of the following, which would *not* be used in a chronologic file?
    (A) Daily reports.
    (B) Freight bills.
    (C) A miscellaneous folder.
    (D) Deposit slips.

17. The chronologic filing system may be used as a supplement to all but which of the following filing systems?
    (A) Alphabetic.
    (B) Numeric.
    (C) Geographic.
    (D) Terminal digital.

18. What is the major advantage of using a chronologic reading file with a subject file system?
    (A) It allows you to find documents with very little information known.
    (B) It allows you to determine where a document is to be filed.
    (C) It lets you know the receiver of the document has read it.
    (D) It makes it easier to separate documents for filing.

19. The papers in a filing folder are arranged with the most recently dated one in front. You have been instructed to arrange them according to date in a binder but with the paper of most recent date at the back. The most efficient of the following methods which you might use in performing this task is to
    (A) begin at the back of the folder and remove the papers in groups of convenient size for binding, laying each group face down on top of the group pulled just before.
    (B) begin at the back of the folder and pull the papers one by one, laying each paper face up on top of the one pulled just before.
    (C) begin at the front of the folder and pull the papers one by one, laying each paper face up on top of the one pulled just before.
    (D) begin at the front of the folder and pull the papers one by one, laying each paper face down on top of the one pulled just before.

20. Of the following, for which reason are cross-references necessary in filing?
    (A) There is a choice of terms under which the correspondence may be filed.
    (B) The only filing information contained in the correspondence is the name of the writer.
    (C) Records are immediately visible without searching through the files.
    (D) Persons other than file clerks can easily locate material.

END OF POSTTEST

Answer Key for Posttest

1. C	5. E	9. C	13. A	17. D
2. D	6. D	10. C	14. D	18. A
3. D	7. A	11. A	15. E	19. C
4. C	8. D	12. B	16. C	20. A

Office Procedures and Terminology Answer Sheet

Pretest

1 Ⓐ Ⓑ Ⓒ Ⓓ   5 Ⓐ Ⓑ Ⓒ Ⓓ   9 Ⓐ Ⓑ Ⓒ Ⓓ   13 Ⓐ Ⓑ Ⓒ Ⓓ   17 Ⓐ Ⓑ Ⓒ Ⓓ
2 Ⓐ Ⓑ Ⓒ Ⓓ   6 Ⓐ Ⓑ Ⓒ Ⓓ   10 Ⓐ Ⓑ Ⓒ Ⓓ   14 Ⓐ Ⓑ Ⓒ Ⓓ   18 Ⓐ Ⓑ Ⓒ Ⓓ
3 Ⓐ Ⓑ Ⓒ Ⓓ   7 Ⓐ Ⓑ Ⓒ Ⓓ   11 Ⓐ Ⓑ Ⓒ Ⓓ   15 Ⓐ Ⓑ Ⓒ Ⓓ   19 Ⓐ Ⓑ Ⓒ Ⓓ
4 Ⓐ Ⓑ Ⓒ Ⓓ   8 Ⓐ Ⓑ Ⓒ Ⓓ   12 Ⓐ Ⓑ Ⓒ Ⓓ   16 Ⓐ Ⓑ Ⓒ Ⓓ   20 Ⓐ Ⓑ Ⓒ Ⓓ

Business Terminology Test

1 Ⓐ Ⓑ Ⓒ Ⓓ   3 Ⓐ Ⓑ Ⓒ Ⓓ   5 Ⓐ Ⓑ Ⓒ Ⓓ   7 Ⓐ Ⓑ Ⓒ Ⓓ   9 Ⓐ Ⓑ Ⓒ Ⓓ
2 Ⓐ Ⓑ Ⓒ Ⓓ   4 Ⓐ Ⓑ Ⓒ Ⓓ   6 Ⓐ Ⓑ Ⓒ Ⓓ   8 Ⓐ Ⓑ Ⓒ Ⓓ   10 Ⓐ Ⓑ Ⓒ Ⓓ

Telephone Techniques Test

1 Ⓐ Ⓑ Ⓒ Ⓓ   3 Ⓐ Ⓑ Ⓒ Ⓓ   5 Ⓐ Ⓑ Ⓒ Ⓓ   7 Ⓐ Ⓑ Ⓒ Ⓓ   9 Ⓐ Ⓑ Ⓒ Ⓓ
2 Ⓐ Ⓑ Ⓒ Ⓓ   4 Ⓐ Ⓑ Ⓒ Ⓓ   6 Ⓐ Ⓑ Ⓒ Ⓓ   8 Ⓐ Ⓑ Ⓒ Ⓓ   10 Ⓐ Ⓑ Ⓒ Ⓓ

Courtesies Test

1 Ⓐ Ⓑ Ⓒ Ⓓ   3 Ⓐ Ⓑ Ⓒ Ⓓ   5 Ⓐ Ⓑ Ⓒ Ⓓ   7 Ⓐ Ⓑ Ⓒ Ⓓ   9 Ⓐ Ⓑ Ⓒ Ⓓ
2 Ⓐ Ⓑ Ⓒ Ⓓ   4 Ⓐ Ⓑ Ⓒ Ⓓ   6 Ⓐ Ⓑ Ⓒ Ⓓ   8 Ⓐ Ⓑ Ⓒ Ⓓ   10 Ⓐ Ⓑ Ⓒ Ⓓ

Correspondence Test

1 Ⓐ Ⓑ Ⓒ Ⓓ   3 Ⓐ Ⓑ Ⓒ Ⓓ   5 Ⓐ Ⓑ Ⓒ Ⓓ   7 Ⓐ Ⓑ Ⓒ Ⓓ   9 Ⓐ Ⓑ Ⓒ Ⓓ
2 Ⓐ Ⓑ Ⓒ Ⓓ   4 Ⓐ Ⓑ Ⓒ Ⓓ   6 Ⓐ Ⓑ Ⓒ Ⓓ   8 Ⓐ Ⓑ Ⓒ Ⓓ   10 Ⓐ Ⓑ Ⓒ Ⓓ

Judgment Test

1 Ⓐ Ⓑ Ⓒ Ⓓ   3 Ⓐ Ⓑ Ⓒ Ⓓ   5 Ⓐ Ⓑ Ⓒ Ⓓ   7 Ⓐ Ⓑ Ⓒ Ⓓ   9 Ⓐ Ⓑ Ⓒ Ⓓ
2 Ⓐ Ⓑ Ⓒ Ⓓ   4 Ⓐ Ⓑ Ⓒ Ⓓ   6 Ⓐ Ⓑ Ⓒ Ⓓ   8 Ⓐ Ⓑ Ⓒ Ⓓ   10 Ⓐ Ⓑ Ⓒ Ⓓ

Mail Services and Shipping Test

1 Ⓐ Ⓑ Ⓒ Ⓓ   3 Ⓐ Ⓑ Ⓒ Ⓓ   5 Ⓐ Ⓑ Ⓒ Ⓓ   7 Ⓐ Ⓑ Ⓒ Ⓓ   9 Ⓐ Ⓑ Ⓒ Ⓓ
2 Ⓐ Ⓑ Ⓒ Ⓓ   4 Ⓐ Ⓑ Ⓒ Ⓓ   6 Ⓐ Ⓑ Ⓒ Ⓓ   8 Ⓐ Ⓑ Ⓒ Ⓓ   10 Ⓐ Ⓑ Ⓒ Ⓓ

Equipment Test

1 Ⓐ Ⓑ Ⓒ Ⓓ   3 Ⓐ Ⓑ Ⓒ Ⓓ   5 Ⓐ Ⓑ Ⓒ Ⓓ   7 Ⓐ Ⓑ Ⓒ Ⓓ   9 Ⓐ Ⓑ Ⓒ Ⓓ
2 Ⓐ Ⓑ Ⓒ Ⓓ   4 Ⓐ Ⓑ Ⓒ Ⓓ   6 Ⓐ Ⓑ Ⓒ Ⓓ   8 Ⓐ Ⓑ Ⓒ Ⓓ   10 Ⓐ Ⓑ Ⓒ Ⓓ

Communications Test

1 Ⓐ Ⓑ Ⓒ Ⓓ   3 Ⓐ Ⓑ Ⓒ Ⓓ   5 Ⓐ Ⓑ Ⓒ Ⓓ   7 Ⓐ Ⓑ Ⓒ Ⓓ   9 Ⓐ Ⓑ Ⓒ Ⓓ
2 Ⓐ Ⓑ Ⓒ Ⓓ   4 Ⓐ Ⓑ Ⓒ Ⓓ   6 Ⓐ Ⓑ Ⓒ Ⓓ   8 Ⓐ Ⓑ Ⓒ Ⓓ   10 Ⓐ Ⓑ Ⓒ Ⓓ

Procedures Test

1 Ⓐ Ⓑ Ⓒ Ⓓ   3 Ⓐ Ⓑ Ⓒ Ⓓ   5 Ⓐ Ⓑ Ⓒ Ⓓ   7 Ⓐ Ⓑ Ⓒ Ⓓ   9 Ⓐ Ⓑ Ⓒ Ⓓ
2 Ⓐ Ⓑ Ⓒ Ⓓ   4 Ⓐ Ⓑ Ⓒ Ⓓ   6 Ⓐ Ⓑ Ⓒ Ⓓ   8 Ⓐ Ⓑ Ⓒ Ⓓ   10 Ⓐ Ⓑ Ⓒ Ⓓ

Posttest

1 Ⓐ Ⓑ Ⓒ Ⓓ   5 Ⓐ Ⓑ Ⓒ Ⓓ   9 Ⓐ Ⓑ Ⓒ Ⓓ   13 Ⓐ Ⓑ Ⓒ Ⓓ   17 Ⓐ Ⓑ Ⓒ Ⓓ
2 Ⓐ Ⓑ Ⓒ Ⓓ   6 Ⓐ Ⓑ Ⓒ Ⓓ   10 Ⓐ Ⓑ Ⓒ Ⓓ   14 Ⓐ Ⓑ Ⓒ Ⓓ   18 Ⓐ Ⓑ Ⓒ Ⓓ
3 Ⓐ Ⓑ Ⓒ Ⓓ   7 Ⓐ Ⓑ Ⓒ Ⓓ   11 Ⓐ Ⓑ Ⓒ Ⓓ   15 Ⓐ Ⓑ Ⓒ Ⓓ   19 Ⓐ Ⓑ Ⓒ Ⓓ
4 Ⓐ Ⓑ Ⓒ Ⓓ   8 Ⓐ Ⓑ Ⓒ Ⓓ   12 Ⓐ Ⓑ Ⓒ Ⓓ   16 Ⓐ Ⓑ Ⓒ Ⓓ   20 Ⓐ Ⓑ Ⓒ Ⓓ

OFFICE PROCEDURES AND TERMINOLOGY

Introductory Pretest and Answers

Directions: For each of the following questions, select the choice which best answers the question or completes the statement. Mark the answer sheet with the letter of that answer.

Allow 5 minutes for this pretest.

1. If your supervisor wanted to send a remittance to a satellite office in another city, which of the following would the supervisor use?
   - (A) Money order.
   - (B) Cash.
   - (C) Traveler's check.
   - (D) Certified check.

2. When an individual calls an office, the person answering the phone is a representative of that office to the person calling. This statement implies which of the following?
   - (A) Only one person should be responsible for answering the telephone.
   - (B) A person with a pleasing, courteous telephone manner is an asset to the office.
   - (C) An efficient person knows how to end the conversation politely.
   - (D) The distribution of the calls to the individuals will be slowed down.

3. Of the following the most appropriate greeting a clerical employee should use in addressing a visitor is
   - (A) Yes! Would you please state your business?
   - (B) Hello! May I help you?
   - (C) Do you want to see someone?
   - (D) Yes! What is your problem?

4. When a correspondent inquires in writing about the purchase of a specific product, it is your responsibility to respond in writing. Which of the following should *not* be included in your reply?
   - (A) An answer to the question asked.
   - (B) Detailed explanations.
   - (C) Offering additional services.
   - (D) Telling them to whom they should rewrite the letter for the information.

5. If your handwriting is poor and you are instructed to use your own handwriting on a questionnaire, which of the following should you do?
   - (A) Type it as it will present a neater appearance.
   - (B) Type some of the information and print the rest.
   - (C) Use your own handwriting on the questionnaire but take a little more time to be neater.
   - (D) Ask someone else whose handwriting is neater to complete the questionnaire for you.

6. Which of the following forms of address is *incorrectly* written?
   - (A) Rabbi Saul Weinstein, D.D.
   - (B) The Most Reverend Archibald Leason.
   - (C) The Reverend Dr. David I. Sotak.
   - (D) The Right Rev. Mons. James Monahan.

7. Which of the following is the proper name given to a machine that is used for making revisions and correcting typewritten errors?
   - (A) Text-editing machine.
   - (B) Telex typewriter.
   - (C) Correction-tapers.
   - (D) Facsimile machine.

8. "A secretary should realize each letter sent out in response to a letter of inquiry represents an expenditure of time and money." Which of the following is the most valid implication of this quotation?
   (A) Use the telephone to answer letters of inquiry directly and promptly.
   (B) Answer mail inquiries with lengthy letters to eliminate the need for further correspondence.
   (C) Prevent the accumulation of many similar inquiries by answering each of these letters promptly.
   (D) Use simple, concise language in answering letters of inquiry.

9. Which of the following should *not* be included in an office procedures manual?
   (A) Care of your word processor.
   (B) The letter styles.
   (C) How to repair your word processor.
   (D) Techniques in formatting columns and revising them.

10. Which of the following should *not* be included in a word processing procedures manual for those who dictate?
    (A) Stating whether it is a draft or a finished copy.
    (B) How to use indexing slips, program disks, or electronic cuing.
    (C) What marks of punctuation you should mention.
    (D) How to change your voice to show pauses within a sentence.

11. As part of a successful secretary-manager team building program, which of the following would *not* be an objective?
    (A) To provide strategies to increase the effectiveness of the secretary-manager team.
    (B) To identify the negative elements that hinder the secretary-manager team.
    (C) To define the roles of each member of the team.
    (D) To inform secretaries that managers are in charge.

12. Which of the following is *not* one of the major communication skills?
    (A) Writing.
    (B) Reading.

(C) Speaking
(D) Thinking.

13. EMS is a term used in the modern-day messenger services. What does the term EMS mean?
    (A) Electronic Mail Service.
    (B) Electric Mailing Service.
    (C) Electronic Marketing Service.
    (D) Electronic Management Systems.

14. Every year since 1930, the Dartnell Institute of Business Research informs us what the cost of an average business letter is that year. Of the following, which is *not* one of the breakdown factors?
    (A) Dictator's time.
    (B) Secretary's time.
    (C) Unfixed charges.
    (D) Fixed charges.

15. Of the following statements, which one do you think will be the strongest change in the secretarial profession in the year 2020?
    (A) There will no longer be sexual harassment.
    (B) Every secretarial desk will have a personal computer or terminal on it.
    (C) Every secretary will have a personal robot.
    (D) The work week will consist of only 25 hours.

16. The term electronic publishing or desktop publishing may be one of the greatest production tools used in offices today. Which of the following is *not* one of the advantages of desktop publishing?
    (A) It enables offices and individuals to produce their own brochures, pamphlets, newsletters, etc.
    (B) It writes sentences correctly without your having to worry about grammar or spelling.
    (C) It doesn't require a great deal of artistic talent on the part of the user.
    (D) It provides a new job market for individuals to explore.

17. In order to reduce office stress, which of the following would be a useful exercise?
    (A) Use elevators.
    (B) Rest after lunch.

(C) Do forward stretches.

(D) Remain at your desk as much as possible to get your work done.

18. Which of the following industries has had the greatest demand for clerical employees?

    (A) Manufacturing companies.

    (B) Publishing companies.

    (C) Natural resource companies.

    (D) Service oriented companies.

19. In order to achieve personal success, every clerical worker should have a personal goal setting plan. Which of the following is *not* an effective goal setting step in your plan?

    (A) Once you have set your goals, do not change them.

    (B) Keep your goals to yourself or your immediate family.

    (C) Be definite.

    (D) Use positive terminology rather than negative.

20. If your supervisor asked you to evaluate a graphics system, which of the following would *not* be an important question to ask?

    (A) Will it help me and my supervisor on the job?

    (B) Will it be used 100 percent of the time?

    (C) Will it work with the computer system we presently have?

    (D) How soon do I need to install the system?

END OF PRETEST

Answer Key for Pretest

1. B	5. C	9. C	13. A	17. C
2. B	6. D	10. D	14. C	18. D
3. B	7. A	11. D	15. B	19. A
4. D	8. D	12. D	16. B	20. B

Study Hints

Have you ever heard the expression, "Books are judged by their cover"? So, too, office workers are judged by the orderliness of their office and especially their work desk and area. Work of greater quality and quantity can be done with less effort, if the work area is orderly.

Safety is important, too. A desk or file drawer left open or out or extended into the aisle when no one is at the desk can cause bruised skin, blackened eye, bruised shoulder, injured hip or knee, or even a broken bone. A waste basket left in the aisle can also cause a fall. Too many file drawers opened at the same time will cause the cabinet to tip over dumping its contents on anyone who happens to be in the way. Remember, that person could be you!

Telephone Techniques

Tact, courtesy, and efficiency in handling telephone contacts are of vital importance to public relations, as well as to efficient work. Rules cannot be made to cover every situation, but you will not need a set of rules if you:

1. Handle every call with tact and courtesy, regardless of its importance.

2. Do everything you can to tell the caller what he or she wants to know or to find the person he or she wants.

3. Handle the instrument itself correctly.

The suggestions given here are based on recommendations of the telephone company and on usage in better office procedures.

The office telephone should be used *as little as possible* for personal calls. When you must use an office phone for a personal call, make the call brief. Discourage your friends and family from calling you at the office unless it is an emergency. Personal calls take time from your work and tie up the telephone when it may be needed for business calls. Too many personal calls make an unfavorable impression.

DO: —Speak clearly.
　　 —Pay close attention.
　　 —Be concise and courteous.
　　 —Answer promptly—by the third ring.
　　 —Have a pad and pencil on hand to take down information.
　　 —Screen calls for your supervisor.

DON'T: —Scream.
　　 —Talk with the transmitter away from your mouth.
　　 —Guess who is calling.
　　 —Give out confidential information.
　　 —Slam the receiver back on the hook or on the desk.
　　 —Neglect to use your supervisor's title.
　　 —Neglect to cover the mouthpiece or use the hold key.
　　 —Transfer a call without asking permission or informing the caller you are doing so.
　　 —Keep people waiting more than 15 to 20 seconds at a time without coming back on the line.

Here are some other points to remember:

1. Familiarize yourself thoroughly with the office and local telephone directories.

2. Call numbers in groups of two figures.

3. Call "Information" or 411 for inquiries not listed in the directories.

4. Dial 1 + Area Code + 555-1212 for long distance directory assistance for numbers outside your area code.

5. Dial operator for:
Collect calls. You want the charge for an out-of-town call to be put on the bill of the party called. If someone at the called telephone agrees to accept the charges, you will be connected.
Third-number calls. You make a call from another telephone and bill it to your own telephone number or another number if that party agrees to pay for the call.
Person-to-person calls. This is the most expensive type of call. Use it when you wish to reach a particular person or extension number.
Mobile and marine calls. When you are calling someone who has a phone in an automobile, truck, aircraft, boat, or ship.
Conference calls. You can talk with several people in different places at the same time.
Calling card calls. You have a special number that allows you to place long distance calls economically and they are charged to your calling card telephone number.
International calls. To make a call to another country.
Time and charge. When placing a call, you may ask the operator to tell you the length of time you talked and how much it cost.
Sequence calling. If you wish to make a large number of out-of-town calls in rapid succession with little waiting between calls, you should file ahead in writing or give the operator the telephone listing of numbers.

6. Telegraph and Cable Service:
Fast telegram. A full-rate rush service which reaches its destinations within a few hours.
Day letters. A deferred day service costing less than the fast telegram rate.

Night letter. Accepted until 2 a.m. to be sent during the night and delivered not earlier than the morning of the next business day.

Serial service. A low-rate service for transmission of words in bulk, a day's telegraphic correspondence from one individual or concern to another individual or concern may be combined into one message, sent in a section of a series or serial.

Words counted. In land telegrams the words in the body of the message only are counted; the place of origin, date, address, and signature are sent free. Common expressions, such as OK, c.o.d., f.o.b., a.m., and p.m. are counted as one word.

Mailgrams. Both the U.S. Postal Service (role is to deliver) and Western Union (role is to transmit) working together.

Western Union money orders. The ability to wire money to someone at another office.

Telex and TWX networks. Make possible to have a typed conversation sent which is cheaper than the telephone.

Courtesies

Almost everyone in an office has to show courtesies at least occasionally. Whether working with peers, supervisors, subordinates, or receiving callers you must use tact, courtesy, and efficiency.

When receiving callers you should treat them as if they are your guests, for that is what they really are, even in an office. Find out who they want to see. If they are strangers and do not have an appointment, find out the purpose of their call. Someone other than the person they ask for may be the person they should see. If they seem hesitant about asking for someone, ask if you can help them.

If it is not possible for callers to see the person they ask for, (because the individual has previous appointments, conferences, or is out) ask if they will call later for an appointment or offer to call them. This overcomes much disappointment in being turned away.

If callers must wait, see that they have a chair, even if you have to get one from another office. Don't try to entertain them, many callers prefer to sit and think.

If callers make conversation, talk only about things in general. If they ask anything about the business of your office, be courteous in answering, but give only such information they are entitled to.

If the callers regularly do business with your office, discussions do not have to be quite so general; but be sure any information you give them is what your supervisor would want them to have. Have an understanding with your supervisor, don't guess, about the way he or she wants callers received.

As a general rule, if the person the callers want to see is busy:

1. Callers without an appointment should wait until the person they are calling on is free or they should see someone else.

2. Callers with an appointment should be announced immediately. If the person they are calling on is only temporarily busy, they are expected to wait a few minutes before being admitted.

3. Announce important visitors immediately, whether they have an appointment or not, unless the person they are calling on is busy with someone equally important. In that case ask them to wait a few minutes until the conference is over.

Correspondence

Preparing correspondence means not only writing but also using the proper styles and parts of letters, memos, envelopes, reports, and column work.

The basics of all correspondence should include the C's of the office:

1. Completeness.
2. Conciseness.
3. Clarity.
4. Correctness.
5. Courtesy.
6. Conversational.

Letters

There are eight basic parts to a letter:

1. Return address or letterhead.
2. Date.
3. Inside address.
4. Salutation.
5. Body or message.
6. Complimentary close.
7. Signature and title.
8. Reference initials.

There are other parts to a letter that may be included. These are:

1. Reference notation.
2. Attention line.
3. Subject line.
4. Second page heading.
5. Notations:
   a. Enclosure (usually used on a letter) or attachment (usually used on a memo).
   b. Copy notation.
   c. Blind copy notation.
   d. Postscript.
   e. Mailing notation.
   f. Confidential notation.

6. Company signature.
   Letter styles include:

   1. Modified-block style.
   2. Full-block style.
   3. Indented paragraph style.
   4. Block style.
   5. The NOMA or AMA or simplified style.
   6. Reversed indented style.

Memos

Use a printed form, if at all possible, for interoffice memorandums. Follow the guide words but do not use personal titles in the TO: and FROM: position. Memos should be one page long; however, if a second page is necessary, you should type the name of the person receiving the memo, the page number, and the date. Memos are usually single spaced and double spaced between paragraphs. No signature line is necessary on a memo.

Judgment

No preparation for office work could be considered complete without reference to a kind of question which is rapidly gaining favor on examinations. This kind of question minimizes factual information; it puts you into a practical situation, and requires you to think your way out. The questions presented here are a representative sampling of judgment questions. The process of answering them will acquaint you with their form and difficulty. The main point to remember in answering other judgment questions is that you must identify the *best* answer to the situation from among the given choices.

Mail Services and Shipping

Although the majority of the mail is handled through the U.S. Postal Service, there are other special types of mail service available through private concerns.

1. *First-class mail.* These are letters, post cards and postal cards, greeting cards, personal notes, bills and statements of account, notebooks or account books, canceled and uncanceled checks, and written matter (including copies) and sealed matter, addressed for out-of-town delivery and/or locally at letter carrier offices. Twelve ounces is the maximum weight allowed.

    Business reply mail pays the postage for the response.

    Mailgram service is an electronic communications service offered by Western Union and the Postal Service.

    Business reply mailgrams are available for customers who require a quick turnaround response.

    Special services which may be included are: special delivery, registry, certification, insurance, COD, certificates of mailing, and merchandise returns.

    All first-class mail weighing over 12 ounces is called Priority Mail.

2. *Second-class mail.* These are newspapers, magazines, and other periodicals when mailed unsealed by others than publishers or news agents.

3. *Third-class mail.* These are regular (weight less than one pound) items including advertisements, circulars and other printed matter (including processed personalized fill-in letters in quantities of 20 or more), letters, booklets, newsletters, corrected proof sheets, and such items as farm and factory products, photographs, keys, and merchandise not sealed against postal inspection; books and catalogues of 24 pages or more, seeds, bulbs, cuttings, etc. There are two rate structures for this class—*single piece* and *bulk rate.*

    Special services available when using third-class mail include: insurance, special handling, special delivery, COD, certificate of mailing, and merchandise returns.

4. *Fourth-class mail.* It includes domestic parcel post, bound printed matter, special fourth-class rate items as books, 16mm or narrower width films, sound recordings, manuscripts, and library rate material, etc., weighing over one pound and

less than 70 pounds with a maximum size of 108 inches in length and girth combined, and not sealed against postal inspection. Some material can be labeled:

> Book Rate.
> Library Rate.
> Special Fourth-Class Rate.
> Bulk Rate Fourth-Class Mail.
> Bound Printed Matter.
> Special Fourth-Class Rate Mail such as films, recordings, etc.
> Special Fourth-Class Presort Rates.

5. *Express mail service.* The fastest service provides several options for both private and business customers who require overnight delivery of letters and packages.

Express mail next day service is designed for mailers whose need for reliable overnight delivery of important items are not on a recurring basis.
(a) Post office to addressee.
(b) Post office to post office.

Express mail custom designed service is offered under an agreement and is designed to meet the needs of customers with regularly scheduled shipments.

Express mail same day airport service provides services between major airports within the United States.

Express mail international service is offered under a service agreement to the United Kingdom, Belgium, and a number of other foreign countries.

6. *Special express mail services.* These include the following:

Express reshipment. Addressed to a customer's P.O. box and then at a designated time of day sent to a specified address.

Express dropship. Used to rush the movement of other classes of mail to a postal facility where the Express Mail pouch is opened and the contents delivered to various addresses in accordance with the standards appropriate for the enclosed class of mail.

7. *Priority mail.* Zone-rated first-class mail weighing more than 12 ounces. It is used when fast transportation and expeditious handling are desired.

8. *Special services.* These include the following:

Special delivery. Any type of domestic mail may be sent by special delivery, a service that expedites transmission.

Registered. Any mailable articles, except unsealed fourth class matter for domestic destinations, may be registered.

Insured mail. Domestic third and fourth class matter, mailed at or addressed to any post office in the U.S. or its possessions, or to U.S. Naval vessels, may (except when addressed to the Philippine Islands) be insured against loss, rifling, or damage in an amount equivalent to its value or the cost of repairs.

COD mail. Mail an article for which you have not been paid and have the price and the cost of the postage collected from the addressee when the article is delivered.

Certified mail. Provides a receipt to the sender and a record of delivery at the office of address.

Special handling. Provides prompt delivery.

Return receipts. Proof of delivery.

Restricted delivery. Delivery is made only to the addressee or to an individual authorized by the addressee to receive this type of mail.

Merchandise return service. Provides a method for a merchandise return permit holder to authorized individuals and organizations to send parcels to the permit holder and have the return postage and fees paid by the permit holder.

Certificates of mailing. Provides evidence of mailing only.

9. *Money orders.* These include the following:

Domestic money orders. These may be purchased at all post offices, branches, and stations, and from rural carriers in the U.S. and its possessions, except for certain offices in Alaska.

International money orders. These may be purchased at most of our larger post offices and some of the smaller ones.

Sample Question and Explanation

Example: When starting a new assignment in a new job location, you should be *least* interested in obtaining immediate information on
(A) the health and hospitalization insurance benefits available.
(B) the expected arrival and departure times and the designated lunch hour.
(C) who your immediate superior will be.
(D) what your major duties will be.

The key word is *immediate*. Although fringe benefits should be important to one starting a new job, it should not be the most important consideration. Choice (A) should be initially considered and held simply because it is an (A) choice. Choice (B) is important; arrival and departure time as well as your lunch hour are necessary to know when beginning a new job. Choice (C) whom you are responsible to, is very important as is (D), the knowledge of the work you will be doing. So select choice (A) as the *least* important consideration.

Tests and Answers

Correct answer key will be found at the end of these practice tests.

Business Terminology Test

Directions: For each of the following questions, select the choice which best answers the question or completes the statement. Mark the answer sheet with the letter of that answer.

Allow 5 minutes for this test.

1. The economic term for the exclusive right to publish or sell written matter is
   (A) competition.
   (B) standardization.
   (C) affiliate.
   (D) copyright.

2. The business organization term for the process by which management and an organized group of workers seek agreement on working terms is
   (A) collective bargaining.
   (B) competition.
   (C) syndicate.
   (D) article of agreement.

3. The communication term for a part of a telephone directory listing addresses and telephone numbers of businesses grouped by type is
   (A) directory service.
   (B) directory.
   (C) classified section.
   (D) postal zone.

4. A real estate term for one who designs and oversees the construction of homes and other buildings is a(n)
   (A) landlord.
   (B) grantor.
   (C) broker.
   (D) architect.

5. The insurance term which means a sum of money returned to the policy holder based on the private sector's earnings is a(n)
   (A) annuity.
   (B) dividend.
   (C) endowment.
   (D) warranty.

6. The transportation term which means a building where bulk goods are stored is
   (A) drayage.
   (B) wharfage.
   (C) warehouse.
   (D) bulkhouse.

7. A banking term which means a place where checks drawn on different banks, sorted and returned for charge against the proper accounts is
   (A) depository.
   (B) clearinghouse.
   (C) commercial bank.
   (D) savings and loan bank.

8. A travel term which means an outline or schedule of a trip is
   (A) tour.
   (B) excursion.
   (C) steerage.
   (D) itinerary.

9. An investment term which means the list of security holdings of a person or firm is a(n)
   (A) portfolio.
   (B) earned surplus.
   (C) compound interest.
   (D) quotation.

10. A marketing term which means one who owes another for merchandise or services purchased is
    (A) consumer.
    (B) retailer.
    (C) debtor.
    (D) middleman.

END OF TEST

Telephone Techniques Test

Allow 5 minutes for this test.

1. If you hear a beep and want to end your first call, hang up. Your telephone will immediately ring with a second call. This feature is referred to as
   (A) call waiting.
   (B) three-way call.
   (C) control call.
   (D) recall waiting.

2. A service offered by the telephone company that allows an individual to call a particular number at considerably lower rates is called
   (A) sequence calling.
   (B) third number calling.
   (C) LARA calls.
   (D) restricted calling card.

3. Before you can screen calls effectively for your supervisor, which of the following must you know?
   (A) The company and the area called from.
   (B) The caller's name and reason for calling.
   (C) The caller's name and title.
   (D) The caller's company and name.

4. When placing a telephone call, you use DDD. What does DDD mean?
   (A) Directory Dialing Distance.
   (B) Day Direct Dollars.
   (C) Daily Direct Dialing.
   (D) Direct Distance Dialing.

5. The telephone company also offers to business firms at a discount price WATS service. What does WATS mean?
   (A) Wide Area Telephone Service.
   (B) Weekdays Available Telephone Specials.
   (C) Western Area Type Service.
   (D) With Appointment Telephone Specials.

6. Which of the following usually costs the least?
   (A) Zero-plus calls.
   (B) One-plus calls.
   (C) EDDD calls.
   (D) Two-plus calls.

7. It is 12 noon in Boston, Massachusetts, where you work, and you have to call Los Angeles. What time is it in California?
   (A) 12 noon.
   (B) 11 a.m.
   (C) 10 a.m.
   (D) 9 a.m.

8. Of the following which is the best way to answer an incoming telephone call?
   (A) "Maryann here."
   (B) "Hello."
   (C) "Grant Advertising, Miss Wilson speaking."
   (D) "Good morning, Grant Advertising, Personnel Office, Mr. Hartman speaking."

9. When you complete a telephone message form for someone else, which of the following is the most important fact to record?
    (A) The telephone number and person's name.
    (B) The telephone number from the phone you answered.
    (C) The correct pronunciation of the person's name.
    (D) The city and state the person called from.

10. The type of call that permits you to speak to anyone who answers the telephone is
    (A) Conference call.
    (B) Collect call.
    (C) Three-way call.
    (D) Station-to-station call.

END OF TEST

Courtesies Test

Allow 5 minutes for this test.

1. Getting along with your fellow workers is very important in the office. Of the following fundamentals, which will help you improve your opportunities for advancement?
    (A) If someone asks you a question you don't know, guess at the answer.
    (B) Listen only to what people say and not the written order.
    (C) Learn the proper techniques of listening and follow these procedures.
    (D) Be friends with everyone and try to settle all disputes.

2. The relationship between you and your supervisor is very important in an office. Of the following, which is the most important quality you or other employees owe your supervisor?
    (A) Sincerity.
    (B) Interest.
    (C) Acceptance.
    (D) Trust.

3. As a newly appointed employee, you are doing a task according to a method your supervisor has told you to use. You believe that you would be less likely to make errors if you were to do the task by a different method, although the method your supervisor has told you to use is faster. For you to discuss your ideas with your supervisor would be
    (A) desirable; your supervisor may not know the value of your method.
    (B) undesirable; your supervisor may know of your method and prefer the faster one.
    (C) desirable; your method may show your supervisor you are able to do accurate work.
    (D) undesirable; your method may not be as helpful to you as you believe it to be.

4. A visitor asks you for information in a very arrogant and rude manner. Which of the following is the best reason for you to give this person the requested information politely?
    (A) The person may not mean to be rude; it may just be the manner of speech.
    (B) It is your duty to teach the person to be polite.
    (C) The person will probably apologize for his/her manner when he/she sees you are polite.
    (D) You are expected to be courteous no matter what.

5. As an employee you come into frequent contact with the public. You can gain public approval of your work most effectively by:
    (A) distributing pamphlets describing your office's objectives and work to the people.
    (B) encouraging employees to behave properly when off duty to impress people favorably.
    (C) making certain employees perform their daily services efficiently and courteously.
    (D) having officials give lectures to groups, describing your office's efficiency and accomplishments.

6. A visitor to your office tells you he has an appointment with your supervisor whom you expect shortly. The visitor asks to wait in your supervisor's private office. For you to allow the visitor to do this is
    (A) desirable; the visitor would be less likely to disturb the other employees or to be disturbed by them.
    (B) undesirable; it is not courteous to permit a visitor to be left alone in an office.
    (C) desirable; your supervisor may wish to speak to the visitor in private.
    (D) undesirable; your supervisor may have left confidential papers on his/her desk.

7. You are newly appointed to an office. While your supervisor is at a conference that may last for several hours, an individual enters the office and asks you for information with which you are not familiar. Of the following which is the best action for you to take?
    (A) Ask the person to return to the office later in the day when your supervisor will have returned.
    (B) Ask the person to wait in the office until your supervisor returns.
    (C) Ask a more experienced person in your office to answer the person's questions.
    (D) Advise the person that the information will be given when she/he writes a letter.

8. You work in an office with many people. Since your desk is closest to the entrance, most visitors direct their inquiries to you. Visitors enter your office and ask you for readily available information; however, you and the other individuals are extremely busy. Which of the following is the best action for you to take?
    (A) Ignore the question in hopes they will turn to someone else.
    (B) Inform visitors politely that you are busy now and ask them to return later.
    (C) Give the requested information concisely but courteously and then continue with your work.
    (D) Advise visitors to write a letter for the information and you will send it through the mail.

9. Which of the following traits is most important for an employee who is in continuous contact with visitors?
    (A) Technical training.
    (B) Courage.
    (C) Ability to read and follow instructions.
    (D) Courtesy.

10. You are a public sector employee and should realize that in contacts with the public
    (A) you should always agree with what a visitor says because "The visitor is always right."
    (B) you should not give any information over the telephone unless the caller identifies him/herself.
    (C) how you treat a visitor may determine the visitor's opinion of your office in general.
    (D) visitors should be furnished with all the information they request.

END OF TEST

Correspondence Test

Directions: Match the sentence or statement in Column I (statements about letters) with the correct word or phrase in Column II (parts of letters). Mark the answer sheet with the letter of that answer.

Allow 5 minutes for this test.

Column I	Column II
1. The signer's name and title.	1. (A) Salutation. (B) Inside address. (C) Writer's identification. (D) Letterhead.
2. A filing code used by the letter writer or the addressee.	2. (A) Reference notation. (B) Message. (C) Salutation. (D) Postscript.
3. An indication that a letter should be read only by the person addressed.	3. (A) Subject. (B) Reference notation. (C) Confidential notation. (D) Closing.
4. It may include the department, division, slogan, telephone number, or office.	4. (A) Company signature. (B) Message. (C) Inside address. (D) Letterhead
5. Replaces the salutation and is typed in all capital letters.	5. (A) Subject. (B) Attention. (C) Closing. (D) Signature.
6. Part that routes the letter to a particular individual or office.	6. (A) Inside address. (B) Attention. (C) Subject. (D) Personal notation.
7. Part of the letter that indicates it has been sent a special way.	7. (A) Reference notation. (B) Subject. (C) Postscript. (D) Mailing notation.
8. Part of the letter that indicates who the typist is and the writer separate from the signer.	8. (A) Writer's identification. (B) Reference initials. (C) Reference notation. (D) Postscript.
9. Part of the letter which shows other people are receiving it as well.	9. (A) Postscript. (B) Reference initials. (C) Copy. (D) Subject.
10. Part of a letter directed to a third person who will deliver it to the addressee.	10. (A) In care of. (B) Attention. (C) Personal. (D) Blind copy.

END OF TEST

Judgment Test

Allow 5 minutes for this test.

1. When everything seems to be going wrong and you realize another problem may occur, which of the following course of action should you take?
   - (A) Tell your supervisor you can't handle it and she/he must decide what to do.
   - (B) Avoid getting upset and emotional about the problem.
   - (C) Listen to what everyone else suggests and let them handle it.
   - (D) Don't answer the phone or open the door until things calm down.

2. Each person who works for someone represents his/her employer. Which of the following shows a total lack of judgment on an employee's part?
   - (A) Making a visitor wait until he/she has completed his/her typing project.
   - (B) Bragging to visitors about his/her skills and abilities.
   - (C) Talking loudly on the telephone.
   - (D) Greeting friends.

3. Which of the following would be the most efficient way to verify a long list of figures?
   - (A) Use a computer.
   - (B) Use a calculator.
   - (C) Reverse the order of the figures and read them.
   - (D) Check the column with someone else.

4. If you want to keep the mailing costs down in your office, of the following which is the best way?
   - (A) Send all the mail first class.
   - (B) Send each letter separately.
   - (C) Use a No. 10 envelope instead of a No. 6 1/2.
   - (D) Keep an up-to-date list of addresses.

5. If an individual calls and wants confidential information you know is not to be given out, which of the following is the best reply?
   - (A) I am sorry but our office procedures manual states that we are not permitted to give out such information over the phone.
   - (B) I am sorry but I am not familiar with that information.
   - (C) I'll transfer you to my supervisor who will give it to you.
   - (D) I am sorry but we are not permitted to release that information.

6. If by mistake you opened your supervisor's mail marked ''Confidential,'' which of the following is the best action to take?
   - (A) Immediately take the letter and envelope to your supervisor and explain your error.
   - (B) Read the letter to see if it is really ''confidential,'' and then handle accordingly.
   - (C) Just deliver the letter and opened envelope as is without any explanation.
   - (D) Type up a new envelope, seal it, and say nothing.

7. Your supervisor asked you to interview some typists from another section who are candidates for the word processing center. You know one of the individuals has a record of tardiness and excessive absenteeism. Of the following, which is the best action for you to take?
   - (A) Not say anything to the applicant or to your supervisor.
   - (B) Tell the applicant you know his/her record and you think it is better she/he doesn't apply.
   - (C) Refer the applicant to your supervisor giving him/her your information and let the supervisor make the decision.
   - (D) Tell the applicant you know of a better position elsewhere.

8. You have been transferred to a new office in another city. You must familiarize yourself with all your fellow workers. If you are not sure of the proper way to address an individual, which of the following should you do?
   - (A) Ask one of your fellow workers.
   - (B) Be very informal and watch and listen to what others say and do.
   - (C) Be very formal until told otherwise.
   - (D) Ask your immediate supervisor for the correct procedures.

9. Using your time wisely is highly commendable in the office. Which of the following would demonstrate your outstanding time management ability?
   - (A) Watching the clock.
   - (B) Meeting assigned deadlines.
   - (C) Emphasizing the importance of productivity.
   - (D) Making suggestions to others on how to improve their time.

10. While your supervisor is at lunch, a visitor approaches you and asks for information regarding an important matter. Although you have no information about the matter, you know your supervisor has just received a confidential report on the subject and the report is still in your supervisor's desk. The most appropriate of the following actions for you to take is?
    - (A) Obtain the report from your supervisor's desk and permit the visitor to read it in your presence.
    - (B) Tell the visitor your supervisor has just received a report on this matter and suggest that the visitor ask your supervisor for permission to read it.
    - (C) Inform the visitor you have no information on the matter and suggest that the visitor return later when your supervisor is back from lunch.
    - (D) Obtain the report from your supervisor's desk and answer the visitor's questions from information contained in the report.

END OF TEST

Mail Services and Shipping Test

Allow 5 minutes for this test.

1. Western Union's role is still to transmit messages. Which of the following is *not* a service of Western Union?
   - (A) Mailgrams.
   - (B) Telex/TWX.
   - (C) Telegrams.
   - (D) Expressgrams.

2. Of the services offered by Western Union, which of the systems provides delivery within hours?
   - (A) Mailgram.
   - (B) Telex/TWX.
   - (C) Telegram.
   - (D) Expressgram.

3. What is the name of the system by which remote offices can send and receive printed messages?
   - (A) Mailgram.
   - (B) Telex/TWX.
   - (C) Telegram.
   - (D) Expressgram.

4. Which one of the four services offered by Western Union works together with the U.S. Postal Service?
   - (A) Mailgram.
   - (B) Telex/TWX.
   - (C) Telegram.
   - (D) Expressgram.

5. What is the name of the service that provides proof of mailing given by the U.S. Postal Service?
   - (A) Certified.
   - (B) COD.
   - (C) Special handling.
   - (D) Special delivery.

6. The best way to send valuable items by first class or priority through the mail is
   - (A) insured.
   - (B) registered.
   - (C) special handling.
   - (D) special delivery.

7. The U.S. Postal Service has installed in major post offices an electronic scanner called an OCR. What is the major function of this machine?
   (A) Speed up the sorting of the mail.
   (B) Speed up the stamping of the mail.
   (C) Speed up the coding of the mail.
   (D) None of the above.

8. The post office classifies mail as first, second, third, and fourth. What does first-class mail consist of?
   (A) Magazines.
   (B) Handwritten material.
   (C) Packages up to 70 lbs.
   (D) Periodicals.

9. As a mail clerk, your supervisor has instructed you to send certain items by "parcel post." How should you send them?
   (A) Fourth-class mail.
   (B) Railway express.
   (C) Registered first-class mail.
   (D) Second-class mail.

10. When a letter is attached to a parcel post package, the rate for the letter is
    (A) First class.
    (B) Second class.
    (C) Third class.
    (D) Fourth class.

END OF TEST

Equipment Test

Allow 5 minutes for this test.

1. Small offices use either face-to-face dictation or dictation-transcribing machines. The chief advantage of a dictation machine over a secretary is
   (A) it eliminates the need for stenographers and saves their salaries for new up-to-date equipment.
   (B) fewer errors are made when using a machine rather than a secretary to take dictation.
   (C) the secretary can be performing other job functions while the dictator is using the machine.
   (D) the machine eliminates outside interruptions—telephone, noise, people talking, typewriter, etc.

2. What is the name of the equipment that is an information handling unit and contains a keyboard, a screen, a magnetic storage unit, and a printer?
   (A) Work station.
   (B) Word processor.
   (C) Text editor.
   (D) Mash.

3. What is the name of the piece of equipment that reduces the size of an original document to very small forms that are then used as records for storage of information?
   (A) Microfilms.
   (B) Microflite.
   (C) Microrecording.
   (D) Microprocessing.

4. If your supervisor is away from the office a great deal and you must contact him/her often, you might suggest a device that helps your supervisor keep in touch with the office. Which of the following would you recommend?
   (A) Messenger.
   (B) Mobile service.
   (C) Pager.
   (D) Mother.

5. There are a variety of devices that produce copy on paper. Which of the following is *not* a printing device?
   (A) Impact printer.
   (B) Letter-quality printer.
   (C) Bidirectional printer.
   (D) Train-track printer.

6. A word processor consists of a CPU, a keyboard, a display screen, a form of magnetic storage, and a printer. Which of the following is *not* a word processor?
   (A) Blind word processor.
   (B) Window word processor.

(C)   Communicating word processor.
(D)   Dedicated word processor.

7.   Which of the following is *not* an assortment or type or style that is used on typewriters, word processor, printers, or data processors?
(A)   Font.
(B)   Daisy wheel.
(C)   Element.
(D)   Chip.

8.   Which of the following is *not* a part of a typewriter?
(A)   Byte.
(B)   Line justification.
(C)   Character.
(D)   Pitch.

9.   When you are typing and need to print one or more characters slightly above the regular line of type by a half or quarter of a line, this is called
(A)   subscript.
(B)   superscript.
(C)   standscript.
(D)   scrolling.

10.   Of the following, the main reason for using a calculating machine is
(A)   a lesser knowledge of arithmetic.
(B)   a more attractive product is obtained.
(C)   greater speed and accuracy are obtained.
(D)   it is not difficult to learn how to operate.

END OF TEST

Communications Test

Allow 5 minutes for this test.

1.   Communications on the job are very important. Of the following, which would help you to improve office communications?
(A)   Read the body language of the person communicating.
(B)   Evaluate the individual communicating.
(C)   Increase your vocabulary and use larger sentence.
(D)   Repeat information to verify its accuracy and clarity.

2.   "A typed letter should resemble a picture properly framed." This statement emphasizes
(A)   accuracy.
(B)   speed.
(C)   convenience.
(D)   neatness.

3.   "Many individuals dictate business correspondence so rapidly that they often pay little attention to matters of punctuation and English. They expect their stenographers to correct their errors." This statement implies most clearly that stenographers should be
(A)   able to write acceptable original reports when required.
(B)   good typists as well as good stenographers.
(C)   efficient clerks as well as good stenographers.
(D)   proficient in language usage.

4.   The chief value of showing enclosures beneath the identification marks on the lower left side of a letter is
(A)   it acts as a check upon the contents before mailing and upon receiving a letter.
(B)   it helps to determine the weight for mailing.
(C)   it is useful in checking the accuracy of typed material.
(D)   it requires an efficient mailing clerk.

5. Which of the following is not an advantage of a window envelope?
   (A) It saves time since the inside address serves also as an outside address.
   (B) It gives protection to the address from being handled by the mailing service.
   (C) It lessens the possibility of mistakes since the address is written only once.
   (D) It is much easier to seal than the plain envelopes.

6. The usual reason for endorsement of a check is
   (A) to transfer ownership of the check.
   (B) to identify the drawer of the check.
   (C) to indicate the check is genuine.
   (D) to prevent payment of the check until a specific time.

7. The way you communicate with people reveals a great deal about your self-concepts. Which of the following communication patterns would *not* reveal your true self?
   (A) Vocabulary and tone of voice.
   (B) Self-image.
   (C) Interpersonal relationship.
   (D) Your goals.

8. Which of the following is *not* part of the communications process?
   (A) Originator.
   (B) Self-image.
   (C) Message.
   (D) Receiver.

9. Another method of communicating is through nonverbal communications. Which of the following would *not* be an example of nonverbal communications?
   (A) Time.
   (B) Space.
   (C) Color.
   (D) Noise.

10. In order for your office to function properly, there must be communication between individuals. Many times due to different backgrounds, education, etc., barriers exist. Which of the following would *not* be a barrier to communications?
    (A) Noise.
    (B) Language usage.
    (C) Inference.
    (D) Time.

END OF TEST

Procedures Test

Allow 5 minutes for this test.

1. When you need additional material and supplies from the central stock room, which of the following should you complete?
   (A) Purchase order.
   (B) Request form.
   (C) Sales form.
   (D) Budget request.

2. Word processing centers in most large offices are centralized. Of the following, what is the greatest advantage of centralization?
   (A) Work is performed more efficiently and effectively.
   (B) More flexibility in work distribution and handling.
   (C) Security controls are intact.
   (D) Work is kept more confidential.

3. If your supervisor travels interstate a great deal, it is recommended you have on your desk which of the following?
   (A) The Blue book.
   (B) The Red book.
   (C) Billingers' Guide book.
   (D) The local telephone directory.

4. If you want to improve your visibility in the office as a productive, effective employee, which of the following is the best method?
   (A) Take your time and complete each assignment very precisely.
   (B) Plan your daily tasks and complete them effectively and efficiently according to your peak periods.
   (C) Learn new office automation techniques.
   (D) Make suggestions on ways to cut costs.

5. A letter should be proofread for corrections by the typist
   (A) as each sentence is typed.
   (B) when the letter has been completed and before it is removed from the typewriter or saved on the diskette.
   (C) immediately after each paragraph.
   (D) after it has been approved by the dictator.

6. Automating for efficiency means most nearly
   (A) performing an assignment despite all the interruptions.
   (B) leaving difficult assignments for someone who is more proficient with the new equipment.
   (C) using the most up-to-date means for performing certain tasks.
   (D) trying to do a few tasks on each new machine at a time.

7. "If the method used in your office seems to be outdated, you should offer constructive suggestions instead of mere criticism of the method." On the basis of this statement, which of the following is the most accurate conclusion?
   (A) The methods used in your office should be criticized only if they cannot be improved.
   (B) Most of the problems can be overcome satisfactorily by your suggestions.
   (C) You should suggest improvements for existing poor methods rather than only finding fault with them.
   (D) The quality of suggestions submitted by employees depends upon the methods used in an office.

8. You keep the payroll records in your office and are instructed by your supervisor to use a new method for keeping the records. You think the new method will be less effective than the one you are now using. In this situation it would be most advisable for you to
   (A) use the new method to keep the records even if you think it may be less effective.
   (B) continue to use the method you consider to be more effective without saying anything to your supervisor.
   (C) use the method you consider to be more effective and then tell your supervisor your reasons for doing so.
   (D) use the new method only if you can improve its effectiveness.

9. Part of your job description is to handle the supplies for your office. Of the following practices, the one that would be least advisable for you to follow is
   (A) use up the supply of an article first before a new supply is ordered.
   (B) keep articles requested frequently in an accessible place.
   (C) use the oldest stock up first.
   (D) everyone should use a requisition slip to obtain supplies.

10. Your supervisor has asked that everyone try to reduce the wasteful use of supplies. You note you have on hand 3,000 legal sized envelopes that have your old mailing address on them. Of the following the most appropriate action for you to take with the envelopes would be
    (A) send them only to individuals who know your new address.
    (B) use them to store small items in like paper clips or rubber bands.
    (C) use them only for first-class mail.
    (D) cross out the old address and either stamp, type, or overlap it with the new address.

END OF TEST

Answer Key for Practice Tests

Business Terminology Test

1. D	3. C	5. B	7. B	9. A
2. A	4. D	6. C	8. D	10. C

Telephone Techniques Test

1. A	3. B	5. A	7. D	9. A
2. D	4. D	6. B	8. C	10. D

Courtesies Test

1. C	3. A	5. C	7. C	9. D
2. A	4. D	6. D	8. C	10. C

Correspondence Test

1. C	3. C	5. A	7. D	9. C
2. A	4. D	6. B	8. B	10. A

Judgment Test

1. B	3. D	5. D	7. C	9. B
2. A	4. D	6. A	8. D	10. C

Mail Services and Shipping Test

1. D	3. B	5. A	7. A	9. A
2. C	4. A	6. B	8. B	10. A

Equipment Test

1. C	3. A	5. D	7. D	9. B
2. B	4. C	6. B	8. A	10. C

Communications Test

1. D	3. D	5. D	7. D	9. D
2. D	4. A	6. A	8. B	10. D

Procedures Test

1. B	3. B	5. B	7. C	9. A
2. B	4. B	6. C	8. A	10. D

Posttest and Answers

Directions: For each of the following questions, select the choice which best answers the question or completes the statement. Mark the answer sheet with the letter of that answer.

Allow 5 minutes for this posttest.

1. What is the business term that means a single letter, figure, space, or symbol produced by a keystroke on a typewriter, a word processor, or a data-entry keyboard?
   - (A) Character.
   - (B) Byte.
   - (C) Document.
   - (D) Insertion.

2. Part of your job as a file clerk is to answer all incoming telephone calls. You receive a telephone call for Emily Hodges, who has resigned. Which of the following should you do?
   - (A) Tell the caller Miss Hodges can now be reached at her home phone.
   - (B) Tell the caller "Miss Hodges is no longer in this office," and then disconnect the caller.
   - (C) Ask the caller whether someone else may help him/her as Miss Hodges has resigned.
   - (D) Tell the caller Miss Hodges isn't permitted to receive personal calls.

3. You notice a visitor has entered your office but the other employees who handle this assignment are not aware of the visitor's presence. Even though it is not part of your job, which of the following actions should you take?
   - (A) Continue with your work and wait for the other employees whose job it is to handle the visitor.
   - (B) Recognize and attend to the visitor immediately.
   - (C) Cough loudly to get one of the other employee's attention.
   - (D) Continue working and wait for the visitor to say something.

4. You are typing a report or manuscript and you need to identify the source of a statement quoted or cited in the text. This function is called a
   - (A) code.
   - (B) subordinate clause.
   - (C) thesis.
   - (D) note.

5. If your immediate supervisor gives you a task to complete that you do not consider a part of your job description, which of the following would you do?
   - (A) Refuse to do any work not listed on your job description.
   - (B) Assign it to one of your other peers.
   - (C) Do it, but be sure you complain to everyone it is not part of your job duties.
   - (D) Accept the task willingly and do it as quickly as possible.

6. If a room or suite number accompanies the building name and is to be typed in the inside address, where is it to be typed?
   - (A) Both the building and room or suite on the same line.
   - (B) The building name only and not the room or suite number.
   - (C) The building name only after the street address.
   - (D) The room or suite in the lower left-hand corner.

7. What is the name of the electric semiautomatic typewriter that permits the use of several styles and sizes of type on the same page just by removable plates or typefaces?
   - (A) Proportional typewriter.
   - (B) Linotype.
   - (C) Statistical typewriter.
   - (D) Varityper.

8. The term referring to the physical specification that affects the appearance and arrangement of a document (the margins, lines, spacing, etc.) is called
   - (A) global.
   - (B) format.
   - (C) menu.
   - (D) playout.

9. When you create a document on one page and a list of addresses on another page and you want to put them together, the term used is
   (A) merge.
   (B) originator.
   (C) printer.
   (D) wraparound.

10. The part of a letter which has a reference number or filing code is called
    (A) message.
    (B) personal notation.
    (C) subject line.
    (D) postscript.

11. Which of the following best describes "office work simplification"?
    (A) An attempt to increase the rate of production by speeding up the movement of employees.
    (B) Eliminating wasteful steps in order to increase efficiency.
    (C) Making jobs as easy as possible for employees so they will not be overworked.
    (D) Eliminating all difficult tasks from an office and leaving only simple ones.

12. The type of speech used by an office employee in telephone conversations greatly affects the communication. Of the following, the best way to express your ideas when telephoning is with a vocabulary that consists mainly of
    (A) formal, intellectual sounding words.
    (B) often used colloquial words.
    (C) technical, emphatic words.
    (D) simple, descriptive words.

13. While speaking on the telephone to someone who called you, you are disconnected. The first thing you should do is
    (A) hang up, but try to keep your line free to receive the caller back.
    (B) immediately get the dialtone and continually dial the person.
    (C) signal the Centrex or switchboard operator and ask to reestablish the connection.
    (D) press "O" for Operator and explain that you were disconnected.

14. A typist would most likely be most productive if the supervisor
    (A) shows that his/her most important interest is in schedules and production goals.
    (B) consistently pressures his/her staff to get the work out.
    (C) never fails to let the typist know she/he is in charge.
    (D) considers the typist's ability and needs while requiring that production goals be met.

15. Of the following types of letters, the most difficult to trace if lost after mailing is
    (A) special delivery letter.
    (B) registered letter.
    (C) insured letter.
    (D) certified letter.

16. Which of the following actions should a supervisor find most effective as a method of determining whether subordinates need additional training in performing their work?
    (A) Compiling a list of absences and latenesses of subordinates.
    (B) Observing how subordinates carry out their various tasks.
    (C) Reviewing the grievances submitted by subordinates.
    (D) Reminding subordinates to consult him/her if they experience difficulty in completing an assignment.

17. The cash fund on hand for the payment of minor office expenses is known as
    (A) petty cash.
    (B) a sinking fund.
    (C) a drawing account.
    (D) net assets.

18. The term "v.v." means most nearly
    (A) namely.
    (B) various places.
    (C) vice versa.
    (D) value indicated above.

19. The CPS Examination has six areas that test one's education, experience, and knowledge. Which of the following areas is not tested?
    (A) Business Law.
    (B) Economics and Management.
    (C) Office Administration and Communications.
    (D) Bookkeeping.

20. If your supervisor asked you to consider leasing word processing equipment from a major distributor, which of the following would *not* be a major point for you to consider?
    (A) The cost of installation.
    (B) Any shipping or handling charges.
    (C) The amount of maintenance down time.
    (D) The amount of depreciation on the printer.

END OF POSTTEST

Answer Key for Posttest

1. A	5. D	9. A	13. A	17. A
2. C	6. A	10. C	14. D	18. C
3. B	7. D	11. B	15. A	19. D
4. D	8. B	12. D	16. B	20. D

Mathematics Review Answer Sheet

Pretest

1 Ⓐ Ⓑ Ⓒ Ⓓ   5 Ⓐ Ⓑ Ⓒ Ⓓ   9 Ⓐ Ⓑ Ⓒ Ⓓ   13 Ⓐ Ⓑ Ⓒ Ⓓ   17 Ⓐ Ⓑ Ⓒ Ⓓ
2 Ⓐ Ⓑ Ⓒ Ⓓ   6 Ⓐ Ⓑ Ⓒ Ⓓ   10 Ⓐ Ⓑ Ⓒ Ⓓ   14 Ⓐ Ⓑ Ⓒ Ⓓ   18 Ⓐ Ⓑ Ⓒ Ⓓ
3 Ⓐ Ⓑ Ⓒ Ⓓ   7 Ⓐ Ⓑ Ⓒ Ⓓ   11 Ⓐ Ⓑ Ⓒ Ⓓ   15 Ⓐ Ⓑ Ⓒ Ⓓ   19 Ⓐ Ⓑ Ⓒ Ⓓ
4 Ⓐ Ⓑ Ⓒ Ⓓ   8 Ⓐ Ⓑ Ⓒ Ⓓ   12 Ⓐ Ⓑ Ⓒ Ⓓ   16 Ⓐ Ⓑ Ⓒ Ⓓ   20 Ⓐ Ⓑ Ⓒ Ⓓ

Computation Test 1

1 Ⓐ Ⓑ Ⓒ Ⓓ Ⓔ   3 Ⓐ Ⓑ Ⓒ Ⓓ Ⓔ   5 Ⓐ Ⓑ Ⓒ Ⓓ Ⓔ   7 Ⓐ Ⓑ Ⓒ Ⓓ Ⓔ   8 Ⓐ Ⓑ Ⓒ Ⓓ Ⓔ
2 Ⓐ Ⓑ Ⓒ Ⓓ Ⓔ   4 Ⓐ Ⓑ Ⓒ Ⓓ Ⓔ   6 Ⓐ Ⓑ Ⓒ Ⓓ Ⓔ

Computation Test 2

1 Ⓐ Ⓑ Ⓒ Ⓓ Ⓔ   3 Ⓐ Ⓑ Ⓒ Ⓓ Ⓔ   5 Ⓐ Ⓑ Ⓒ Ⓓ Ⓔ   7 Ⓐ Ⓑ Ⓒ Ⓓ Ⓔ   8 Ⓐ Ⓑ Ⓒ Ⓓ Ⓔ
2 Ⓐ Ⓑ Ⓒ Ⓓ Ⓔ   4 Ⓐ Ⓑ Ⓒ Ⓓ Ⓔ   6 Ⓐ Ⓑ Ⓒ Ⓓ Ⓔ

Word Problems Test 1

1 Ⓐ Ⓑ Ⓒ Ⓓ   3 Ⓐ Ⓑ Ⓒ Ⓓ   5 Ⓐ Ⓑ Ⓒ Ⓓ   7 Ⓐ Ⓑ Ⓒ Ⓓ   8 Ⓐ Ⓑ Ⓒ Ⓓ
2 Ⓐ Ⓑ Ⓒ Ⓓ   4 Ⓐ Ⓑ Ⓒ Ⓓ   6 Ⓐ Ⓑ Ⓒ Ⓓ

Word Problems Test 2

1 Ⓐ Ⓑ Ⓒ Ⓓ   3 Ⓐ Ⓑ Ⓒ Ⓓ   5 Ⓐ Ⓑ Ⓒ Ⓓ   7 Ⓐ Ⓑ Ⓒ Ⓓ   8 Ⓐ Ⓑ Ⓒ Ⓓ
2 Ⓐ Ⓑ Ⓒ Ⓓ   4 Ⓐ Ⓑ Ⓒ Ⓓ   6 Ⓐ Ⓑ Ⓒ Ⓓ

Posttest

1 Ⓐ Ⓑ Ⓒ Ⓓ Ⓔ   5 Ⓐ Ⓑ Ⓒ Ⓓ Ⓔ   9 Ⓐ Ⓑ Ⓒ Ⓓ Ⓔ   13 Ⓐ Ⓑ Ⓒ Ⓓ Ⓔ   17 Ⓐ Ⓑ Ⓒ Ⓓ Ⓔ
2 Ⓐ Ⓑ Ⓒ Ⓓ Ⓔ   6 Ⓐ Ⓑ Ⓒ Ⓓ Ⓔ   10 Ⓐ Ⓑ Ⓒ Ⓓ Ⓔ   14 Ⓐ Ⓑ Ⓒ Ⓓ Ⓔ   18 Ⓐ Ⓑ Ⓒ Ⓓ Ⓔ
3 Ⓐ Ⓑ Ⓒ Ⓓ Ⓔ   7 Ⓐ Ⓑ Ⓒ Ⓓ Ⓔ   11 Ⓐ Ⓑ Ⓒ Ⓓ Ⓔ   15 Ⓐ Ⓑ Ⓒ Ⓓ Ⓔ   19 Ⓐ Ⓑ Ⓒ Ⓓ Ⓔ
4 Ⓐ Ⓑ Ⓒ Ⓓ Ⓔ   8 Ⓐ Ⓑ Ⓒ Ⓓ Ⓔ   12 Ⓐ Ⓑ Ⓒ Ⓓ Ⓔ   16 Ⓐ Ⓑ Ⓒ Ⓓ Ⓔ   20 Ⓐ Ⓑ Ⓒ Ⓓ Ⓔ

MATHEMATICS

Introductory Pretest and Answers

Computations

Directions: For each of the following questions, select the choice which best answers the question or completes the statement. Mark the answer sheet with the letter of that answer.

Allow 5 minutes for this pretest.

1. Add 28, 19, 17, 24 =
   - (A) 87
   - (B) 88
   - (C) 90
   - (D) 89

2. Subtract $48.98 from $1,250.37 =
   - (A) $1,201.39
   - (B) $1,201.49
   - (C) $1,200.39
   - (D) $1,201.38

3. Multiply 7962.27 times .06 =
   - (A) 4777.362
   - (B) 477.6732
   - (C) 4787.632
   - (D) 477.7362

4. Divide 2339.86 by 3.7 =
   - (A) 632.4
   - (B) 62.34
   - (C) 642.3
   - (D) 63.24

5. 3723 plus 14 plus 936 =
   - (A) 4773
   - (B) 4699
   - (C) 4673
   - (D) 4763

6. 3021 minus 447 minus 386 =
   - (A) 2188
   - (B) 2682
   - (C) 2061
   - (D) 3854

7. 12 times 19 times 43 =
   - (A) 9724
   - (B) 10703
   - (C) 9804
   - (D) 8904

8. 43281 divided by 3 divided by 7 =
   - (A) 14427
   - (B) 2061
   - (C) 2188
   - (D) 1982

9. 25 percent of 48 =
   - (A) 14
   - (B) 24
   - (C) 16
   - (D) 12

10. The sum of 1/3, 4/6, 3/4, 1/2, and 1/12 =
    - (A) 3 1/4
    - (B) 2 1/2
    - (C) 2 1/16
    - (D) 2 1/3

Word Problems

11. If you receive $36.70 a day and you worked 13 days, what would your total earnings be?
    - (A) $477.30
    - (B) $477.20
    - (C) $477.10
    - (D) $477.40

12. If you worked from 8:23 a.m. to 2:53 p.m., how many hours did you work?
    (A) 6 hours 16 minutes
    (B) 6 hours 30 minutes
    (C) 7 hours 16 minutes
    (D) 6 hours 40 minutes

13. If paper costs $5.92 a ream and you are allowed 5 percent discount for cash, how many reams can you purchase for $282.50 cash? Do not disregard fractional parts of a cent.
    (A) 49 reams
    (B) 50 reams
    (C) 60 reams
    (D) 53 reams

14. Your supervisor hands you 800 cards to be filed. You can file 80 cards an hour, and you work 7 hours. How many cards will you have left to be filed at the end of the day?
    (A) 40
    (B) 140
    (C) 250
    (D) 240

15. If you earn $12,000 a year and receive a bonus of $1,050 plus your regular yearly increment of $750, what will your new salary be?
    (A) $13,800
    (B) $12,750
    (C) $13,500
    (D) $14,100

16. If four typists can type 600 letters in three days, how many letters can two typists complete in one day?
    (A) 100
    (B) 90
    (C) 120
    (D) 150

17. Your office purchased six gross of stenographic pads. If the pads were used at the rate of 24 a week, what is the maximum number of weeks the six gross would last?
    (A) 6 weeks
    (B) 24 weeks
    (C) 12 weeks
    (D) 36 weeks

18. Your department had 69 employees on the staff in January. This is a decrease of 8 percent from the number of employees on the payroll in June. How many employees were on the payroll in June?
    (A) 75
    (B) 76
    (C) 74
    (D) 77

19. You purchased a computer for your office that cost $12,000. It depreciated in value 45 percent the first year, 20 percent of the reduced value the second year, and 20 percent of the reduced value the third year. What is it now worth after the third year?
    (A) $4,250
    (B) $4,328
    (C) $1,800
    (D) $4,224

20. If 12 word processing center employees can produce 12,000 documents in 20 days, how many documents can 18 word processors produce in 50 days?
    (A) 37,500
    (B) 35,000
    (C) 32,500
    (D) 45,000

END OF PRETEST

Answer Key for Pretest

1.	B	5.	C	9.	D	13.	B	17.	D
2.	A	6.	A	10.	D	14.	D	18.	A
3.	D	7.	C	11.	C	15.	A	19.	D
4.	A	8.	B	12.	B	16.	A	20.	D

Study Hints

This section provides practice through a series of tests modeled on the different question types that have actually appeared on examinations. An important tip from years of experience with the self-tutored test-takers: *Study the directions!* We have included those you are most likely to meet on your examination. Control over them will gain precious minutes for you. This doesn't mean you can skip reading directions on your actual examination, but does mean that you will be ahead of the game for knowing the language examiners use. A misunderstood direction can lead to a run of incorrect answers. Avoid this costly carelessness.

1. Plan on taking different types of computation tests. Keep alert to the differences and complications. That will help keep you bright and interested.

2. Review your errors. This is an important step for every study session. Allow time for redoing every incorrect answer. The good self-tutor is a good self-critic. You learn most from your mistakes; then you should never make them again.

3. Study the sample solutions. Note how carefully we have worked out each step. Get into this habit when doing all the practice tests.

Rules

Sample Questions and Explanations

Here are some basic types of problems explained and solved in this section. Each of the basic problems are solved in a step-by-step fashion. Most of the problems you will face on an actual examination are either like one of these types or a variation of one.

Problem 1. Staplers are bought for $18 a dozen. In order to gain 40 percent, what must the selling price of a stapler be?

Solution To find the selling price, you must multiply the cost by the rate of profit or loss.

$18 times 1.40 (140 percent) equals $25.20 divided by 12 = $2.10

Problem 2. Staplers are bought for $30 a dozen and sold at $3.50 each. What is the rate of profit on the transaction?

Solution Multiply $3.50 by 12 to find the selling price of a dozen staplers.

$3.50 x 12 = $42 less $30 = $12 profit. Subtract the cost from the selling price to find the actual profit; to find what percent of the cost the profit is involves converting a fraction into a percent. Multiply the fraction $12 over 30 x 100 = 1200 divided by 30 = 40%.

Problem 3. If you add 8⅕, 45 ⅝, 2 ¹⁷⁄₂₀, 14½, and 1 ²¹⁄₄₀, will the answer be?

Solution In adding mixed numbers like these, you perform three additions—the addition of the whole numbers, the addition of the fractions, and combinations of the added whole numbers and fractions.

The whole numbers total 70. To add the fractions, you must first find the least common denominator which is 40. Then for each separate fraction you divide the denominator into the common denominator and multiply the resulting quotient by the numerator. You add all these products and divide by the common denominator:

⅕ = 8; ⅝ = 25; ¹⁷⁄₂₀ = 34; ½ = 20; ²¹⁄₄₀ = 21

108 divided by 40 = 2⁷⁄₁₀ plus 70 = 72⁷⁄₁₀

Problem 4. 233.404 divided by 4.6 = (A) 50.74 (B) 52.24 (C) 57.30 (D) 58.24

Solution

```
       50.74
46 /2334.04
     230
      340
      322
      184
      184
```

Since the answer is clearly 50.74, mark (A) on the answer sheet. Do not mark any of the other letter choices. There is only one correct answer.

Problem 5. Multiply 2946 × 7.007 = (A) 21,642.622 (B) 20,642.622

(C) 41,244.001   (D) 20,641.622

Solution

2946	The answer is
×7.007	20,642.622, which is
20622	answer choice B. This
0000	answer is similar to
0000	answer choices (A) and
20622	(D), but it is not the
20642.622	same. So you must be

careful not to let the (A) and (D) choices confuse you. Mark only (B) on your answer sheet.

Problem 6. A certain kind of diskette can be bought for $2 each or in packages of 12 for $20. How much more would it cost to buy 240 diskettes singly than to buy them in the 12-diskette packages? (A) $4 (B) $80 (C) $400 (D) $480

Solution ''How much more would it cost to buy 240 diskettes individually than to buy them in the 12-diskette packages?'' asks the question, and

you are given clues to work with. The first step is to figure the cost of both methods and find the difference. Buying 240 diskettes at $2 each would cost $480 ($2 × 240 = $480). Buying the diskettes in packages of 12 would mean buying 20 packages (240 divided by 12 = $20); at $20 a package they would cost $400 ($20 × 20 = $400). The difference is $80 ($480–$400 = $80), and the answer is (B).

Each of the following tests presents the kind of questions you may expect on your examination. Don't try to take all the tests at once. Rather, schedule yourself so you take a few at each session, and spend about the same time on them at each session. Score yourself honestly and date each test. You should be able to detect improvement in your performance on successive sessions.

If you continue to have difficulty, purchase a basic mathematics textbook and review all the rules.

Tests and Answers

The answer key will be found at the end of these practice tests.

Computation Test

Directions: In this test you are to do the basic mathematical operations in arithmetic—addition, subtraction, multiplication, and division. For each of the following questions, select the choice which best answers the question or completes the statement. Mark the space (E) only if your answer for a question does not exactly agree with any of the first four suggested answers. Mark the answer sheet with the letter of that answer.

Allow 2 minutes for this test.

1. Add 68, 30, 46, 52 =
   (A) 169
   (B) 189
   (C) 196
   (D) 198
   (E) None of these.

2. Add 44, 57, 60, 32 =
   (A) 193
   (B) 139
   (C) 161
   (D) 138
   (E) None of these.

3. Subtract 191 minus 59 =
   (A) 133
   (B) 132
   (C) 131
   (D) 122
   (E) None of these.

4. Subtract 86 minus 47 =
   (A) 49
   (B) 29
   (C) 38
   (D) 39
   (E) None of these.

5. Multiply 39 x 7 =
   (A) 273
   (B) 312
   (C) 234
   (D) 237
   (E) None of these.

6. Multiply 173 x 4 =
   (A) 292
   (B) 692
   (C) 629
   (D) 682
   (E) None of these.

7. Divide 54 by 9 =
   (A) 5
   (B) 6
   (C) 7
   (D) 8
   (E) None of these.

8. Divide 497 by 7 =
   (A) 73
   (B) 68
   (C) 69
   (D) 70
   (E) None of these.

END OF TEST

Computation Test 2

Allow 2 minutes for this test.

1. Which is incorrect?
   (A) 24 + 80 + 12 + 69 = 185
   (B) 13 + 22 + 82 + 41 = 158
   (C) 71 + 14 + 35 + 18 = 138
   (D) 56 + 71 + 59 + 63 = 248
   (E) 68 + 85 + 59 + 92 = 304

2. Which is incorrect?
   (A) 54 + 36 + 19 + 27 = 146
   (B) 42 + 16 + 72 + 66 = 196
   (C) 20 + 35 + 78 + 53 = 186
   (D) 56 + 95 + 53 + 71 = 275
   (E) 75 + 14 + 49 + 87 = 225

3. Which is incorrect?
   (A) 91 − 59 = 32
   (B) 78 − 39 = 39
   (C) 36 − 19 = 27
   (D) 65 − 37 = 28
   (E) 37 − 19 = 18

4. Which is incorrect?
   (A) 92 − 57 = 35
   (B) 71 − 37 = 44
   (C) 94 − 27 = 67
   (D) 72 − 39 = 33
   (E) 64 − 49 = 15

5. Which is incorrect?
   (A) 73 × 4 = 292
   (B) 39 × 6 = 234
   (C) 17 × 5 = 95
   (D) 14 × 9 = 126
   (E) 99 × 2 = 198

6. Which is incorrect?
   (A) 43 × 8 = 344
   (B) 12 × 9 = 108
   (C) 19 × 5 = 95
   (D) 29 × 9 = 261
   (E) 44 × 7 = 318

7. Which is incorrect?
   (A) 355 ÷ 5 = 71
   (B) 217 ÷ 31 = 7
   (C) 576 ÷ 8 = 73
   (D) 194 ÷ 2 = 97
   (E) 438 ÷ 6 = 73

8. Which is incorrect?
   (A) 279 ÷ 9 = 31
   (B) 184 ÷ 4 = 47
   (C) 375 ÷ 5 = 75
   (D) 675 ÷ 9 = 75
   (E) 623 ÷ 7 = 89

END OF TEST

Word Problems Test 1

The questions in this part are provided as practice for the type of questions you will be asked on your examination. Do them all carefully and then compare your answers with those given at the end of this section. These questions have been designed to bring out all the tricks and difficulties you may expect to meet on your examination. When you have practiced with them, you will be better able to cope with the actual examination questions. Try to work quickly and accurately. If your score on the first trial is less than 70 percent right, plan to do the section over at some later date. When you do it over, you should note an improvement in your score. Let at least two weeks elapse before trying this section for the second time.

Directions: Each question in this test is followed by four suggested answers. Indicate the letter preceding your answer choice and mark the answer sheet with the letter of that answer.

Allow 3 minutes for this test.

1. A file clerk's weekly salary is increased from $200 to $225. What is the percentage of increase?
    (A) 10%
    (B) 12½%
    (C) 11⅛%
    (D) 14½%

2. If there are 245 offices in your company, the average number of offices for each of the five departments is
    (A) 48
    (B) 47
    (C) 50
    (D) 49

3. If you had 45 folders to file and 9 file clerks to do the job, what is the average each file clerk should do?
    (A) 7
    (B) 6
    (C) 8
    (D) 5

4. If your photocopy machine's cooling fan runs 5 minutes a day for 10 days in a given month, it would run how long during this month?
    (A) 50 minutes
    (B) 1½ hours
    (C) 1 hour
    (D) 30 minutes

5. If your company uses 1,500 employees in clerical jobs and half as many more to do management jobs, the total number of people is
    (A) 2,000
    (B) 2,520
    (C) 2,050
    (D) 2,250

6. If the stenographic pool produces 1,820 documents in 7 hours, what is the average hourly documents produced?
    (A) 230
    (B) 260
    (C) 250
    (D) 280

7. If, of the 1,820 documents issued, 100 were memos, then how many letters were produced?
    (A) 60
    (B) 260
    (C) 1,720
    (D) 1,270

8. If the fluid used for the main printing press is stored in a 100 gallon barrel, and your supervisor said it is ⅗ full, how many gallons do you need to order to fill the barrel?
    (A) 20
    (B) 60
    (C) 40
    (D) 80

END OF TEST

Word Problems Test 2

Allow 3 minutes for this test.

1. If 15 typists complete 2,800 work projects in 18 days, how many projects will 8 typists complete in 25 days?
   (A) 2,900
   (B) 2,074
   (C) 1,843
   (D) 2,650

2. You are responsible for the supplies and you have 600 lined tablets on hand. If you give personnel 3/8 of them, administration 1/4 of them, and payroll 1/6 of them, how many pads do you have left?
   (A) 48
   (B) 125
   (C) 240
   (D) 475

3. If a certain job can be performed by 18 file clerks in 26 days, how many file clerks would you need to complete the job in 12 days?
   (A) 24
   (B) 30
   (C) 39
   (D) 52

4. If 10 secretaries can do a certain task in 10 hours, how long will it take 5 secretaries to do the same task?
   (A) 5 hours
   (B) 10 hours
   (C) 15 hours
   (D) 20 hours

5. Your office uses an average of 25 twenty-five cent stamps, 35 forty cent stamps, and 350 twenty-two cent stamps a day. The total cost of stamps used by your office in a five-day period is
   (A) $97.25
   (B) $486.25
   (C) $468.25
   (D) $352.40

6. A clerk is assigned to check the accuracy of the entries on 490 forms. The clerk checks 40 forms an hour. After working one hour on this task, the clerk is joined by another clerk who checks the form at the rate of 35 an hour. The total number of hours required to do the entire assignment is
   (A) 5
   (B) 6
   (C) 7
   (D) 8

7. There are a total of 420 employees in your department; 30 percent are clerks and 1/7 are typists. The difference between the number of clerks and the number of typists is
   (A) 126
   (B) 66
   (C) 186
   (D) 80

8. Your photocopy machine produces copies of a memo at a cost of 2 cents a copy, and the machine produces 120 copies a minute. If the cost of producing these memos was $12, how many minutes of operation did it take the machine to produce this number of copies?
   (A) 5
   (B) 2
   (C) 10
   (D) 6

END OF TEST

Answer Key for Practice Tests

Computation Test 1

1. C	3. B	5. A	7. B
2. A	4. D	6. B	8. E

Computation Test 2

1. D	3. C	5. C	7. C
2. A	4. B	6. E	8. B

Word Problems Test 1

1. B	3. D	5. D	7. C
2. D	4. A	6. B	8. B

Word Problems Test 2

1. B	3. C	5. B	7. B
2. B	4. D	6. C	8. A

Posttest and Answers

Computations

Directions: For each of the following questions, select the choice which best answers the question or completes the statement. Mark the answer sheet with the letter of that answer.

Allow 5 minutes for this posttest.

1. Add the following: $40, $2.75, $186.21, $24,865, $.74, $8.42, $2,475.28, $11,998.24 =
   - (A) $38,537.04
   - (B) $39,537.04
   - (C) $38,533.40
   - (D) $39,573.40
   - (E) None of these.

2. Add the following: 7 years, 3 months; 5 years, 6 months; 8 years, 11 months =
   - (A) 20 years
   - (B) 20 years 8 months
   - (C) 21 years 9 months
   - (D) 21 years 8 months
   - (E) None of these.

3. The difference between 2876 and 1453 =
   - (A) 1342
   - (B) 1324
   - (C) 1234
   - (D) 1423
   - (E) None of these.

4. Perform the indicated operation and express your answer in inches: 12 feet, minus 7 inches, plus 2 feet 1 inch, minus 7 feet, minus 1 yard, plus 2 yards 1 foot 3 inches =
   - (A) 130 inches
   - (B) 129 inches
   - (C) 128
   - (D) 131 inches
   - (E) None of these.

5. Perform the following: .020301 times 2.15 divided by .00000063 =
   - (A) 69218.19
   - (B) 69821.19
   - (C) 69281.91
   - (D) 69281.19
   - (E) None of these.

6. Multiply 454,286 times 4 ⅕ =
   - (A) 190,021 ⅕
   - (B) 190,234
   - (C) 190,201 ⅕
   - (D) 190,202 ⅖
   - (E) None of these.

7. Find 5½ percent of $2,800 =
   - (A) 140
   - (B) 154
   - (C) 160
   - (D) 172
   - (E) None of these.

8. If 12 percent of a number is 48, what is the number?
   - (A) 12
   - (B) 60
   - (C) 144
   - (D) 192
   - (E) None of these.

9. If the product of 8.3 multiplied by .42 is subtracted from the product of 156 multiplied by .09, the result is most nearly =
   - (A) 10.6
   - (B) 13.7
   - (C) 17.5
   - (D) 20.8
   - (E) None of these.

10. Find 3 ⅓ divided by 2/3 =
    - (A) 2
    - (B) 3
    - (C) 4
    - (D) 5
    - (E) None of these.

Word Problems

11. If each of the 5 divisions have 15 typists, the total number of typists for all 5 division is?
    - (A) 70
    - (B) 65
    - (C) 60
    - (D) 80
    - (E) None of these.

12. If you work 8 hours a day for 6 days, how many hours will you have worked?
    (A) 40
    (B) 45
    (C) 50
    (D) 47
    (E) None of these.

13. If you earn $12,000 a year, approximately how much do you earn a week?
    (A) $230
    (B) $220
    (C) $240
    (D) $200
    (E) None of these.

14. If you divide 56 employees equally among 8 divisions, each division will get how many employees?
    (A) 6
    (B) 7
    (C) 8
    (D) 5
    (E) None of these.

15. If two numbers are multiplied together, the result is 3752. If one of the two numbers is 56, what is the other number?
    (A) 41
    (B) 15
    (C) 109
    (D) 76
    (E) None of these.

16. One percent of your salary of $23,000 goes for savings bonds. How much is saved each year?
    (A) $.023
    (B) $23
    (C) $2.30
    (D) $2,300
    (E) None of these.

17. Your new office is 10 feet by 8 feet. How many square feet will you have in your new office?
    (A) 80 square feet
    (B) 92 square feet
    (C) 800 square feet
    (D) 18 square feet
    (E) None of these.

18. If a secretary takes 13 letters of dictation a day for 15 days, how many letters will she have taken?
    (A) 165
    (B) 190
    (C) 200
    (D) 175
    (E) None of these.

19. What is the cost of 2 dozen boxes of pens at $3.60 a ¼ dozen pens?
    (A) $28.80
    (B) $29.50
    (C) $20.88
    (D) $28.08
    (E) None of these.

20. If the new computer being delivered weighs 3 tons, how many pounds will it weigh?
    (A) 3000 pounds
    (B) 1500 pounds
    (C) 1200 pounds
    (D) 6000 pounds
    (E) None of these.

END OF POSTTEST

Answers Key for Posttest

1.	E	5.	D	9.	A	13.	A	17.	A
2.	D	6.	E	10.	D	14.	B	18.	E
3.	D	7.	B	11.	E	15.	E	19.	A
4.	B	8.	E	12.	E	16.	E	20.	D

Clerical Performance Ability Answer Sheet

Pretest

1 (A) (B) (C) (D) (E)	11 (A) (B) (C) (D) (E)	21 _____	31 (A) (B) (C) (D) (E)	41 (A) (B) (C) (D) (E)
2 (A) (B) (C) (D) (E)	12 (A) (B) (C) (D) (E)	22 _____	32 (A) (B) (C) (D) (E)	42 (A) (B) (C) (D) (E)
3 (A) (B) (C) (D) (E)	13 (A) (B) (C) (D) (E)	23 _____	33 (A) (B) (C) (D) (E)	43 (A) (B) (C) (D) (E)
4 (A) (B) (C) (D) (E)	14 (A) (B) (C) (D) (E)	24 _____	34 (A) (B) (C) (D) (E)	44 (A) (B) (C) (D) (E)
5 (A) (B) (C) (D) (E)	15 (A) (B) (C) (D) (E)	25 _____	35 (A) (B) (C) (D) (E)	45 (A) (B) (C) (D) (E)
6 (A) (B) (C) (D) (E)	16 (A) (B) (C) (D) (E)	26 _____	36 (A) (B) (C) (D) (E)	46 (A) (B) (C) (D) (E)
7 (A) (B) (C) (D) (E)	17 (A) (B) (C) (D) (E)	27 _____	37 (A) (B) (C) (D) (E)	47 (A) (B) (C) (D) (E)
8 (A) (B) (C) (D) (E)	18 (A) (B) (C) (D) (E)	28 _____	38 (A) (B) (C) (D) (E)	48 (A) (B) (C) (D) (E)
9 (A) (B) (C) (D) (E)	19 (A) (B) (C) (D) (E)	29 _____	39 (A) (B) (C) (D) (E)	49 (A) (B) (C) (D) (E)
10 (A) (B) (C) (D) (E)	20 (A) (B) (C) (D) (E)	30 _____	40 (A) (B) (C) (D) (E)	50 (A) (B) (C) (D) (E)

Coding Test 1

1 (A) (B) (C) (D)	3 (A) (B) (C) (D)	5 (A) (B) (C) (D)	7 (A) (B) (C) (D)	9 (A) (B) (C) (D)
2 (A) (B) (C) (D)	4 (A) (B) (C) (D)	6 (A) (B) (C) (D)	8 (A) (B) (C) (D)	10 (A) (B) (C) (D)

Coding Test 2

1 _____	9 _____	17 _____	25 _____	33 _____
2 _____	10 _____	18 _____	26 _____	34 _____
3 _____	11 _____	19 _____	27 _____	35 _____
4 _____	12 _____	20 _____	28 _____	36 _____
5 _____	13 _____	21 _____	29 _____	37 _____
6 _____	14 _____	22 _____	30 _____	38 _____
7 _____	15 _____	23 _____	31 _____	39 _____
8 _____	16 _____	24 _____	32 _____	40 _____

Coding Test 3

1 (A) (B) (C) (D)	4 (A) (B) (C) (D)	7 (A) (B) (C) (D)	10 (A) (B) (C) (D)	13 (A) (B) (C) (D)
2 (A) (B) (C) (D)	5 (A) (B) (C) (D)	8 (A) (B) (C) (D)	11 (A) (B) (C) (D)	14 (A) (B) (C) (D)
3 (A) (B) (C) (D)	6 (A) (B) (C) (D)	9 (A) (B) (C) (D)	12 (A) (B) (C) (D)	15 (A) (B) (C) (D)

Name and Number Comparison Test 1

1 (A) (B) (C) (D) (E)	4 (A) (B) (C) (D) (E)	7 (A) (B) (C) (D) (E)	10 (A) (B) (C) (D) (E)	13 (A) (B) (C) (D) (E)
2 (A) (B) (C) (D) (E)	5 (A) (B) (C) (D) (E)	8 (A) (B) (C) (D) (E)	11 (A) (B) (C) (D) (E)	14 (A) (B) (C) (D) (E)
3 (A) (B) (C) (D) (E)	6 (A) (B) (C) (D) (E)	9 (A) (B) (C) (D) (E)	12 (A) (B) (C) (D) (E)	15 (A) (B) (C) (D) (E)

Name and Number Comparison Test 2

1 (A) (B) (C) (D) (E)	4 (A) (B) (C) (D) (E)	7 (A) (B) (C) (D) (E)	10 (A) (B) (C) (D) (E)	13 (A) (B) (C) (D) (E)
2 (A) (B) (C) (D) (E)	5 (A) (B) (C) (D) (E)	8 (A) (B) (C) (D) (E)	11 (A) (B) (C) (D) (E)	14 (A) (B) (C) (D) (E)
3 (A) (B) (C) (D) (E)	6 (A) (B) (C) (D) (E)	9 (A) (B) (C) (D) (E)	12 (A) (B) (C) (D) (E)	15 (A) (B) (C) (D) (E)

Name and Number Comparison Test 3

1 (A) (B) (C) (D) (E)	5 (A) (B) (C) (D) (E)	9 (A) (B) (C) (D) (E)	13 (A) (B) (C) (D) (E)	17 (A) (B) (C) (D) (E)
2 (A) (B) (C) (D) (E)	6 (A) (B) (C) (D) (E)	10 (A) (B) (C) (D) (E)	14 (A) (B) (C) (D) (E)	18 (A) (B) (C) (D) (E)
3 (A) (B) (C) (D) (E)	7 (A) (B) (C) (D) (E)	11 (A) (B) (C) (D) (E)	15 (A) (B) (C) (D) (E)	19 (A) (B) (C) (D) (E)
4 (A) (B) (C) (D) (E)	8 (A) (B) (C) (D) (E)	12 (A) (B) (C) (D) (E)	16 (A) (B) (C) (D) (E)	20 (A) (B) (C) (D) (E)

Data Interpretation Test 1

1 _____   3 _____   5 _____   7 _____   8 _____
2 _____   4 _____   6 _____

Data Interpretation Test 2

1 _____   3 _____   5 _____   7 _____   8 _____
2 _____   4 _____   6 _____

Matching Letters and Numbers Test 1

1 Ⓐ Ⓑ Ⓒ Ⓓ Ⓔ   4 Ⓐ Ⓑ Ⓒ Ⓓ Ⓔ   7 Ⓐ Ⓑ Ⓒ Ⓓ Ⓔ   10 Ⓐ Ⓑ Ⓒ Ⓓ Ⓔ   13 Ⓐ Ⓑ Ⓒ Ⓓ Ⓔ
2 Ⓐ Ⓑ Ⓒ Ⓓ Ⓔ   5 Ⓐ Ⓑ Ⓒ Ⓓ Ⓔ   8 Ⓐ Ⓑ Ⓒ Ⓓ Ⓔ   11 Ⓐ Ⓑ Ⓒ Ⓓ Ⓔ   14 Ⓐ Ⓑ Ⓒ Ⓓ Ⓔ
3 Ⓐ Ⓑ Ⓒ Ⓓ Ⓔ   6 Ⓐ Ⓑ Ⓒ Ⓓ Ⓔ   9 Ⓐ Ⓑ Ⓒ Ⓓ Ⓔ   12 Ⓐ Ⓑ Ⓒ Ⓓ Ⓔ   15 Ⓐ Ⓑ Ⓒ Ⓓ Ⓔ

Matching Letters and Numbers Test 2

1 Ⓐ Ⓑ Ⓒ Ⓓ Ⓔ   4 Ⓐ Ⓑ Ⓒ Ⓓ Ⓔ   7 Ⓐ Ⓑ Ⓒ Ⓓ Ⓔ   10 Ⓐ Ⓑ Ⓒ Ⓓ Ⓔ   13 Ⓐ Ⓑ Ⓒ Ⓓ Ⓔ
2 Ⓐ Ⓑ Ⓒ Ⓓ Ⓔ   5 Ⓐ Ⓑ Ⓒ Ⓓ Ⓔ   8 Ⓐ Ⓑ Ⓒ Ⓓ Ⓔ   11 Ⓐ Ⓑ Ⓒ Ⓓ Ⓔ   14 Ⓐ Ⓑ Ⓒ Ⓓ Ⓔ
3 Ⓐ Ⓑ Ⓒ Ⓓ Ⓔ   6 Ⓐ Ⓑ Ⓒ Ⓓ Ⓔ   9 Ⓐ Ⓑ Ⓒ Ⓓ Ⓔ   12 Ⓐ Ⓑ Ⓒ Ⓓ Ⓔ   15 Ⓐ Ⓑ Ⓒ Ⓓ Ⓔ

Letter Series Test 1

1 Ⓐ Ⓑ Ⓒ Ⓓ   4 Ⓐ Ⓑ Ⓒ Ⓓ   7 Ⓐ Ⓑ Ⓒ Ⓓ   10 Ⓐ Ⓑ Ⓒ Ⓓ   13 Ⓐ Ⓑ Ⓒ Ⓓ Ⓔ
2 Ⓐ Ⓑ Ⓒ Ⓓ   5 Ⓐ Ⓑ Ⓒ Ⓓ   8 Ⓐ Ⓑ Ⓒ Ⓓ   11 Ⓐ Ⓑ Ⓒ Ⓓ Ⓔ   14 Ⓐ Ⓑ Ⓒ Ⓓ Ⓔ
3 Ⓐ Ⓑ Ⓒ Ⓓ   6 Ⓐ Ⓑ Ⓒ Ⓓ   9 Ⓐ Ⓑ Ⓒ Ⓓ   12 Ⓐ Ⓑ Ⓒ Ⓓ Ⓔ   15 Ⓐ Ⓑ Ⓒ Ⓓ Ⓔ

Letter Series Test 2

1 Ⓐ Ⓑ Ⓒ Ⓓ Ⓔ   5 Ⓐ Ⓑ Ⓒ Ⓓ Ⓔ   9 Ⓐ Ⓑ Ⓒ Ⓓ Ⓔ   13 Ⓐ Ⓑ Ⓒ Ⓓ Ⓔ   17 Ⓐ Ⓑ Ⓒ Ⓓ Ⓔ
2 Ⓐ Ⓑ Ⓒ Ⓓ Ⓔ   6 Ⓐ Ⓑ Ⓒ Ⓓ Ⓔ   10 Ⓐ Ⓑ Ⓒ Ⓓ Ⓔ   14 Ⓐ Ⓑ Ⓒ Ⓓ Ⓔ   18 Ⓐ Ⓑ Ⓒ Ⓓ Ⓔ
3 Ⓐ Ⓑ Ⓒ Ⓓ Ⓔ   7 Ⓐ Ⓑ Ⓒ Ⓓ Ⓔ   11 Ⓐ Ⓑ Ⓒ Ⓓ Ⓔ   15 Ⓐ Ⓑ Ⓒ Ⓓ Ⓔ   19 Ⓐ Ⓑ Ⓒ Ⓓ Ⓔ
4 Ⓐ Ⓑ Ⓒ Ⓓ Ⓔ   8 Ⓐ Ⓑ Ⓒ Ⓓ Ⓔ   12 Ⓐ Ⓑ Ⓒ Ⓓ Ⓔ   16 Ⓐ Ⓑ Ⓒ Ⓓ Ⓔ   20 Ⓐ Ⓑ Ⓒ Ⓓ Ⓔ

Matching Pairs Test

1 Ⓐ Ⓑ Ⓒ Ⓓ Ⓔ   4 Ⓐ Ⓑ Ⓒ Ⓓ Ⓔ   7 Ⓐ Ⓑ Ⓒ Ⓓ Ⓔ   10 Ⓐ Ⓑ Ⓒ Ⓓ Ⓔ   13 Ⓐ Ⓑ Ⓒ Ⓓ Ⓔ
2 Ⓐ Ⓑ Ⓒ Ⓓ Ⓔ   5 Ⓐ Ⓑ Ⓒ Ⓓ Ⓔ   8 Ⓐ Ⓑ Ⓒ Ⓓ Ⓔ   11 Ⓐ Ⓑ Ⓒ Ⓓ Ⓔ   14 Ⓐ Ⓑ Ⓒ Ⓓ Ⓔ
3 Ⓐ Ⓑ Ⓒ Ⓓ Ⓔ   6 Ⓐ Ⓑ Ⓒ Ⓓ Ⓔ   9 Ⓐ Ⓑ Ⓒ Ⓓ Ⓔ   12 Ⓐ Ⓑ Ⓒ Ⓓ Ⓔ   15 Ⓐ Ⓑ Ⓒ Ⓓ Ⓔ

Posttest

1 Ⓐ Ⓑ Ⓒ Ⓓ   11 Ⓐ Ⓑ Ⓒ Ⓓ Ⓔ   21 Ⓐ Ⓑ Ⓒ Ⓓ Ⓔ   31 Ⓐ Ⓑ Ⓒ Ⓓ   41 Ⓐ Ⓑ Ⓒ Ⓓ Ⓔ
2 Ⓐ Ⓑ Ⓒ Ⓓ   12 Ⓐ Ⓑ Ⓒ Ⓓ Ⓔ   22 Ⓐ Ⓑ Ⓒ Ⓓ Ⓔ   32 Ⓐ Ⓑ Ⓒ Ⓓ Ⓔ   42 Ⓐ Ⓑ Ⓒ Ⓓ Ⓔ
3 Ⓐ Ⓑ Ⓒ Ⓓ   13 Ⓐ Ⓑ Ⓒ Ⓓ Ⓔ   23 Ⓐ Ⓑ Ⓒ Ⓓ Ⓔ   33 Ⓐ Ⓑ Ⓒ Ⓓ Ⓔ   43 Ⓐ Ⓑ Ⓒ Ⓓ Ⓔ
4 Ⓐ Ⓑ Ⓒ Ⓓ   14 Ⓐ Ⓑ Ⓒ Ⓓ Ⓔ   24 Ⓐ Ⓑ Ⓒ Ⓓ Ⓔ   34 Ⓐ Ⓑ Ⓒ Ⓓ Ⓔ   44 Ⓐ Ⓑ Ⓒ Ⓓ Ⓔ
5 Ⓐ Ⓑ Ⓒ Ⓓ   15 Ⓐ Ⓑ Ⓒ Ⓓ Ⓔ   25 Ⓐ Ⓑ Ⓒ Ⓓ Ⓔ   35 Ⓐ Ⓑ Ⓒ Ⓓ Ⓔ   45 Ⓐ Ⓑ Ⓒ Ⓓ Ⓔ
6 Ⓐ Ⓑ Ⓒ Ⓓ   16 Ⓐ Ⓑ Ⓒ Ⓓ Ⓔ   26 Ⓐ Ⓑ Ⓒ Ⓓ   36 Ⓐ Ⓑ Ⓒ Ⓓ Ⓔ   46 Ⓐ Ⓑ Ⓒ Ⓓ Ⓔ
7 Ⓐ Ⓑ Ⓒ Ⓓ   17 Ⓐ Ⓑ Ⓒ Ⓓ Ⓔ   27 Ⓐ Ⓑ Ⓒ Ⓓ   37 Ⓐ Ⓑ Ⓒ Ⓓ Ⓔ   47 Ⓐ Ⓑ Ⓒ Ⓓ Ⓔ
8 Ⓐ Ⓑ Ⓒ Ⓓ   18 Ⓐ Ⓑ Ⓒ Ⓓ Ⓔ   28 Ⓐ Ⓑ Ⓒ Ⓓ   38 Ⓐ Ⓑ Ⓒ Ⓓ Ⓔ   48 Ⓐ Ⓑ Ⓒ Ⓓ Ⓔ
9 Ⓐ Ⓑ Ⓒ Ⓓ   19 Ⓐ Ⓑ Ⓒ Ⓓ Ⓔ   29 Ⓐ Ⓑ Ⓒ Ⓓ   39 Ⓐ Ⓑ Ⓒ Ⓓ Ⓔ   49 Ⓐ Ⓑ Ⓒ Ⓓ Ⓔ
10 Ⓐ Ⓑ Ⓒ Ⓓ   20 Ⓐ Ⓑ Ⓒ Ⓓ Ⓔ   30 Ⓐ Ⓑ Ⓒ Ⓓ   40 Ⓐ Ⓑ Ⓒ Ⓓ Ⓔ   50 Ⓐ Ⓑ Ⓒ Ⓓ Ⓔ

CLERICAL PERFORMANCE ABILITY

Introductory Pretest and Answers

Coding

Directions: The codes given in Column I below begin and end with a capital letter and have an eight digit number in between. You are to arrange the codes in Column I according to the following rules:

1. Arrange the codes in alphabetical order, according to the first letter.

2. When two or more codes have the same first letter, arrange the codes in alphabetical order according to the last letter.

3. When two or more of the codes have the same first and last letters, arrange the codes in numerical order, beginning with the lower number.

The codes in Column I are numbered (1) through (5). Column II gives you a selection of four possible answers. You are to choose from Column II the lettered choice which gives the correct listing of the codes in Column I arranged according to the above rules. Mark the answer sheet with the letter of that answer.

Allow 10 minutes for this pretest.

	COLUMN I: Set of Codes		COLUMN II: Possible Answers

1. (1) S55126179E   (A) 1, 5, 2, 3, 4
   (2) R55136177Q   (B) 3, 4, 1, 5, 2
   (3) P55126177R   (C) 3, 5, 2, 1, 4
   (4) S55126178R   (D) 4, 3, 1, 5, 2
   (5) R55126180P   (E) None of these

2. (1) T64217813Q   (A) 4, 1, 3, 2, 5
   (2) I642178170   (B) 2, 4, 3, 1, 5
   (3) T642178180   (C) 4, 1, 5, 2, 3
   (4) I64217811Q   (D) 2, 3, 4, 1, 5
   (5) T64217816Q   (E) None of these

3. (1) L51138101K   (A) 1, 5, 3, 2, 4
   (2) S51138001R   (B) 1, 3, 5, 2, 4
   (3) S51188111K   (C) 1, 5, 2, 4, 3
   (4) S5118311OR   (D) 2, 5, 1, 4, 3
   (5) L51188100R   (E) None of these

4. (1) J28475336D   (A) 5, 1, 2, 3, 4
   (2) T28775363D   (B) 4, 3, 5, 1, 2
   (3) J27843566P   (C) 1, 5, 2, 4, 3
   (4) T27834563P   (D) 5, 1, 3, 2, 4
   (5) J28435536D   (E) None of these

5. (1) G42786441J   (A) 2, 5, 4, 3, 1
   (2) H45665413J   (B) 5, 4, 1, 3, 2
   (3) G43117690J   (C) 4, 5, 1, 3, 2
   (4) G43546698I   (D) 1, 3, 5, 4, 2
   (5) G41679942I   (E) None of these

6. (1) P18736652U   (A) 1, 3, 4, 5, 2
   (2) P18766352V   (B) 1, 5, 2, 3, 4
   (3) T17686532U   (C) 3, 4, 5, 1, 2
   (4) T17865523U   (D) 5, 2, 1, 3, 4
   (5) P18675332V   (E) None of these

7. (1) H32548137E   (A) 2, 4, 5, 1, 3
   (2) H35243178A   (B) 1, 5, 2, 3, 4
   (3) H35284378F   (C) 1, 5, 2, 4, 3
   (4) H35288337A   (D) 2, 1, 5, 3, 4
   (5) H32883173B   (E) None of these

8. (1) D89077275M   (A) 3, 2, 5, 4, 1
   (2) D98073724N   (B) 1, 4, 3, 2, 5
   (3) D90877274N   (C) 4, 1, 5, 2, 3
   (4) D98877275M   (D) 1, 3, 2, 5, 4
   (5) D98873725N   (E) None of these

9. (1) P44343313Y   (A) 2, 3, 1, 4, 5
   (2) P44141341S   (B) 1, 5, 3, 2, 4
   (3) P41143431W   (C) 4, 2, 3, 5, 1
   (4) P41143413W   (D) 5, 3, 2, 4, 1
   (5) P44313433H   (E) None of these

10. (1) W22746920A   (A) 2, 1, 3, 4, 5
    (2) W22743720A   (B) 2, 1, 5, 3, 4
    (3) W32987655A   (C) 1, 2, 3, 4, 5
    (4) W43298765A   (D) 1, 2, 5, 3, 4
    (5) W30987433A   (E) None of these

Name and Number Comparison

Directions: Each of the following questions consists of three names or numbers which are much alike. For each question compare the names or numbers to decide which ones, if any, are exactly alike. Mark the answer sheet with the letter of that answer.

(A) if *ALL THREE* are exactly *ALIKE*.
(B) if only the *FIRST* and *SECOND* are exactly *ALIKE*.
(C) if only the *FIRST* and *THIRD* are exactly *ALIKE*.
(D) if only the *SECOND* and *THIRD* are exactly *ALIKE*.
(E) if ALL THREE *are DIFFERENT*.

11. Atherton R. Warde
    Asheton R. Warde
    Atherton P. Warde

14. 2312793
    2312793
    2312793

17. Grace O'Brien
    Grace O'Brien
    Grace O'Brein

19. 63233
    63233
    62333

12. H. Merritt Audubon
    H. Merriott Audubon
    H. Merritt Audubon

15. 1065407
    1065407
    1065047

18. 23848
    28384
    23848

20. 56658
    55668
    55668

13. 6219354
    6219354
    6219354

16. Wm. Oates
    Wm. Oates
    Wm. Oates

Data Interpretation

Directions: All the questions in this test refer to the following chart. Read each question carefully and answer it on the basis of this chart. Select the best case and mark the answer sheet with the letter of that answer.

Hospital Care for Patients

Case	Rent	Food	Shelter	Light	Fuel	Milk	Clothing	Household Supplies	Medical Care	Medicine	Hospitalization	Fare	Cash Allowance
A	X	X	X		X		X				X		
B	X	X		X	X	X		X					
C		X		X		X		X	X	X			
D	X	X	X		X		X	X					
E		X			X		X		X			X	X
F		X		X		X		X					
G	X	X	X	X		X	X				X		
H	X		X				X					X	

Which case received   **Consolidate your answers here**

21. food, light, and hospitalization?   21. _____

22. medical care, shelter, clothing, and fuel?   22. _____

                                                        23. _____
23. rent, food, shelter, fuel, and household sup-
    plies?   24. _____

24. fuel, shelter, clothing, no hospitalization, but   25. _____
    medical care?
                                                        26. _____
25. rent, shelter, no household supplies, no hospi-   27. _____
    talization, but fare?
                                                        28. _____
26. food, milk, household supplies, no fuel, but
    medical care?   29. _____

27. shelter, clothing, light, no medicine, but hospi- 30. _____
    talization?

28. shelter, clothing, no medical care, no cash al-
    lowance, but light?

29. food, shelter, fuel, but no hospitalization?

30. rent, fuel, milk, and household supplies?

Matching Letter and Numbers

COLUMN I: Set of Questions	COLUMN II: Possible Answers
32. 5 T 8 N 2 9 V L	(A) 4, 9, L, V
	(B) 4, 5, N, Z
	(C) 5, 8, L, Z
	(D) 8, 9, N, V
	(E) none of these

Directions: In this test of clerical ability, Column I consists of a set of numbered questions which you are to answer one at a time. Column II consists of possible answers to the set of questions in Column I. Select from Column II the one possible answer which contains only the numbers and letters, regardless of their order, which appear in the question in Column I. If none of the four possible answers is correct, mark E on your answer sheet.

COLUMN I: Set of Questions	COLUMN II: Possible Answers
33. 7 8 L 5 Z 9 P V	(A) 9 V 4 L N 3
34. N 6 4 L 3 Z G 9	(B) N 4 5 Z 3 9
35. V 9 3 4 K N 5 L	(C) 8 5 Z L 9 P
36. L V 9 2 N 8 T 5	(D) N 9 8 V L T
37. 5 Z L 9 P V 2 8	(E) none of these

COLUMN I: Set of Questions	COLUMN II: Possible Answers
31. 4 K 2 9 N 5 T G	(A) 4, 5, K, T
	(B) 4, 7, G, K
	(C) 2, 5, G, L
	(D) 2, 7, L, T
	(E) none of these

COLUMN I: Set of Questions	COLUMN II: Possible Answers
38. L 2 4 8 V P 7 N	(A) N 2 7 L 8 V
39. V 4 7 8 N T Z 6	(B) 2 V T 8 G 7
40. T L 5 N 6 8 7 V	(C) 8 6 T L N 4
	(D) V 7 6 N T 8
	(E) none of these

Letter Series

Directions: Each question consists of a series of letters which follow some definite order. Study each series to determine the order. Then look at the answer choices. Select the one answer that will complete the set in accordance with the pattern established.

Suggestion: In solving alphabetic series, it is helpful to write out the alphabet and keep it in front of you as you work. This makes it easier to spot the key to a letter series.

a b c d e f g h i j k l m n o p q r s t u v w x y z

41. c d f g j k o . . . . .
   (A) p t
   (B) p u
   (C) t x
   (D) t z
   (E) s x

42. f d h f j h l . . . . .
   (A) j m
   (B) i n
   (C) j n
   (D) k m
   (E) i m

43. r n p t p r v . . . . .
   (A) s u
   (B) r t
   (C) x z
   (D) z x
   (E) t r

44. d f h h e g i i f h j . . . . .
   (A) j g
   (B) g g
   (C) g i
   (D) j i
   (E) l l

45. y x v t s q o n l j i . . . . .
   (A) h f
   (B) h g
   (C) g e
   (D) f e
   (E) g f

46. f r h t j v l . . . . .
   (A) m n
   (B) w y
   (C) x n
   (D) n w
   (E) x m

47. m p n q o r p . . . . .
   (A) s q
   (B) q r
   (C) t q
   (D) q s
   (E) s r

48. g i k h j l i . . . . .
   (A) k l
   (B) j k
   (C) j l
   (D) j m
   (E) k m

49. a c f h k m p . . . . .
   (A) s v
   (B) r t
   (C) r u
   (D) s u
   (E) q r

50. c d f g j k m . . . . .
   (A) n q
   (B) p q
   (C) o p
   (D) n p
   (E) o r

END OF PRETEST

Answer Key for Pretest

1. C	6. B	11. E	16. A	21. G
2. B	7. A	12. C	17. B	22. E
3. A	8. B	13. A	18. C	23. D
4. D	9. E	14. A	19. B	24. E
5. B	10. B	15. B	20. D	25. H

26.	C	31.	A	36.	D	41.	B	46.	C
27.	G	32.	D	37.	C	42.	C	47.	A
28.	G	33.	C	38.	A	43.	B	48.	E
29.	D	34.	E	39.	D	44.	A	49.	C
30.	B	35.	A	40.	D	45.	C	50.	A

Study Hints

Clerical performance examinations are used to predict success in some occupations or courses of training. They are not really different in form from other types of examinations. However, they may be used to forecast your success in some future course or job.

You cannot prepare for these examinations, but you can practice by being as familiar as possible with the kinds of questions that will be asked. Thus, practicing these questions improves your score. This section provides that kind of familiarity and practice. Many of your competitors may already have gained this advantage.

These examinations are designed to measure clerical performance that demonstrates your ability to understand a task and to do it speedily. Your score will depend mostly on your speed. Usually, you will be penalized for errors, but our advice is that you work as fast as you can. Strive to work as rapidly and as accurately as possible.

Tests and Answers

The answer key will be found at the end of these practice tests.

Coding

Directions: The codes given in Column I below begin and end with a capital letter and have an eight digit number in between. You are to arrange the codes in Column I according to the following rules:

1. Arrange the codes in alphabetical order, according to the first letter.

2. When two or more codes have the same first letter, arrange the codes in alphabetical order according to the last letter.

3. When two or more of the codes have the same first and last letters, arrange the codes in numerical order, beginning with the lower number.

The codes in Column I are numbered (1) through (5). Column II gives you a selection of four possible answers. You are to choose from Column II the lettered choice which gives the correct listing of the codes in Column I arranged according to the above rules. Mark the answer sheet with the letter of that answer.

Example:

	COLUMN I: Set of Codes	COLUMN II: Possible Answers
1. (1)	E75044127B	(A) 4, 1, 3, 2, 5
(2)	B96399104A	(B) 4, 1, 2, 3, 5
(3)	B93939086A	(C) 4, 3, 2, 5, 1
(4)	B47064465H	(D) 3, 2, 5, 4, 1
(5)	B99040922A	

In the sample question, the four codes starting with B should be placed before the code starting with E. The codes starting with B and ending with A should be placed before the code starting with B and ending with H. Then the codes starting with B and ending with A should be listed in numerical order, beginning with the lowest number. The correct way to arrange the codes, therefore, is:

(3) B93939086A
(2) B96399104A
(5) B99040922A
(4) B47064465H
(1) E75044127B

Since the order of arrangement is 3, 2, 5, 4, 1—the answer to the sample question is (D). Now proceed to answer the following test questions according to the above instructions.

CODING TEST 1

Allow 10 minutes for this test.

	COLUMN I: Set of Codes	COLUMN II: Possible Answers		COLUMN I: Set of Codes	COLUMN II: Possible Answers
1. (1)	C83261824G	(A) 2, 4, 1, 5, 3	6. (1)	N74663826M	(A) 2, 4, 5, 3, 1
(2)	C78361833C	(B) 4, 2, 1, 3, 5	(2)	M74633286M	(B) 2, 5, 4, 1, 3
(3)	G83261732G	(C) 3, 1, 5, 2, 4	(3)	N76633228N	(C) 1, 2, 5, 3, 4
(4)	C88361823C	(D) 2, 3, 5, 1, 4	(4)	M76483686N	(D) 2, 5, 1, 4, 3
(5)	G83261743C		(5)	M74636688M	
2. (1)	A11710107H	(A) 2, 1, 4, 3, 5	7. (1)	P97560324B	(A) 1, 5, 2, 3, 4
(2)	H17110017A	(B) 3, 1, 5, 2, 4	(2)	R97663024B	(B) 3, 1, 4, 5, 2
(3)	A11170707A	(C) 3, 4, 1, 5, 2	(3)	P97503024E	(C) 1, 5, 3, 2, 4
(4)	H17170171H	(D) 3, 5, 1, 2, 4	(4)	R97563240E	(D) 1, 5, 2, 3, 4
(5)	A11710177A		(5)	P97652304B	
3. (1)	R26794821S	(A) 3, 2, 4, 1, 5	8. (1)	H92411165G	(A) 2, 5, 3, 4, 1
(2)	O26794821T	(B) 3, 4, 2, 1, 5	(2)	A92141465G	(B) 3, 4, 2, 5, 1
(3)	M26794827Z	(C) 4, 2, 1, 3, 5	(3)	H92141165C	(C) 3, 2, 1, 5, 4
(4)	Q26794821R	(D) 5, 4, 1, 2, 3	(4)	H92444165C	(D) 3, 1, 2, 5, 4
(5)	S26794821P		(5)	A92411465G	
4. (1)	D89143888P	(A) 3, 5, 2, 1, 4	9. (1)	X90637799S	(A) 4, 3, 5, 2, 1
(2)	D98143838B	(B) 3, 1, 4, 5, 2	(2)	N90037696S	(B) 5, 4, 2, 1, 3
(3)	D89113883B	(C) 4, 2, 3, 1, 5	(3)	Y90677369B	(C) 5, 2, 4, 1, 3
(4)	D89148338P	(D) 4, 1, 3, 5, 2	(4)	X09677693B	(D) 5, 2, 3, 4, 1
(5)	D89148388B		(5)	M09673699S	
5. (1)	W62455599E	(A) 2, 4, 3, 1, 5	10. (1)	K78425174L	(A) 4, 2, 1, 3, 5
(2)	W62455090F	(B) 3, 1, 5, 2, 4	(2)	K78452714C	(B) 2, 3, 5, 4, 1
(3)	W62405099E	(C) 5, 3, 1, 4, 2	(3)	K78547214N	(C) 1, 4, 2, 3, 5
(4)	V62455097F	(D) 5, 4, 3, 1, 2	(4)	K78442774C	(D) 4, 2, 1, 5, 3
(5)	V62405979E		(5)	K78547724M	

END OF TEST

CODING TEST 2

Directions: In this test of speed and accuracy, you are asked to make the kind of code changes that are required when Code Words and Numbers are changed. An office used the following to code cost prices secretly:

```
w   r   i   t   e   s   a   b   l   y
1   2   3   4   5   6   7   8   9   0
```

This entailed changing all the price tags. In Column I you are given a list of tag prices in the old code marks, and you are asked to change them to the new code marks. In Column II you are able to write the letters called for by the New Code.

```
f   i   n   d   b   y   z   e   a   l
1   2   3   4   5 6   7   8 9 0
```

The office then decides to switch the code to:

Sample Questions and Explanations

COLUMN I: COLUMN II:
Old Code   New Code

A. fzl   _____
B. yen   _____

In converting the Old Code letters to the letters required by the New Code, you must note carefully the numbers corresponding to each. For question A the Old Code letters "fzl" correspond to the numbers 1, 7, and 0 respectively. The letters in the New Code corresponding to those same numbers are: w, a, and y. Therefore, the correct answer to question A is: *way*. For question B the letters "yen" of the Old Code correspond to the numbers 6, 8, and 3. The New Code letters corresponding to those same numbers are: *sbi*.

Now proceed to answer the following test questions on the basis of the instructions given above.

Allow 20 minutes for this test.

COLUMN I: COLUMN II:
Old Code   New Code

1. dnb   _____
2. nba   _____
3. blz   _____
4. lzdy   _____
5. ife   _____
6. fye   _____
7. alzd   _____
8. nel   _____
9. ilza   _____
10. blz   _____

COLUMN I: COLUMN II:
Old Code   New Code

11. fzi   _____
12. dey   _____
13. nyid   _____
14. lzey   _____
15. dfl   _____
16. bea   _____
17. bnd   _____
18. zyd   _____
19. eidf   _____
20. byi   _____
21. bend   _____
22. dial   _____
23. fil   _____
24. iny   _____
25. lie   _____
26. nye   _____
27. zeb   _____
28. deal   _____
29. nez   _____
30. fie   _____
31. bald   _____
32. lye   _____
33. lean   _____
34. bin   _____
35. nil   _____
36. yea   _____
37. zen   _____
38. den   _____
39. line   _____
40. ale   _____

END OF TEST

CODING TEST 3

Directions: In this test of speed and accuracy, you are given a three-line Code Table consisting of corresponding letters and numbers. In the first line you are given a Code Name. In the second line, the letters of the Code Word are given directly below the Code Name. In the third line, the Code Numbers are listed directly below the Code Word. For each question in this test, you will use the Code Table to determine if the code letters in Column II and the Code Numbers in Column III correspond to the Code Name printed in capital letters in Column I. Study each question carefully, and mark the answer sheet as follows:

(A) if there is an error in Column II only.
(B) if there is an error in Column III only.
(C) if there is an error in both Columns II and III.
(D) if both columns II and III are correct.

Sample Question and Explanation

CODE TABLE

CODE NAME	R I C H M E D A L
CODE WORD	i n s u l a t e d
CODE NUMBERS	0 1 2 3 4 5 6 7 8

	Column I Code Name	Column II Code Word	Column III Code Numbers
Example	MIRED	lniat	41058

In answering this sample question, your task is to determine if the letters given in Column II and the numbers listed in Column III are, according to the CODE TABLE given above, the letters and numbers that appear directly below the capital letters given in Column I. In the sample question, for example, do the letters lniat appear directly below the capital letters MIRED, according to the CODE TABLE? And, likewise, do the numbers 41058 appear directly below the capital letters MIRED? As you can see, the letters lniat in Column II are correctly coded to the capital letters MIRED. The numbers in Column III, however, are incorrectly coded: the numbers appearing directly below MIRED are 41056—not 41058. Since there is an error only in Column III, the correct answer to the sample question is B.

Allow 20 minutes for this test.

CODE TABLE

CODE NAME	G A L D B R U C H
CODE WORD	c o m p l i a n t
CODE NUMBERS	1 2 3 4 5 6 7 8 9

	Column I Code Name	Column II Code Word	Column III Code Numbers
1.	BRALD	liomp	56234
2.	LAGUC	mocan	32168
3.	HURAD	taiop	97623
4.	CHUBA	ntali	89752
5.	DULGH	panct	47318

CODE TABLE

CODE NAME	S H U M A C K E R
CODE WORD	f a v o r i t e s
CODE NUMBERS	0 1 2 3 4 5 6 7 8

6.	SUMAC	fvoai	02345
7.	MAKER	ortev	34658
8.	CRAMS	isrof	57430
9.	HARMS	arsof	14832
10.	UKRAH	vtsra	26841

CODE TABLE

CODE NAME	S I M O N D A L E
CODE WORD	e d u c a t i o n
CODE NUMBERS	4 5 7 9 6 8 3 1 2

11.	MESON	uneca	72496
12.	DILES	tdoie	85124
13.	LEMON	onuct	12795
14.	OAESN	conea	93246
15.	IDMEA	dtuni	58923

END OF TEST

Name and Number Comparisons

Name and Number Comparison tests are one of the most popular means of testing clerical aptitude. These tests demonstrate your ability to quickly recognize similarities and differences. Although people differ greatly in this ability, it is possible for you to practice and to improve your skill in this type of question. Your score depends on both accuracy and speed. Therefore, you must work out for yourself a balance between the two. In your practice you must try different approaches to find out which one is best for you.

Sample Questions and Explanations

1. Davis Hazen	4. Jno. M. Dea	7. 34212	10. 23544
David Hozen	Jno. M. Dea	34212	25344
David Hazen	Jno. M. Dea	34112	25344

2. Lois Appel	5. Ann K. Dove	8. 10235
Lois Appel	Ann H. Dove	10235
Lois Apfel	Ann K. Dove	10235

3. June Allen	6. 21107	9. 32614
Jane Allan	21017	32164
Jane Allan	21117	32614

In question 1, all three names are different; therefore, the answer is (E). In question 2 only the first and second names are the same; therefore, the answer is (B). In the third question only the second and third names are exactly alike; therefore, the answer is (D). The other answers are 4 (A); 5 (C); 6 (E); 7 (B); 8 (A); 9 (C); and 10 (D).

Name and Number Comparison Test 1

Directions: Each of the following questions consists of three names or numbers which are much alike. For each question compare the names or numbers to decide which ones, if any, are exactly alike. Mark the answer sheet with the letter of that answer.

(A) if *all three are exactly alike.*
(B) if only the *first* and *second* are exactly *alike.*
(C) if only the *first* and *third* are exactly *alike.*
(D) if only the *second* and *third* are exactly *alike.*
(E) if *all three* are *different.*

Allow 4 minutes for this test.

1. Francis Ransdell Frances Ramsdell Francis Ramsdell	5. Ella Burk Newham Ella Burk Newnham Elena Burk Newnham	9. 4695682 4695862 4695682	13. 1592514 1592574 1592574
2. Cornelius Detwiler Cornelius Detwiler Cornelius Detwiler	6. Jno. K. Ravencroft Jno. H. Ravencroft Jno. H. Ravencoft	10. Stricklund Kanedy Stricklund Kanedy Stricklund Kanedy	14. 2010202 2010202 2010220
3. 6452054 6452654 6452054	7. Martin Wills Pullen Martin Wills Pulen Martin Wills Pullen	11. Joy Harlor Witner Joy Harloe Witner Joy Harloe Witner	15. 6177396 6177936 6177396
4. 8501268 8501268 8501286	8. 3457988 3457986 3457986	12. R. M. O. Uberroth R. M. O. Uberroth R. N. O. Uberroth	

END OF TEST

Name and Number Comparison Test 2

Allow 4 minutes for this test.

1. Lee Berlin Lea Berlin Les Berlin	2. Webster Cayne Webster Cayne Webster Cain	3. Charles Danis Charles Donis Charles Danis	4. Frank Collyer Frank Collyer Frank Collyer

5. Sylvia Gross	8. Irene Crawford	11. John Finn	14. Harold Friedberg
Sylvia Grohs	Irene Crowford	John Fin	Harold Friedberg
Sylvia Grohs	Irene Crawford	John Finn	Harold Freedberg
6. Thomas O'Neill	9. Charles Duggan	12. Ray Finkelstein	15. Trude Friedl
Thomas O'Neil	Charles Duggan	Ray Finklestein	Trude Freidl
Thomas O'Neal	Charles Dugan	Ray Finkelstien	Trude Freidl
7. Jess M. Olsen	10. Frank Dudley	13. Sam Freedman	
Jess N. Olson	Frank Dudlee	Sam Friedman	
Jess M. Olsen	Frank Dudley	Sam Freedman	

END OF TEST

Name and Number Comparison Test 3

Allow 5 minutes for this test.

1. Morris Mutterperl	6. Ellis Nichols	11. 38312	16. 63381
Morris Muterperl	Ellis Nichols	31283	63381
Morris Mutterpurl	Ellis Nicols	31283	63318
2. Helen Mutter	7. Reed Newsom	12. 90020	17. 81585
Helen Mutter	Reed Newsome	92000	85185
Helen Mutter	Reed Newsom	90200	85185
3. Jack Neiderman	8. Anna O'Brien	13. 94343	18. 90463
Jack Neiderman	Anna O'Brein	94343	90426
Jack Niederman	Anna O'Brein	94343	90463
4. Donald Nearney	9. Chas. Nuzzolo	14. 83536	19. 22249
Donald Nurney	Chas. Nuzzolo	83536	22249
Donald Nurney	Chas. Nuzolo	85336	22294
5. Adeline Neice	10. John Nystrom	15. 96632	20. 57422
Adeline Neice	John Niestrom	93266	52742
Adeline Niece	John Nystrom	93266	57224

END OF TEST

Data Interpretation

The Data Interpretation questions take various forms: charts, tables, and graphs. Also there are various types of each; for example, a graph may be the circle-type, the line-type, the bar-type, or a combination of these types.

These questions are all from actual, previous examinations. Please note the tables and charts cover a variety of fields of work, and require no previous knowledge of the subject. Each set of questions is to be answered solely on the basis of the table or chart shown. Before answering each set of questions, look over the data given to you and get a general idea of what it means. Then, in answering the questions, refer back to the given data.

Sample Question and Explanation

VELOCITY
Ft./Sec.

Look at the two columns
of data below:

Time sec.	Velocity ft./sec.
0	2
2	3
4	4
6	5
8	6
10	7

TIME-SEC.

Example: Which one of the lines on the graph above left most closely represents the data in the two columns above right?

An examination of the graph shows that time values are indicated along the horizontal scale, and velocity values along the vertical scale. If you observe the velocity value at zero time, you see that the A line has a value of 0 velocity, and the C line has a value of 2 ft./sec. No values are shown at 0 time for lines B and D. Hence line C is the only one which shows a velocity of 2 ft./sec. at 0 time.

Similarly, at 2 sec., the velocity value for line B is 0, for line A is 2.5, and for line C, 3. Here again C is the only line which corresponds to the data in the table. At 4 sec. the velocity value for line D is 0, for line B is 1.9, for line C is 4, and for line A is 5. Also line C is the only one that gives the value shown in the table. The same process can be repeated for time values 6, 8, and 10 sec., all of which show that line C is the only one corresponding to the values given in the above table.

Data Interpretation Test 1

Directions: All the questions in this test refer to the following chart. Read each question carefully and answer it on the basis of the chart. Select the best answer and mark the correct letter on the answer sheet.

Allow 5 minutes for this test.

Dept.	Total No. of Employees	No of Office Stations Oper.	Total No. of Stations	No. of Stations of Each Type				
				M	*N*	*O*	*P*	*Q*
A	2540	21	20	10	1	3	1	5
B	8733	35	32	3	7	6	12	4
C	225	5	5	1	1	1	0	2
D	12489	12	12	1	1	0	9	1
E	3465	18	20	6	3	5	2	4
F	40375	56	49	30	8	11	0	0
G	2870	7	8	1	1	1	3	2
H	2850	22	14	5	4	2	2	1
J	465	11	11	3	0	1	5	2
K	3600	36	26	4	9	6	5	2

1. Which department has the greatest number of station operators?

2. Which department would have two stations not in operation even when all the office station operators are working?

3. Which department has eight fewer stations than operators?

4. Which department has the greatest number of type "N" stations?

5. Which department has the greatest number of type "P" stations?

6. Which department has exactly 1 percent of its employees operating office stations?

7. Which department would be unable to perform any work requiring an "N" type station?

8. Which department is the fifth largest in the total number of employees?

END OF TEST

Data Interpretation Test 2

Allow 5 minutes for this test.

Bureau	Type	No. of Persons	In Stock	FORM I Requisitioned	In Stock	FORM II Requisitioned
A	CENTRAL	24	188	500	175	300
B	DISTRICT	15	176	250	202	175
C	DISTRICT	12	167	200	133	150
D	DISTRICT	11	194	200	271	175
E	CENTRAL	29	216	600	179	800
F	DISTRICT	10	189	150	138	200
H	DISTRICT	10	139	105	165	240
I	CENTRAL	25	324	450	313	450
K	CENTRAL	21	277	850	290	150
L	DISTRICT	13	112	280	109	225
M	DISTRICT	14	148	310	246	300
N	DISTRICT	19	165	225	175	475
O	CENTRAL	29	298	785	147	285
P	DISTRICT	19	110	240	178	175
R	CENTRAL	28	317	255	309	185
S	CENTRAL	31	330	270	137	200
T	DISTRICT	11	155	180	149	250
U	DISTRICT	14	138	170	215	155
X	DISTRICT	12	199	160	512	125
Z	DISTRICT	15	171	100	378	135

1. Which district bureau has the greatest number of Form I's in stock?

2. Which central bureau is requisitioning the smallest number of Form II's?

3. Which district bureau is requisitioning the smallest number of Form I's?

4. Which district bureau is requisitioning the greatest number of Form II's?

5. Which district bureau with fewer than 13 persons is requisitioning the smallest number of Form I's?

6. Which central bureau with more than 22 persons has the largest number of Form II's in stock?

7. Which central bureau with more than 200 Form I's in stock has the greatest number of Form II's in stock?

8. Which central bureau that has requisitioned more than 200 Form II's has the smallest number of persons?

END OF TEST

Matching Letters and Numbers

Directions: In this test of clerical ability, Column I consists of a set of numbered questions which you are to answer one at a time. Column II consists of possible answers to the set of questions in Column I. Select from Column II the one possible answer which contains only the numbers and letters, regardless of their order, which appear in the question in Column I. If none of the four possible answers is correct, mark (E) on your answer sheet.

Sample Question and Explanation

Example:

COLUMN I: Set of questions	COLUMN II: Possible Answers
2 Q P 5 T G 4 7	(A) 5 G 8 P 4 Q
	(B) P R 7 Q 4 2
	(C) Q 5 P 9 G 2
	(D) 2 5 P 7 Q
	(E) none of these

The correct answer to the sample question is (D). How did we arrive at that solution? First, remember that the instructions tell you to select as your answer the choice that contains only the numbers and letters, regardless of their order, which appear in the question. The answer choice in Column II does not have to contain all of the letters and numbers that appear in the question. But the answer cannot contain a number or letter that does not appear in the question. Thus, begin by checking the numbers and letters that appear in answer (A). You will note that while 5 G P 4 Q all appear in the sample question, the number 8, which is included in answer (A), does *not* appear in the question. Answer (A) is incorrect. Answer (B) is incorrect as the letter R does not appear in the sample question. Answer (C) is incorrect as 9 does not appear in the question. In checking answer (D), however, note that 4 2 5 P 7 Q all appear in the sample question. Thus, (D) is the correct choice. Answer (E) is obviously eliminated.

Now proceed to answer the following test questions on the basis of the instructions given above.

Matching Letters and Numbers Test 1

Allow 5 minutes for this test.

COLUMN I: Set of questions	COLUMN II: Possible Answers
1. N 5 4 7 T K 3 Z	(A) 3 8 K N
2. 8 5 3 V L 2 Z N	(B) 5 8 N V
3. 2 5 N 9 K L V	(C) 3 9 V Z
4. 9 8 L 2 5 Z K V	(D) 5 9 K Z
5. Z 6 5 V 9 3 P N	(E) none of these
6. 6 Z T N 8 7 4 V	(A) 2 7 L N
7. V 7 8 6 N 5 P L	(B) 2 8 T V
8. N 7 P V 8 4 2 L	(C) 6 8 L T
9. 7 8 G 4 3 V L T	(D) 6 7 N V
10. 4 8 G 2 T N 6 L	(E) none of these
11. V 5 7 Z N 9 4 T	(A) 2 5 N Z
12. 4 6 P T 2 N K 9	(B) 4 5 N P
13. 6 4 N 2 P 8 Z K	(C) 2 9 P T
14. 7 P 5 2 4 N K T	(D) 4 9 T Z
15. K T 8 5 4 N 2 P	(E) none of these

END OF TEST

Matching Letters and Numbers Test 2

Allow 5 minutes for this test.

COLUMN I: Set of questions	COLUMN II: Possible Answers
1. 6 4 T G 9 K N 8	(A) Z 8 K G 9 7
2. K 3 L 6 Z 7 9 T	(B) 7 N Z T 9 8
3. N 8 9 3 K G 7 Z	(C) L 3 Z K 7 6
4. L Z G 6 4 9 K 3	(D) 4 K T G 8 6
5. 9 T K 8 3 7 N Z	(E) none of these

COLUMN I: Set of questions	COLUMN II: Possible Answers		
6. 2 3 P 6 V Z 4 L	(A) 3 6 G P 7 N	11. Q 1 6 R L 9 7 V	(A) F 3 N K J 4
7. T 7 4 3 P Z 9 G	(B) 3 7 P V 4 T	12. 8 W 2 Z P 4 H O	(B) Q H 4 0 5 M
8. 6 N G Z 3 9 P 7	(C) 4 6 V Z 2 L	13. N J 3 T K 5 F M	(C) O W 2 Z 4 8
9. 9 6 P 4 N G Z 2	(D) T 7 G Z T 3	14. 5 T H M O 4 Q J	(D) R 9 V 1 Q 6
10. 4 8 G 2 T N 6 L	(E) none of these	15. 4 Z X 8 W O 2 L	(E) none of these

END OF TEST

Letter Series

Sample Question and Explanation

Directions: In each of these questions, there is a series of letters which follow some definite order, and below there are five sets of two letters each. Look at the letters in the series and determine the order; then from the suggested answers at the right, select the set that gives the next two letters in the series in their correct order.

Example:

1. x c x d x e x . . .
   (A) f x
   (B) f g
   (C) x f
   (D) e f
   (E) x g

The series consists of x's alternating with letters in alphabetical order. The next two letters would be f and x; therefore, (A) is the correct answer.

Example:

2. a b d c e f h . . .
   (A) g h
   (B) i g
   (C) g i
   (D) k l
   (E) i h

If you compare this series with the alphabet, you will find that it goes along in pairs. The first pair is in their usual order and the second pair is in reverse order. The last letter given in the series is the second letter of the pair g h, which is in reverse order. The first missing letter must, therefore, be g. The next pair of letters would be i j, in that order. The second of the missing letters is i. The alternative you look for, then, is g i, which is letter (C).

Suggestion: In solving alphabetic series and progressions, it is helpful to write out the alphabet and keep it in front of you as you work. This makes it easier to spot the key to a letter series.

a b c d e f g h i j k l m n o p q r s t u v w x y z

Letter Series Test 1

Allow 13 minutes for this test.

1. b a c a d a e a f a g a...
   - (A) h a
   - (B) a h
   - (C) k a
   - (D) l a

2. a b d b b d c b d d b d e b d f b...
   - (A) h d
   - (B) q x
   - (C) d b
   - (D) d g

3. j i h g f e d c...
   - (A) b c
   - (B) q p
   - (C) b a
   - (D) n p

4. z y x w v u t s r...
   - (A) p q
   - (B) q p
   - (C) o p
   - (D) d h

5. x x w x v x u x t x s x r...
   - (A) x o
   - (B) c b
   - (C) x q
   - (D) a b

6. k l n m o p r q s t...
   - (A) v u
   - (B) u v
   - (C) w v
   - (D) v w

7. a b c f e d g h i l k j m...
   - (A) o n
   - (B) n o
   - (C) o m
   - (D) m o

8. z y w x v u s t r q o p n m...
   - (A) k j
   - (B) j k
   - (C) k l
   - (D) l k

9. y z x w u v t s q r p o m n...
   - (A) k j
   - (B) l k
   - (C) k l
   - (D) j k

10. z y x u v w t s r o p q n m l...
    - (A) i k
    - (B) k i
    - (C) i j
    - (D) k j

11. m n o m n o m...
    - (A) m n
    - (B) n o
    - (C) n m
    - (D) o n
    - (E) o m

12. f g g f h h f...
    - (A) f f
    - (B) f i
    - (C) i i
    - (D) i f
    - (E) j j

13. l c d l e f l...
    - (A) l g
    - (B) g h
    - (C) l e
    - (D) f g
    - (E) g g

14. r l s m t n u...
    - (A) o v
    - (B) u v
    - (C) v w
    - (D) o w
    - (E) v o

15. a b z c d y e...
    - (A) x g
    - (B) x w
    - (C) f w
    - (D) f x
    - (E) f g

END OF TEST

Letter Series Test 2

Directions: Each question consists of a series of letters which follow some definite order. Study each series to determine what the order is. Then look at the answer choices. Select the one answer that will complete the set in accordance with the pattern established. Mark the answer sheet with the letter of the answer.

Allow 10 minutes for this test.

Series	Answers (A) (B) (C) (D) (E)	Series	Answers (A) (B) (C) (D) (E)
1. a c e g	h i j k l	11. j c k c	a c e h l
2. a b d e g	c d h i k	12. g j e l c	m n o p q
3. m n p s	t v w x z	13. c c d f	e f g h i
4. a z b y c	d g j n x	14. s g p h m i	j k l m n
5. z w t	q r s t u	15. o p n q m	a e n r s
6. c c d d r	a d e h r	16. a b d h	b f j l p
7. a r b s c	d r s t x	17. s d b t e c u f	a d e r v
8. n p m o	i j k l m	18. c d c c e c c c	c d e f g
9. z y w v t	r s t u v	19. q r s r s t	q r s t u
10. a m c p e	b r s w z	20. a e i m	a i o q u

END OF TEST

Matching Pairs Test

Directions: Each of the questions in this test consists of five pairs of names or numbers. You are asked to compare them and to decide which of the pairs are exactly alike. Count the number of identical pairs in each list of five. Mark the answer sheet to show the number of identical pairs in each list according to the following:

(A) if only one pair is identical.
(B) if only two pairs are identical.
(C) if only three pairs are identical.
(D) if only four pairs are identical.
(E) if only five pairs are identical.

Sample Question and Explanation

Example:

QUESTION	EXPLANATION
Adelphi College—Adelphi College	SAME
Braxton Corp.—Braxeton Corp	Extra "e" in "Braxeton"
	No period in Corp
Wassaic State School—Wassaic State School	SAME
Islip Hospital—Islup Hospital	Islip vs. Islup
Greenwich House—Greenwich House	SAME

The correct answer is (C) for three identical pairs. Now begin the following test questions. Mark your answers on the answer sheet.

Allow 13 minutes for this test.

1. Diagnostic Clinic—Diagnostic Clinic
   Yorkville Health—Yorkville Health
   Meinhard Clinic—Meinhart Clinic
   Tremont Diagnostic—Tremont Diagnostic
   Griscom Infirmary—Griscom Infirmiry

2. 73526—73526
   7283627198—7283627198
   627—637
   728352617183—728352617282
   6281—6281

3. Jefferson Clinic—Jeffersen Clinic
   Mott Haven Center—Mott Haven Center
   Bronx Hospital—Bronx Hospital
   Montefiore Hospital—Montifeore Hospital
   Mercer Hospital—Mercor Hospital

4. 936271826—926371826
   5271—5291
   82637192037—82637192037
   726354256—72634256
   527182—5271882

5. Trinity Hospital—Trinity Hospital
   Central Harlem—Centrel Harlem
   St. Luke's Hospital—St. Lukes' Hospital
   N.Y. Dispensery—N. Y. Dispensary
   Mt. Sinai Hospital—Mt. Sinia Hospital

6. 725361552637—725361555637
   7526378—7526377
   6975—6975
   82637481028—82637481028
   3427—3429

7. Misericordia Hospital—Miseracordia Hospital
   Lebonan Hospital—Lebanon Hospital
   Gouverneur Hospital—Gouverner Hospital
   German Polyclinic—German Policlinic
   French Hospital—French Hospital

8. 63728—63728
   367281—367281
   8277364933251—827364933351
   62733846273—6273846293
   62836—62836

9. King's County Hospital—Kings County Hospital
   St. Johns Long Island—St. John's Long Island
   Bellevue Hospital—Bellvue Hospital
   Beth David Hospital—Beth David Hospital
   Samaritan Hospital—Samaritan Hospital

10. 62836454—6283635
    42738267—42738367
    573829—573829
    738291627874—738291627874
    725—735

11. Bloomingdal Clinc—Bloomingdale Clinic
    Communitty Hospital—Community Hospital
    Metropolitan Hospital—Metropoliton Hospital
    Lenox Hill Hospital—Lenex Hill Hospital
    Lincoln Hospital—Lincoln Hospital

12. 638364728—6283648
    627385—627383
    54283902—54283602
    63352—53554
    7283562781—7283562781

13. Sydenham Hospital—Sydanham Hospital
    Roosevalt Hospital—Roosevelt Hospital
    Vanderbilt Clinic—Vanderbild Clinic
    Women's Hospital—Woman's Hospital
    Flushing Hospital—Flushing Hospital

14. 62738—62738
    727355542321—72735542321
    263849332—263849332
    262837—263837
    47382919—47282912

15. Arietta Crane Farm—Areitta Crane Farm
    Bikur Cholim Home—Bikur Chilm Home
    Burke Foundation—Burke Foundation
    Blythedale Home—Blythdale Home
    Campbell Cottages—Cambell Cottages

END OF TEST

Answer Key For Practice Tests

Coding Test 1

1.	A	3.	A	5.	D	7.	C	9.	C
2.	D	4.	A	6.	B	8.	A	10.	D

Coding Test 2

1.	tie	9.	ryal	17.	eit	25.	yrb	33.	ybli
2.	iel	10.	eya	18.	ast	26.	isb	34.	eri
3.	eya	11.	war	19.	brtw	27.	abe	35.	iry
4.	yats	12.	tbs	20.	esr	28.	tbly	36.	sbl
5.	rwb	13.	isrt	21.	ebit	29.	iba	37.	abi
6.	wsb	14.	yabs	22.	trly	30.	wrb	38.	tbi
7.	lyat	15.	twy	23.	wry	31.	elyt	39.	yrib
8.	iby	16.	ebl	24.	ris	32.	ysb	40.	lyb

Coding Test 3

1.	D	4.	A	7.	C	10.	D	13.	C
2.	B	5.	C	8.	B	11.	D	14.	A
3.	B	6.	A	9.	B	12.	A	15.	B

Name and Number Comparison Test 1

1.	E	4.	B	7.	C	10.	A	13.	D
2.	A	5.	E	8.	D	11.	D	14.	B
3.	C	6.	E	9.	C	12.	B	15.	C

Name and Number Comparison Test 2

1.	E	4.	A	7.	C	10.	C	13.	C
2.	B	5.	D	8.	C	11.	C	14.	B
3.	C	6.	E	9.	B	12.	E	15.	D

Name and Number Comparison Test 3

1.	E	5.	B	9.	B	13.	A	17.	D
2.	A	6.	B	10.	C	14.	B	18.	C
3.	B	7.	C	11.	D	15.	D	19.	B
4.	D	8.	D	12.	E	16.	B	20.	E

Data Interpretation Test 1

1.	F	3.	H	5.	B	7.	J	8.	E
2.	E	4.	K	6.	K				

Data Interpretation Test 2

1.	X	3.	Z	5.	H	7.	I	8.	A
2.	K	4.	N	6.	I				

Matching Letters and Numbers Test 1

1.	E	4.	D	7.	D	10.	C	13.	E
2.	B	5.	C	8.	A	11.	D	14.	B
3.	E	6.	D	9.	E	12.	C	15.	B

Matching Letters and Numbers Test 2

1.	D	4.	E	7.	D	10.	E	13.	E
2.	C	5.	B	8.	A	11.	D	14.	B
3.	A	6.	C	9.	E	12.	C	15.	C

Letter Series Test 1

1.	A	4.	B	7.	B	10.	C	13.	B
2.	D	5.	C	8.	C	11.	B	14.	A
3.	C	6.	A	9.	B	12.	C	15.	D

Letter Series Test 2

1.	B	5.	A	9.	B	13.	E	17.	B
2.	C	6.	E	10.	C	14.	A	18.	D
3.	C	7.	D	11.	E	15.	D	19.	C
4.	E	8.	D	12.	B	16.	E	20.	D

Matching Pairs Test

1.	C	4.	A	7.	A	10.	B	13.	A
2.	C	5.	A	8.	C	11.	A	14.	B
3.	B	6.	B	9.	B	12.	A	15.	A

Posttest and Answers

Allow 13 minutes for this posttest

Coding

Directions: The questions following the chart consist of three lines of code letters and numbers. The numbers on each line should correspond with the line of code letters in the table below:

Code Letter	P	L	I	J	B	O	H	U	C	G
Corresponding Number	0	1	2	3	4	5	6	7	8	9

In some of the questions an error exists in the coding. Compare the letters and numbers in each question carefully. If you find an error or errors, mark the answer sheet with the letter of that answer as follows:

(A) only *one* of the lines in the question contains an error.
(B) any *two* lines in the question contain an error.
(C) all *three* lines in the question contain an error.
(D) none of the lines in the question contain an error.

Sample Question and Explanation

Example:
JHOILCP	3652180
BICLGUP	4286970
UCIBHLJ	5824613

In the above sample, the first line is correct since each code letter listed has the correct corresponding number. On the second line, an error exists because code letter L should have the number 1 instead of the number 6. On the third line an error exists because the code letter U should have the number 7 instead of the number 5. Since there are errors on two of the three lines, the correct answer is (B).

1.
BULJCIP	4713920
HIGPOUL	6290571
OCUHJBI	5876342

2.
CUBLOIJ	8741023
LCLGCLB	1818914
JPUHIOC	3076158

3.
OIJGCBPO	8398405
UHPBLIOP	76041250
CLUIPGPC	81720908

4.
LLOUPJH	1157136
HOBLICG	6041289
IOUPJHC	2570386

5.
LIOCLPJ	1251813
PGOLIHP	0951260
GBLPHUO	9410675

6.
BPCOUOJI	40875732
UOHCIPLB	75682014
GLHUUCBJ	92677843

7.
HOIOHJLH	65256361
IOJJHHBP	25536640
OJHBJOPI	53642502

8.
UGJILPHG	79321609
BOHLULPB	45617104
PIBHUGLJ	02467913

9.
OBJLPCGB	54310894
CULIJBPL	87123401
HOHJCCBG	65638849

10.
UJLLGBOJ	73119453
HOBLPICC	65410288
BHLPJGIB	46103924

Name and Number Comparison

Directions: In the following questions compare the three names or numbers, and mark the answer sheet with the letter of that answer as follows:

(A) if *ALL THREE* are exactly *ALIKE*.
(B) if only the *FIRST* and *SECOND* are exactly *ALIKE*.
(C) if only the *FIRST* and *THIRD* are exactly *ALIKE*.
(D) if only the *SECOND* and *THIRD* are exactly *ALIKE*.
(E) if *ALL THREE* are *DIFFERENT*.

11. Albert Lentz Albert Lentz Albet Lents	15. Hugh Lunny Hugh Luny Hugh Lunny	19. May Marshall May Marshall May Marshall	23. Gloria Moore Gloria Moor Gloria Moore
12. 93476 94376 94376	16. 29522 29522 29522	20. 25816 25816 25816	24. 92889 92889 98289
13. Seymour Lindell Seymour Lindel Seymour Lindell	17. Mal Mallin Mal Mallin Mal Malin	21. Walter Mattson Walter Mattson Walter Matson	25. Leo Musso Leo Muso Leo Muso
14. 90731 90731 90731	18. 50090 50090 50900	22. 71555 75111 75155	

Data Interpretation

The following form is a Payroll Summary of New Employees and lists all employees appointed to the Word Processing Section in the payroll periods indicated. In addition to the payroll period and name, the form includes each new employee's payroll number, title, status, work location, and supervisor's name.

WORD PROCESSING SECTION
Payroll Summary of New Employees — Starting Payroll Period 1

Payroll Period	Name	Payroll Number	Title	Status	Room Number	Supervisor
1	Allen, Roberta	361	Typist	Prov.	312	Macari, J.
1	Ondo, James	545	Clerk	Perm.	532	Dempsey, V.
2	Hoffer, Amy	620	W. Proc.	Perm.	620	Marcy, M.
2	Lee, Sarah	373	Steno.	Prov.	308	Macari, J.
2	Rollon, Carmen	555	W. Proc.	Perm.	530	Dempsey, V.
3	Hodges, Emilie	469	Typist	Perm.	411	Butchko, M.
4	Akpak, Alice	576	Steno.	Prov.	532	Dempsey, V.
5	Egee, John	624	W. Proc.	Perm.	622	Marcy, M.
5	Malderia, Pat	464	Typist	Perm.	411	Butchko, M.

26. In which one of the following payroll periods did two employees in the same title begin work?
    (A) 1
    (B) 2
    (C) 3
    (D) 5

27. To which one of the following supervisors was one typist assigned?
    (A) Macari, J.
    (B) Butchko, M.
    (C) Marcy, M.
    (D) Dempsey, V.

28. Which one of the following supervisors was assigned the greatest number of new employees?
    (A) Marcy, M.
    (B) Macari, J.
    (C) Butchko, M.
    (D) Dempsey, V.

29. Which one of the following employees was assigned three payroll periods after another employee to the same job location?
    (A) Alice Akpak.
    (B) Pat Malderia.
    (C) Carmen Rollon.
    (D) John Egee.

30. The title in which both provisional and permanent appointments were made is
    (A) word processor.
    (B) clerk.
    (C) stenographer.
    (D) typist.

31. The employees who started work in the same payroll period and have the same status but different titles are
    (A) James Ondo and Roberta Allen.
    (B) Amy Hoffer and Carmen Rollon.
    (C) Sarah Lee and Alice Akpak.
    (D) John Egee and Pat Malderia.

Matching Letters and Numbers

Directions: In this test of clerical ability, Column I consists of sets of numbered questions which you are to answer one at a time. Column II consists of possible answers to the set of questions in Column I. Select from Column II the one possible answer which contains only the numbers and letters, regardless of their order, which appear in the question in Column I. If none of the four possible answers is correct, mark (E) on your answer sheet.

COLUMN I: Set of Questions	COLUMN II: Possible Answers
32. Z 5 3 L 7 K 4 G	(A) T 4 K 5 G 2
33. K V 6 T 2 7 4 L	(B) 7 K 4 G Z 5
34. G T V 9 L 4 5 3	(C) L 5 2 G K 7
35. G T 5 N 9 2 K 4	(D) T 2 7 L 6 V
36. K 4 5 T G 2 6 P	(E) none of these
37. V K Z 5 2 L 8 9	(A) N K 8 3 5 7
38. N Z 2 L V 3 5 8	(B) V N 5 8 2 L
39. N P 3 9 V 5 6 Z	(C) 9 Z 3 V P 6
40. Z 3 K T 7 4 5 N	(D) K 5 Z 9 V 8
41. V L K 9 N 5 2 7	(E) none of these

Letter Series

Directions: Each question consists of a series of letters which follow some definite order. Study each series to determine what the order is. Then look at the answer choices. Select the one answer that will complete the set in accordance with the pattern established.
Suggestion: In solving alphabetic series problems, it is helpful to write out the alphabet and keep it in front of you as you work. This makes it easier to spot the key to a letter series.

42. j h n l r p v . . . .
    (A) t x
    (B) s z
    (C) t z
    (D) s y
    (E) z t

43. q g r i s k t . . . .
    (A) u l
    (B) m u
    (C) l u
    (D) m n
    (E) l m

44. e h i f i j g . . . .
    (A) h i
    (B) j k
    (C) i k
    (D) h j
    (E) i j

45. t g h u e f v . . . .
    (A) d c
    (B) d w
    (C) d e
    (D) c d
    (E) c w

46. h g f k j i n . . . .
    (A) m l
    (B) p o
    (C) l m
    (D) o p
    (E) m o

47. r p n l j h f . . . .
    (A) e c
    (B) d c
    (C) e b
    (D) d b
    (E) e d

48. e g t h j t k . . . .
    (A) l t
    (B) m t
    (C) l m
    (D) t l
    (E) m n

49. b d c e g f h . . . .
     (A) g i
     (B) i k
     (C) j i
     (D) j l
     (E) h j

50. e h j m o r t . . . .
     (A) v y
     (B) w z
     (C) v x
     (D) x z
     (E) w y

END OF POSTTEST

Answer Key for Posttest

1. A	11. B	21. B	31. D	41. E
2. C	12. D	22. E	32. B	42. C
3. A	13. C	23. C	33. D	43. B
4. C	14. A	24. B	34. E	44. B
5. A	15. C	25. D	35. A	45. D
6. B	16. A	26. B	36. A	46. A
7. C	17. B	27. A	37. D	47. D
8. A	18. B	28. D	38. B	48. B
9. D	19. A	29. A	39. C	49. C
10. D	20. A	30. D	40. E	50. E

TYPING

Typing Answer Sheet

Typing Format Pretest

1 ⓐ ⓑ ⓒ ⓓ   3 ⓐ ⓑ ⓒ ⓓ   5 ⓐ ⓑ ⓒ ⓓ   7 ⓐ ⓑ ⓒ ⓓ   9 ⓐ ⓑ ⓒ ⓓ
2 ⓐ ⓑ ⓒ ⓓ   4 ⓐ ⓑ ⓒ ⓓ   6 ⓐ ⓑ ⓒ ⓓ   8 ⓐ ⓑ ⓒ ⓓ   10 ⓐ ⓑ ⓒ ⓓ

Typing Performance Pretest

Number of WPM Typed _____
Number of Errors _____

Typing Format Test 1

1 ⓐ ⓑ ⓒ ⓓ   3 ⓐ ⓑ ⓒ ⓓ   5 ⓐ ⓑ ⓒ ⓓ   7 ⓐ ⓑ ⓒ ⓓ   9 ⓐ ⓑ ⓒ ⓓ
2 ⓐ ⓑ ⓒ ⓓ   4 ⓐ ⓑ ⓒ ⓓ   6 ⓐ ⓑ ⓒ ⓓ   8 ⓐ ⓑ ⓒ ⓓ   10 ⓐ ⓑ ⓒ ⓓ

Typing Format Test 2

1 ⓐ ⓑ ⓒ ⓓ   3 ⓐ ⓑ ⓒ ⓓ   5 ⓐ ⓑ ⓒ ⓓ   7 ⓐ ⓑ ⓒ ⓓ   9 ⓐ ⓑ ⓒ ⓓ
2 ⓐ ⓑ ⓒ ⓓ   4 ⓐ ⓑ ⓒ ⓓ   6 ⓐ ⓑ ⓒ ⓓ   8 ⓐ ⓑ ⓒ ⓓ   10 ⓐ ⓑ ⓒ ⓓ

Typing Performance Test 1

Number of WPM Typed _____
Number of Errors _____

Typing Performance Test 2

Number of WPM Typed _____
Number of Errors _____

Typing Performance Test 3

Number of WPM Typed _____
Number of Errors _____

Typing Performance Test 4

Number of WPM Typed _____
Number of Errors _____

Typing Format Posttest

1 ⓐ ⓑ ⓒ ⓓ   3 ⓐ ⓑ ⓒ ⓓ   5 ⓐ ⓑ ⓒ ⓓ   7 ⓐ ⓑ ⓒ ⓓ   9 ⓐ ⓑ ⓒ ⓓ
2 ⓐ ⓑ ⓒ ⓓ   4 ⓐ ⓑ ⓒ ⓓ   6 ⓐ ⓑ ⓒ ⓓ   8 ⓐ ⓑ ⓒ ⓓ   10 ⓐ ⓑ ⓒ ⓓ

Typing Performance Posttest

Number of WPM Typed _____
Number of Errors _____

TYPING

Introductory Pretest and Answers

Typing Format Pretest

Directions: For each of the following questions, select the choice which best answers the question or completes the statement. Mark the answer sheet with the letter of that answer.

Allow 2 minutes for this pretest.

1. Which part of a typed manuscript is typed in all capitals, centered, underscored or not, preceded by roman numerals, and preceded by two blank lines and followed by one blank line?
   - (A) Main subdivisions.
   - (B) Main divisions.
   - (C) Minor subdivisions.
   - (D) Tables.

2. In a report or manuscript, notes serve two functions; namely, to provide comments on the main text and to serve as a bibliographic reference. Of the notes which are used, the note that is a bibliographic reference that appears parenthetically within the main text is a
   - (A) footnote.
   - (B) endnote.
   - (C) headnote.
   - (D) textnote.

3. Which term refers to the arrangement on each page of the various parts of a letter?
   - (A) Letter format.
   - (B) Preface.
   - (C) Message layout.
   - (D) Dedication.

4. Which of the following parts of a letter is *not* a required part?
   - (A) Title of originator.
   - (B) Return address.
   - (C) Complimentary close.
   - (D) Reference initials.

5. Many times, a typist is required to type up minutes of a meeting. Which of the following is *not* a major part of an agenda?
   - (A) Quorum check.
   - (B) Minutes read.
   - (C) Treasurer's report.
   - (D) Reminder system.

6. There comes a time in every typist's job when a line must end with a hyphen. If you do not have an automatic hyphen facility on your machine, which of the following would you *not* do?
   - (A) Use a dictionary.
   - (B) Try not to end two lines in succession with hyphens.
   - (C) Try not to end a page with a hyphen.
   - (D) Try not to divide before a suffix.

7. Which of the following is *not* true when typing tables?
   - (A) Try to keep the table on one page.
   - (B) Try to use leaders more than ruled lines.
   - (C) Try to give each table a title.
   - (D) Try to have column heads.

8. When typing equations and mathematical figures you must slow your motion down and follow certain rules. Of the following, which is *not* a good rule to follow?
   - (A) Do not break up long equations.
   - (B) Space before and after operational mathematical signs connecting two terms of an equation except in subscripts and superscripts.
   - (C) Type all you can of equations.
   - (D) Allow an extra space on either side of symbols, terms, or equations in the text.

9. A typist's procedures manual contains a great deal of information. Of the following, which is the *least* important to be included?
   (A) Letter styles.
   (B) Word division rules.
   (C) Rules of grammar.
   (D) Telephone numbers.

10. If you have to address a letter to the president of a college or university, which of the following is *incorrect*?
   (A) Dr. James L. Herold
       President Rider College
   (B) President James L. Herold
       Rider College
   (C) Dr. James L. Herold, Ph.D.
       Rider College
   (D) James L. Herold, Ph.D.
       President Rider College

END OF PRETEST

Answer Key for Pretest

1. B	3. C	5. D	7. B	9. D
2. D	4. A	6. D	8. A	10. C

Typing Performance Pretest

Directions: Type the copy exactly as it is given below. Spell, space, begin and end each line, paragraph, punctuate, and capitalize precisely as shown. Make no erasures, insertions, or other corrections. Errors are penalized whether they are erased or otherwise corrected. Keep on typing even though you detect an error in your copy. If you finish typing the exercise before the time limit is up, double space once and start typing from the beginning of the pretest exercise. If you fill up one side of the paper, turn it over and continue typing on the other side. Then determine your words a minute (wam).

Allow 5 minutes for this pretest.

Pretest Exercise	words a minute
This pretest exercise is similar in form and	1
in difficulty to the copy you will be required	2
to keystroke for the plain copy test. You are to	3
space, capitalize, punctuate, spell, and begin and	4
end each line precisely as in the copy. Make no	5
erasures, insertions, or other changes in this test	6
because errors will be penalized even if they are	7
erased or otherwise corrected. Practice typewriting	8
this material on scratch paper until the five min-	9
utes are finished, remembering that for your examin-	10
ation it is more important for you to type accu-	11
rately than to try to type too rapidly.	12
The plain copy test consists of a practice ex-	13
ercise and a specific test exercise. The practice	14

```
exercise, usually about ten lines in length, enables      15
you to warm up and to make certain the typewriter is      16
functioning properly. The practice exercise is not        17
scored. After the practice exercise, you are in-          18
structed to put clean paper in your machine for the       19
actual test. You are given time to read both the          20
plain copy directions and the actual test exercise        21
to be typed. Then the actual examination begins.          22
```

Each time you reach this point, double space once and begin again.

END OF PRETEST

Typing Performance

NUMBER OF WPM TYPED _____

NUMBER OF ERRORS _____

SPEED IN WPM	40	42	44	47–49	52–54	56–59	61–64	66–68	71–73	76+
ERRORS PERMITTED	3	4	5	6	7	8	9	10	11	12

Study Hints

In order to improve your typing skill, you must *practice*. You must always keep your eyes on your copy in order to have the maximum efficiency in speed and accuracy. Practice such exercises as:

• Alphabetic drills.
• Rhythm drills.
• Alternate hand drills.
• Concentration drills.
• Individual words, phrases, and then sentences.
• Number and symbol drills.
• Most frequently used word lists.
• Motion patterns.
• Stroke families.
• Double letter drills.
• Home row, upper row, and lower row drills.
• Individual letter drills.

Rules

In the typing test, you are faced with a single task; that is, copying material *exactly* as it is presented. You must demonstrate how rapidly you can do so and with what accuracy.

You will have a specified length of time in which to type, and your score will be based upon the number of words a minute (wpm) you type within that time and upon the number of errors you make. The typing tests given to candidates generally consist of about 20 to 25 lines of copy. Usually 5 minutes are allowed for typing this material. The minimum performance standards for applicants also vary. For some positions a minimum speed of 30 wpm is adequate; for others, 35 wpm, 40 wpm, or even greater speeds are required. The number of errors permitted also varies.

For our purpose here, the information given will help you prepare for your typing examination. You must type at least 40 wpm to meet the minimum speed rating required. Also, at that minimum speed, you may not have more than 3 errors. The following table shows how the copy test is scored:

MINIMUM SPEED IN WPM	40	42	44	47–49	52–54	56–59	61–64	66–68	71–73	76+
ERRORS PERMITTED	3	4	5	6	7	8	9	10	11	12

Write down the total words a minute you typed and the number of errors. Please note in this book that 40 wpm is the minimum amount accepted with a maximum of 3 errors. Then score yourself from the table.

If this speed is not attained, the test is not scored for accuracy. When the speed requirement is satisfied, your test paper is compared with the printed test exercise and marked and charged for typing errors.

When you practice with the typing exercises in this section, score yourself with errors according to the table above and the rules given below for calculating your typing speed.

Here are the basic principles in scoring typing errors. One scoring error is made for each of the following:

1. *Word or Punctuation Mark* incorrectly typed or in which there was an erasure. (An error in spacing which follows an incorrect word or punctuation mark is not further charged.)

2. *Series* of consecutive words omitted, repeated, inserted, transposed, or erased. A charge is made for errors within such series, but the total charge cannot exceed the number of words.

3. *Line* or part of line typed over other material, typed with all capitals, or apparently typed with the fingers on the wrong keys.

4. *Change* from the *Margin* where most lines are begun by you or from the *Paragraph Indention* most frequently used by you.

NOTE: The number of errors allowed in the above table must be increased proportionately for tests which are longer than 5 minutes.

Sample Question and Explanation

Directions: For each of the following questions, select the choice which best answers the question or completes the statement. Mark the answer sheet with the letter of that answer.

Example: When taking the typing speed test, which of the following statements is *incorrect*?
(A) Corrections are permitted.
(B) Errors are penalized whether they are erased or otherwise corrected.
(C) Spell, space, begin and end each line precisely as shown.
(D) Keep on typing even though you finish the exercise.

The directions state: ''Errors are penalized whether they are erased or otherwise corrected.'' Thus, the correct answer has to be (A).

Sample Practice Exercise

Directions: Type the copy exactly as it is given below. Spell, space, begin and end each line, paragraph, punctuate, and capitalize precisely as shown. Make no erasures, insertions, or other corrections. Errors are penalized whether they are erased or otherwise corrected. Keep on typing even though you detect an error in your copy. If you finish typing the exercise before the time limit is up, double space once and start typing from the beginning of the practice exercise. If you fill up one side of the paper, turn it over and continue typing on the other side. Then determine your words a minute (wpm).

Allow 3 minutes for this test.

Practice Exercise	words a minute
The exercises on the following pages provide	1
samples of the kind of copy you must type on actual	2
clerical examinations. You should practice these	3
exercises under ''battle'' conditions—the situation	4

```
you'll be in when taking the actual examination.        5
Carefully follow all copy directions. Time yourself    6
rigorously or, better yet, get someone to hold the     7
watch and time you accurately. Use either scoring      8
table to rate your performance. Don't be discour-      9
aged by low scores. Keep practicing and you will      10
be ready when examination time rolls around.          11
```

Each time you reach this point, double space once and begin again.

END OF TEST

TYPING PERFORMANCE

NUMBER OF WPM TYPED _____

NUMBER OF ERRORS _____

SPEED IN WPM	40	42	44	47–49	52–54	56–59	61–64	66–68	71–73	76+
ERRORS PERMITTED	3	4	5	6	7	8	9	10	11	12

Tests and Answers

The answer key will be found at the end of these practice tests.

Typing Format Questions

Typing Format Test 1

Directions: For each of the following questions, select the choice which best answers the question or completes the statement. Mark the answer sheet with the letter of that answer.

Allow 2 minutes for this test.

1. Which of the following should *not* be included on a personal data sheet?
   (A) Career objectives.
   (B) Work experience.
   (C) Achievements and accomplishments.
   (D) Strong and weak points.

2. Which of the following is *not* considered a time waster?
   (A) Log preparation.
   (B) Disorganization.
   (C) Visiting.
   (D) Procrastination.

3. Having a good memory is very important on the job. You must develop your memory and develop good habits. Which of the following is *not* a good habit to develop?
   (A) Being an attentive listener.
   (B) Taking a picture of visitors.
   (C) Training your mind by using repetition methods.
   (D) Don't clutter your mind with a lot of trivial information.

4. If you worked in a legal office, you would be required to type a lot of legal information. What is the best definition of the common legal term *lien*?
   (A) A statement of truth.
   (B) A legal enforceable agreement between two or more individuals.
   (C) The power to vote for another.
   (D) A claim against a piece of property as payment for a debt.

5. Stress can affect everyone on the job. Which of the following is *not* a contributor to stress?
   (A) Job insecurity.
   (B) Visualization.
   (C) Working conditions.
   (D) Personal problems.

6. If you were asked to place the word "Personal" on an envelope, where is the correct placement?
   (A) Under the stamp.
   (B) Lower left-hand corner.
   (C) In the inside address.
   (D) Below the return address.

7. If you are filling in as a temporary receptionist, which of the following would *not* be one of your duties?
   (A) Welcoming visitors.
   (B) Remembering visitors' names and faces.
   (C) Admitting all visitors.
   (D) Keeping a record of visitors.

8. What is the best proper name given to independently operated machines that are not connected to other machines?
   (A) Repetitive automatic typewriters.
   (B) Display editors.
   (C) Stand-alone machines.
   (D) Memory bank capability machines.

9. Most typists are familiar with the wide range of the quality of bond paper. Which of the following is *not* a term associated with bond paper?
   (A) Cotton-fiber bond.
   (B) Rag fiber bond.
   (C) Watermarks on bond.
   (D) Manifold bond.

10. Businesses have given much attention to providing a favorable working environment for office employees. Which of the following is not a major concern?
    (A) Quality and quantity of equipment and supplies.
    (B) Efficient, comfortable facilities.
    (C) Proper facilities for handicapped individuals.
    (D) Observing OSHA factors for health and safety.

END OF TEST

Typing Format Test 2

Allow 2 minutes for this test.

1. Beginning office workers must develop their office skills in order to meet the standards employers expect of them. Which of the following is *not* an important office skill requirement?
   (A) Trying to be an error-free worker.
   (B) Being willing to understand the office terminology.
   (C) Developing an attitude of cooperation.
   (D) Developing new procedures rather than following established ones.

2. Typists should have an unabridged dictionary at their desk for ready reference. The word unabridged means
   (A) not condensed.
   (B) particular.
   (C) alternative.
   (D) suitable or proper.

3. If you are using a No. 10 envelope, which of the following is *not* a step to follow when folding a letter?
   (A) Last crease goes in envelope first.
   (B) Turn the letter so the last fold is at your left.
   (C) Fold up the bottom third of the letter first.
   (D) Fold right-hand third toward the left.

4. Every typist should have a procedures manual available. Of the following points, which is *not* an important item to place in the procedures manual?
   (A) Mail information.
   (B) Filing information.
   (C) Office layout.
   (D) Personal preference information.

5. What is the best definition for the term *docket file*?
   (A) The decimal system.
   (B) Information arranged by date.
   (C) Information arranged by subject's location.
   (D) Subject filing used by lawyers.

6. An efficient typist should spend the first hour of the day
   (A) handling the most difficult tasks.
   (B) answering telephone messages.
   (C) filing all the previous day's mail.
   (D) gathering needed supplies.

7. The name of the typewriter that is used for making revisions and typing error-free copy is called
   (A) fact finder.
   (B) text-editor.
   (C) facsimile machine.
   (D) type-organizer machine.

8. The graphic illustration that is used by an organization to show the formal structure is called a/an
   (A) organization chart.
   (B) scalar organization.
   (C) line organization.
   (D) chain of command.

9. The trend in office layout that is designed without conventional walls, corridors, and floor-to-ceiling partitions is referred to as?
   (A) marketing.
   (B) arrangement.
   (C) landscaping.
   (D) acoustics.

10. Which of the following is *not* an advantage of an office landscape arrangement?
    (A) Improves oral communications.
    (B) Improves the usage of space.
    (C) Improves the flow of paper.
    (D) Improves the grapevines.

END OF TEST

Answer Key for Practice Tests

Typing Format Test 1

1. D	3. B	5. B	7. C	9. D
2. A	4. D	6. B	8. C	10. A

Typing Format Test 2

1. D	3. D	5. D	7. B	9. C
2. A	4. C	6. A	8. A	10. D

Typing Performance Test

Typing Performance Test 1

Directions: Type the copy exactly as it is given below. Spell, space, begin and end each line, paragraph, punctuate, and capitalize precisely as shown. Make no erasures, insertions, or other corrections. Errors are penalized whether they are erased or otherwise corrected. Keep on typing even though you detect an error in your copy. If you finish typing the exercise before the time limit is up, double space once and start typing from the beginning of the exercise. If you fill up one side of the paper, turn it over and continue typing on the other side.

Allow 5 minutes for this test.

Exercise	words a minute
Thanks to the new world of electronics, Dvorak	1
keyboards may finally make some inroads over Qwerty.	2
The old standard design of typewriter keyboards is	3
called Qwerty after the first letters on the top	4
alphabetic row. It is a really hard arrangement	5
that was first used more than a century ago to slow	6
down fast typists who otherwise might have over-	7
whelmed the creaky machines of the day. August Dvorak	8
designed a better keyboard almost fifty years ago that	9
groups the most frequently used letters on the home	10
row. It also eliminates many awkward "bridges" in	11
which one finger types two consecutive letters across	12
rows. Try typing "pieces" for instance.	13
Everybody seems to agree that Dvorak is faster	14
to learn, easier to type, less tiring, and less	15
likely to cause errors than in Qwerty. But, after	16
all, everyone already knows Qwerty and, in any case,	17
who would want to throw out millions of typewriters?	18
If you are interested in more information, you	19
can write to Dvorak Developments or Freelance Com-	20
munications, Post Office Box 1895, Upland, CA 91785.	21

Each time you reach this point, double space once and begin again.

END OF TEST

Typing Performance Test 2

Directions: Type the copy exactly as it is given below. Spell, space, begin and end each line, paragraph, punctuate, and capitalize precisely as shown. Make no erasures, insertions, or other corrections. Errors are penalized whether they are erased or otherwise corrected. Keep on typing even though you detect an error in your copy. If you finish typing the exercise before the time limit is up, double space once and start typing from the beginning of the exercise. If you fill up one side of the paper, turn it over and continue typing on the other side.

Allow 5 minutes for this test.

Exercise	words a minute
It is of utmost importance that individuals	1
seeking to advance their career in an organization	2
be able to write effectively. The ability to write	3
and speak clearly and to make yourself readily under-	4
stood, are abilities for which there are no substi-	5
tutes. You may have some excellent ideas that could	6
increase productivity or could solve existing pro-	7
blems; but if you are unable to communicate this	8
information to the proper people in your organiza-	9
tion, it may very well be useless. You must listen	10
to your superiors when they communicate directions	11
to you either in writing or verbally. However, your	12
superiors do not have to listen to you, and they	13
probably will not unless you are able to gain their	14
interest quickly. There is no better way to accom-	15
plish this than through well-written memorandums.	16
Individuals who occupy superior positions in	17
organizations have a limited amount of time. They	18
are involved with complex problems and are usually	19
responsible for a number of subordinates. These	20
superiors must budget their limited time and will	21
devote only a portion of it to communicating with	22
their subordinates.	

Each time you reach this point, double space once and begin again.

END OF TEST

Typing Performance Test 3

Directions: Type the copy exactly as it is given below. Spell, space, begin, and end each line, paragraph, punctuate, and capitalize precisely as shown. Make no erasures, insertions, or other corrections. Errors are penalized whether they are erased or otherwise corrected. Keep on typing even though you detect an error in your copy. If you finish typing the exercise before the time limit is up, double space once and start typing from the beginning of the exercise. If you fill up one side of the paper, turn it over and continue typing on the other side.

Allow 5 minutes for this test.

Exercise	words a minute
There are certain guidelines that will help	1
you when typing an envelope. First, most private	2
and public sector offices have preprinted return ad-	3
dress envelopes. If they do not, type the address on	4
the upper left side of the envelope. Only personal	5
stationery carries the return address on the enve-	6
lope flap. You may double space an address that	7
is less than three lines. Type envelopes in block	8
style; that is, the name, address, city, state and	9
ZIP should be flush with each other. The punctuation	10
and form should correspond to the address on the in-	11
side of the letter. Although the city name should be	12
spelled in full, the state should be designated by	13
the two-letter postal abbreviation given by the U.S.	14
Postal Service. Be sure to include the ZIP code num-	15
ber following the state. No comma is required between	16
the state abbreviation and the ZIP code number.	17
If a letter is to be sent in care of someone	18
else, that line is typed as the second line of the	19
address. The notation c/o is acceptable.	20

Each time you reach this point, double space once and begin again.

END OF TEST

Typing Performance Test 4

Directions: Type the copy exactly as it is given below. Spell, space, begin and end each line, paragraph, punctuate, and capitalize precisely as shown. Make no erasures, insertions, or other corrections. Errors are penalized whether they are erased or otherwise corrected. Keep on typing even though you detect an error in your copy. If you finish typing the exercise before the time limit is up, double space once and start typing from the beginning of the exercise. If you fill up one side of the paper, turn it over and continue typing on the other side.

Allow 5 minutes for this test.

Exercise

words a minute

Clerical supervisors are the operating ex-	1
ecutives of management. Their responsibility is	2
second to none. In the last surveys, it is they	3
who influence the organization's labor policies.	4
The exact limits of authority which they are expected	5
to exercise vary from agency to agency. For example,	6
some offices which have installed job evaluations and	7
merit ratings may require that supervisors refer re-	8
quests for reclassification or grievances involving	9
ratings to the wage administration office. Similarly,	10
some large offices have established special discipline	11
boards and may require all disciplinary cases to be	12
handled by this body. Regardless of such administra-	13
tive differences, however, the primary responsibility	14
is theirs. They are the initial contact for the	15
workers. The workers' opinion of an office is often	16
formed largely on the basis of impressions created	17
by their statements and actions. Thus, clerical	18
supervisors must become familiar with labor relation	19
problems and be able to handle them naturally.	20

Each time you reach this point, double space once and begin again.

END OF TEST

Posttest and Answers

Typing Format Posttest

Directions: For each of the following questions, select the choice which best answers the question or completes the statement. Mark the answer sheet with the letter of that answer.

Allow 2 minutes for this posttest.

1. The business letter style that has the date line, the complimentary close, and the writer's identification beginning at the centering point is referred to as?
   (A) Block style.
   (B) Full block style.
   (C) Simplified style.
   (D) Modified style.

2. The stationery size that is 7¼ × 10½ inches is known as
   (A) Standard.
   (B) Baronial.
   (C) Monarch.
   (D) Governmental.

3. The punctuation style of a business letter that uses a colon after the salutation and a comma after the complimentary close is referred to as
   (A) Standard.
   (B) Open.
   (C) Closed.
   (D) Spaced.

4. Which of the following is *not* considered a proper reference notation?
   (A) In reply to:
   (B) Your reference:
   (C) Refer to:
   (D) Yours in replying to:

5. Of the following salutations, which is *incorrect*?
   (A) Dear Messrs. Wilson and Jones:
   (B) Dear Friends:
   (C) Dear Ms. Scott and Mr. Jones:
   (D) My Dear Mrs. Mason:

6. Where is the proper placement of enclosure notations on a letter?
   (A) The line below the reference notation.
   (B) The line below the copy notation.
   (C) The line below the postscript.
   (D) After the inside address.

7. When arranging and typing a one-page report, whichh of the following is *not* a concern?
   (A) Top margin.
   (B) Bottom margin.
   (C) Side margin.
   (D) Balancing.

8. When typing a report using sideheadings, which of the following statements is *not* true regarding them?
   (A) They are preceded by two blank line.
   (B) They are followed by one blank line.
   (C) They are underlined.
   (D) They are typed in all capital letters.

9. Which of the following would *not* be included on a postal card?
   (A) Return address.
   (B) Complimentary closing.
   (C) Reference initials.
   (D) Date.

10. Invoices usually list the materials or services delivered. Which of the following would you *not* type on a printed form?
    (A) Address.
    (B) Date.
    (C) Totals.
    (D) Signature line.

Answer Key for Posttest

1. D	3. A	5. D	7. D	9. B
2. C	4. D	6. A	8. C	10. D

Typing Performance Posttest

Directions: Type the copy exactly as it is given below. Spell, space, begin and end each line, paragraph, punctuate, and capitalize precisely as shown. Make no erasures, insertions, or other corrections. Errors are penalized whether they are erased or otherwise corrected. Keep on typing even though you detect an error in your copy. If you finish typing the exercise before the time limit is up, double space once and start typing from the beginning of the exercise. If you fill up one side of the paper, turn it over and continue typing on the other side.

Allow 5 minutes for this posttest.

Exercise	words a minute
Acquired skills fall into two categories: those	1
that can be forgotten and those which one never for-	2
gets. In general, skills which are entirely mental	3
can be completely forgotten with disuse. If you	4
never speak, read, or listen to a foreign language	5
which you once learned, even one which you knew very	6
well, you may forget it completely. On the other	7
hand, those skills which have some physical compon-	8
ents are rarely totally forgotten. Thus, while you	9
may lose speed, proficiency, and endurance at bicycle	10
riding, swimming, playing the piano, or typing, you	11
can still participate in each activity, however	12
badly. It should be possible to brush up your skills	13
in each of these areas, though you may find that	14
much time and hard work are necessary to regain your	15
original proficiency. If you were once proficient	16
in typing, you should be able to sit at a typewriter	17
right now and touch type very slowly. Try it. Put	18
a piece of paper into your typewriter and, without	19
looking at the keyboard, start typing. Great!	20

Each time you reach this point, double space once and begin again.

END OF POSTTEST

Shorthand

Shorthand Answer Sheet

Shorthand Format Pretest

1 Ⓐ Ⓑ Ⓒ Ⓓ   3 Ⓐ Ⓑ Ⓒ Ⓓ   5 Ⓐ Ⓑ Ⓒ Ⓓ   7 Ⓐ Ⓑ Ⓒ Ⓓ   9 Ⓐ Ⓑ Ⓒ Ⓓ
2 Ⓐ Ⓑ Ⓒ Ⓓ   4 Ⓐ Ⓑ Ⓒ Ⓓ   6 Ⓐ Ⓑ Ⓒ Ⓓ   8 Ⓐ Ⓑ Ⓒ Ⓓ   10 Ⓐ Ⓑ Ⓒ Ⓓ

Stenography Performance Pretest

1 Ⓐ Ⓑ Ⓒ Ⓓ	18 Ⓐ Ⓑ Ⓒ Ⓓ	34 Ⓐ Ⓑ Ⓒ Ⓓ	50 Ⓐ Ⓑ Ⓒ Ⓓ	66 Ⓐ Ⓑ Ⓒ Ⓓ
2 Ⓐ Ⓑ Ⓒ Ⓓ	19 Ⓐ Ⓑ Ⓒ Ⓓ	35 Ⓐ Ⓑ Ⓒ Ⓓ	51 Ⓐ Ⓑ Ⓒ Ⓓ	67 Ⓐ Ⓑ Ⓒ Ⓓ
3 Ⓐ Ⓑ Ⓒ Ⓓ	20 Ⓐ Ⓑ Ⓒ Ⓓ	36 Ⓐ Ⓑ Ⓒ Ⓓ	52 Ⓐ Ⓑ Ⓒ Ⓓ	68 Ⓐ Ⓑ Ⓒ Ⓓ
4 Ⓐ Ⓑ Ⓒ Ⓓ	21 Ⓐ Ⓑ Ⓒ Ⓓ	37 Ⓐ Ⓑ Ⓒ Ⓓ	53 Ⓐ Ⓑ Ⓒ Ⓓ	69 Ⓐ Ⓑ Ⓒ Ⓓ
5 Ⓐ Ⓑ Ⓒ Ⓓ	22 Ⓐ Ⓑ Ⓒ Ⓓ	38 Ⓐ Ⓑ Ⓒ Ⓓ	54 Ⓐ Ⓑ Ⓒ Ⓓ	70 Ⓐ Ⓑ Ⓒ Ⓓ
6 Ⓐ Ⓑ Ⓒ Ⓓ	23 Ⓐ Ⓑ Ⓒ Ⓓ	39 Ⓐ Ⓑ Ⓒ Ⓓ	55 Ⓐ Ⓑ Ⓒ Ⓓ	71 Ⓐ Ⓑ Ⓒ Ⓓ
7 Ⓐ Ⓑ Ⓒ Ⓓ	24 Ⓐ Ⓑ Ⓒ Ⓓ	40 Ⓐ Ⓑ Ⓒ Ⓓ	56 Ⓐ Ⓑ Ⓒ Ⓓ	72 Ⓐ Ⓑ Ⓒ Ⓓ
8 Ⓐ Ⓑ Ⓒ Ⓓ	25 Ⓐ Ⓑ Ⓒ Ⓓ	41 Ⓐ Ⓑ Ⓒ Ⓓ	57 Ⓐ Ⓑ Ⓒ Ⓓ	73 Ⓐ Ⓑ Ⓒ Ⓓ
9 Ⓐ Ⓑ Ⓒ Ⓓ	26 Ⓐ Ⓑ Ⓒ Ⓓ	42 Ⓐ Ⓑ Ⓒ Ⓓ	58 Ⓐ Ⓑ Ⓒ Ⓓ	74 Ⓐ Ⓑ Ⓒ Ⓓ
10 Ⓐ Ⓑ Ⓒ Ⓓ	27 Ⓐ Ⓑ Ⓒ Ⓓ	43 Ⓐ Ⓑ Ⓒ Ⓓ	59 Ⓐ Ⓑ Ⓒ Ⓓ	75 Ⓐ Ⓑ Ⓒ Ⓓ
11 Ⓐ Ⓑ Ⓒ Ⓓ	28 Ⓐ Ⓑ Ⓒ Ⓓ	44 Ⓐ Ⓑ Ⓒ Ⓓ	60 Ⓐ Ⓑ Ⓒ Ⓓ	76 Ⓐ Ⓑ Ⓒ Ⓓ
12 Ⓐ Ⓑ Ⓒ Ⓓ	29 Ⓐ Ⓑ Ⓒ Ⓓ	45 Ⓐ Ⓑ Ⓒ Ⓓ	61 Ⓐ Ⓑ Ⓒ Ⓓ	77 Ⓐ Ⓑ Ⓒ Ⓓ
13 Ⓐ Ⓑ Ⓒ Ⓓ	30 Ⓐ Ⓑ Ⓒ Ⓓ	46 Ⓐ Ⓑ Ⓒ Ⓓ	62 Ⓐ Ⓑ Ⓒ Ⓓ	78 Ⓐ Ⓑ Ⓒ Ⓓ
14 Ⓐ Ⓑ Ⓒ Ⓓ	31 Ⓐ Ⓑ Ⓒ Ⓓ	47 Ⓐ Ⓑ Ⓒ Ⓓ	63 Ⓐ Ⓑ Ⓒ Ⓓ	79 Ⓐ Ⓑ Ⓒ Ⓓ
15 Ⓐ Ⓑ Ⓒ Ⓓ	32 Ⓐ Ⓑ Ⓒ Ⓓ	48 Ⓐ Ⓑ Ⓒ Ⓓ	64 Ⓐ Ⓑ Ⓒ Ⓓ	80 Ⓐ Ⓑ Ⓒ Ⓓ
16 Ⓐ Ⓑ Ⓒ Ⓓ	33 Ⓐ Ⓑ Ⓒ Ⓓ	49 Ⓐ Ⓑ Ⓒ Ⓓ	65 Ⓐ Ⓑ Ⓒ Ⓓ	81 Ⓐ Ⓑ Ⓒ Ⓓ
17 Ⓐ Ⓑ Ⓒ Ⓓ				

Shorthand Format Test 1

1 Ⓐ Ⓑ Ⓒ Ⓓ   3 Ⓐ Ⓑ Ⓒ Ⓓ   5 Ⓐ Ⓑ Ⓒ Ⓓ   7 Ⓐ Ⓑ Ⓒ Ⓓ   9 Ⓐ Ⓑ Ⓒ Ⓓ
2 Ⓐ Ⓑ Ⓒ Ⓓ   4 Ⓐ Ⓑ Ⓒ Ⓓ   6 Ⓐ Ⓑ Ⓒ Ⓓ   8 Ⓐ Ⓑ Ⓒ Ⓓ   10 Ⓐ Ⓑ Ⓒ Ⓓ

Shorthand Format Test 2

1 Ⓐ Ⓑ Ⓒ Ⓓ   3 Ⓐ Ⓑ Ⓒ Ⓓ   5 Ⓐ Ⓑ Ⓒ Ⓓ   7 Ⓐ Ⓑ Ⓒ Ⓓ   9 Ⓐ Ⓑ Ⓒ Ⓓ
2 Ⓐ Ⓑ Ⓒ Ⓓ   4 Ⓐ Ⓑ Ⓒ Ⓓ   6 Ⓐ Ⓑ Ⓒ Ⓓ   8 Ⓐ Ⓑ Ⓒ Ⓓ   10 Ⓐ Ⓑ Ⓒ Ⓓ

Stenography Performance Test 1

1 Ⓐ Ⓑ Ⓒ Ⓓ Ⓔ	17 Ⓐ Ⓑ Ⓒ Ⓓ Ⓔ	33 Ⓐ Ⓑ Ⓒ Ⓓ Ⓔ	49 Ⓐ Ⓑ Ⓒ Ⓓ Ⓔ	65 Ⓐ Ⓑ Ⓒ Ⓓ Ⓔ
2 Ⓐ Ⓑ Ⓒ Ⓓ Ⓔ	18 Ⓐ Ⓑ Ⓒ Ⓓ Ⓔ	34 Ⓐ Ⓑ Ⓒ Ⓓ Ⓔ	50 Ⓐ Ⓑ Ⓒ Ⓓ Ⓔ	66 Ⓐ Ⓑ Ⓒ Ⓓ Ⓔ
3 Ⓐ Ⓑ Ⓒ Ⓓ Ⓔ	19 Ⓐ Ⓑ Ⓒ Ⓓ Ⓔ	35 Ⓐ Ⓑ Ⓒ Ⓓ Ⓔ	51 Ⓐ Ⓑ Ⓒ Ⓓ Ⓔ	67 Ⓐ Ⓑ Ⓒ Ⓓ Ⓔ
4 Ⓐ Ⓑ Ⓒ Ⓓ Ⓔ	20 Ⓐ Ⓑ Ⓒ Ⓓ Ⓔ	36 Ⓐ Ⓑ Ⓒ Ⓓ Ⓔ	52 Ⓐ Ⓑ Ⓒ Ⓓ Ⓔ	68 Ⓐ Ⓑ Ⓒ Ⓓ Ⓔ
5 Ⓐ Ⓑ Ⓒ Ⓓ Ⓔ	21 Ⓐ Ⓑ Ⓒ Ⓓ Ⓔ	37 Ⓐ Ⓑ Ⓒ Ⓓ Ⓔ	53 Ⓐ Ⓑ Ⓒ Ⓓ Ⓔ	69 Ⓐ Ⓑ Ⓒ Ⓓ Ⓔ
6 Ⓐ Ⓑ Ⓒ Ⓓ Ⓔ	22 Ⓐ Ⓑ Ⓒ Ⓓ Ⓔ	38 Ⓐ Ⓑ Ⓒ Ⓓ Ⓔ	54 Ⓐ Ⓑ Ⓒ Ⓓ Ⓔ	70 Ⓐ Ⓑ Ⓒ Ⓓ Ⓔ
7 Ⓐ Ⓑ Ⓒ Ⓓ Ⓔ	23 Ⓐ Ⓑ Ⓒ Ⓓ Ⓔ	39 Ⓐ Ⓑ Ⓒ Ⓓ Ⓔ	55 Ⓐ Ⓑ Ⓒ Ⓓ Ⓔ	71 Ⓐ Ⓑ Ⓒ Ⓓ Ⓔ
8 Ⓐ Ⓑ Ⓒ Ⓓ Ⓔ	24 Ⓐ Ⓑ Ⓒ Ⓓ Ⓔ	40 Ⓐ Ⓑ Ⓒ Ⓓ Ⓔ	56 Ⓐ Ⓑ Ⓒ Ⓓ Ⓔ	72 Ⓐ Ⓑ Ⓒ Ⓓ Ⓔ
9 Ⓐ Ⓑ Ⓒ Ⓓ Ⓔ	25 Ⓐ Ⓑ Ⓒ Ⓓ Ⓔ	41 Ⓐ Ⓑ Ⓒ Ⓓ Ⓔ	57 Ⓐ Ⓑ Ⓒ Ⓓ Ⓔ	73 Ⓐ Ⓑ Ⓒ Ⓓ Ⓔ
10 Ⓐ Ⓑ Ⓒ Ⓓ Ⓔ	26 Ⓐ Ⓑ Ⓒ Ⓓ Ⓔ	42 Ⓐ Ⓑ Ⓒ Ⓓ Ⓔ	58 Ⓐ Ⓑ Ⓒ Ⓓ Ⓔ	74 Ⓐ Ⓑ Ⓒ Ⓓ Ⓔ
11 Ⓐ Ⓑ Ⓒ Ⓓ Ⓔ	27 Ⓐ Ⓑ Ⓒ Ⓓ Ⓔ	43 Ⓐ Ⓑ Ⓒ Ⓓ Ⓔ	59 Ⓐ Ⓑ Ⓒ Ⓓ Ⓔ	75 Ⓐ Ⓑ Ⓒ Ⓓ Ⓔ
12 Ⓐ Ⓑ Ⓒ Ⓓ Ⓔ	28 Ⓐ Ⓑ Ⓒ Ⓓ Ⓔ	44 Ⓐ Ⓑ Ⓒ Ⓓ Ⓔ	60 Ⓐ Ⓑ Ⓒ Ⓓ Ⓔ	76 Ⓐ Ⓑ Ⓒ Ⓓ Ⓔ
13 Ⓐ Ⓑ Ⓒ Ⓓ Ⓔ	29 Ⓐ Ⓑ Ⓒ Ⓓ Ⓔ	45 Ⓐ Ⓑ Ⓒ Ⓓ Ⓔ	61 Ⓐ Ⓑ Ⓒ Ⓓ Ⓔ	77 Ⓐ Ⓑ Ⓒ Ⓓ Ⓔ
14 Ⓐ Ⓑ Ⓒ Ⓓ Ⓔ	30 Ⓐ Ⓑ Ⓒ Ⓓ Ⓔ	46 Ⓐ Ⓑ Ⓒ Ⓓ Ⓔ	62 Ⓐ Ⓑ Ⓒ Ⓓ Ⓔ	78 Ⓐ Ⓑ Ⓒ Ⓓ Ⓔ
15 Ⓐ Ⓑ Ⓒ Ⓓ Ⓔ	31 Ⓐ Ⓑ Ⓒ Ⓓ Ⓔ	47 Ⓐ Ⓑ Ⓒ Ⓓ Ⓔ	63 Ⓐ Ⓑ Ⓒ Ⓓ Ⓔ	79 Ⓐ Ⓑ Ⓒ Ⓓ Ⓔ
16 Ⓐ Ⓑ Ⓒ Ⓓ Ⓔ	32 Ⓐ Ⓑ Ⓒ Ⓓ Ⓔ	48 Ⓐ Ⓑ Ⓒ Ⓓ Ⓔ	64 Ⓐ Ⓑ Ⓒ Ⓓ Ⓔ	80 Ⓐ Ⓑ Ⓒ Ⓓ Ⓔ

81 Ⓐ Ⓑ Ⓒ Ⓓ Ⓔ 91 Ⓐ Ⓑ Ⓒ Ⓓ Ⓔ 100 Ⓐ Ⓑ Ⓒ Ⓓ Ⓔ 109 Ⓐ Ⓑ Ⓒ Ⓓ Ⓔ 118 Ⓐ Ⓑ Ⓒ Ⓓ Ⓔ
82 Ⓐ Ⓑ Ⓒ Ⓓ Ⓔ 92 Ⓐ Ⓑ Ⓒ Ⓓ Ⓔ 101 Ⓐ Ⓑ Ⓒ Ⓓ Ⓔ 110 Ⓐ Ⓑ Ⓒ Ⓓ Ⓔ 119 Ⓐ Ⓑ Ⓒ Ⓓ Ⓔ
83 Ⓐ Ⓑ Ⓒ Ⓓ Ⓔ 93 Ⓐ Ⓑ Ⓒ Ⓓ Ⓔ 102 Ⓐ Ⓑ Ⓒ Ⓓ Ⓔ 111 Ⓐ Ⓑ Ⓒ Ⓓ Ⓔ 120 Ⓐ Ⓑ Ⓒ Ⓓ Ⓔ
84 Ⓐ Ⓑ Ⓒ Ⓓ Ⓔ 94 Ⓐ Ⓑ Ⓒ Ⓓ Ⓔ 103 Ⓐ Ⓑ Ⓒ Ⓓ Ⓔ 112 Ⓐ Ⓑ Ⓒ Ⓓ Ⓔ 121 Ⓐ Ⓑ Ⓒ Ⓓ Ⓔ
85 Ⓐ Ⓑ Ⓒ Ⓓ Ⓔ 95 Ⓐ Ⓑ Ⓒ Ⓓ Ⓔ 104 Ⓐ Ⓑ Ⓒ Ⓓ Ⓔ 113 Ⓐ Ⓑ Ⓒ Ⓓ Ⓔ 122 Ⓐ Ⓑ Ⓒ Ⓓ Ⓔ
86 Ⓐ Ⓑ Ⓒ Ⓓ Ⓔ 96 Ⓐ Ⓑ Ⓒ Ⓓ Ⓔ 105 Ⓐ Ⓑ Ⓒ Ⓓ Ⓔ 114 Ⓐ Ⓑ Ⓒ Ⓓ Ⓔ 123 Ⓐ Ⓑ Ⓒ Ⓓ Ⓔ
87 Ⓐ Ⓑ Ⓒ Ⓓ Ⓔ 97 Ⓐ Ⓑ Ⓒ Ⓓ Ⓔ 106 Ⓐ Ⓑ Ⓒ Ⓓ Ⓔ 115 Ⓐ Ⓑ Ⓒ Ⓓ Ⓔ 124 Ⓐ Ⓑ Ⓒ Ⓓ Ⓔ
88 Ⓐ Ⓑ Ⓒ Ⓓ Ⓔ 98 Ⓐ Ⓑ Ⓒ Ⓓ Ⓔ 107 Ⓐ Ⓑ Ⓒ Ⓓ Ⓔ 116 Ⓐ Ⓑ Ⓒ Ⓓ Ⓔ 125 Ⓐ Ⓑ Ⓒ Ⓓ Ⓔ
89 Ⓐ Ⓑ Ⓒ Ⓓ Ⓔ 99 Ⓐ Ⓑ Ⓒ Ⓓ Ⓔ 108 Ⓐ Ⓑ Ⓒ Ⓓ Ⓔ 117 Ⓐ Ⓑ Ⓒ Ⓓ Ⓔ 126 Ⓐ Ⓑ Ⓒ Ⓓ Ⓔ
90 Ⓐ Ⓑ Ⓒ Ⓓ Ⓔ

Stenography Performance Test 2

1 Ⓐ Ⓑ Ⓒ Ⓓ Ⓔ   26 Ⓐ Ⓑ Ⓒ Ⓓ Ⓔ   51 Ⓐ Ⓑ Ⓒ Ⓓ Ⓔ   76 Ⓐ Ⓑ Ⓒ Ⓓ Ⓔ   101 Ⓐ Ⓑ Ⓒ Ⓓ Ⓔ
2 Ⓐ Ⓑ Ⓒ Ⓓ Ⓔ   27 Ⓐ Ⓑ Ⓒ Ⓓ Ⓔ   52 Ⓐ Ⓑ Ⓒ Ⓓ Ⓔ   77 Ⓐ Ⓑ Ⓒ Ⓓ Ⓔ   102 Ⓐ Ⓑ Ⓒ Ⓓ Ⓔ
3 Ⓐ Ⓑ Ⓒ Ⓓ Ⓔ   28 Ⓐ Ⓑ Ⓒ Ⓓ Ⓔ   53 Ⓐ Ⓑ Ⓒ Ⓓ Ⓔ   78 Ⓐ Ⓑ Ⓒ Ⓓ Ⓔ   103 Ⓐ Ⓑ Ⓒ Ⓓ Ⓔ
4 Ⓐ Ⓑ Ⓒ Ⓓ Ⓔ   29 Ⓐ Ⓑ Ⓒ Ⓓ Ⓔ   54 Ⓐ Ⓑ Ⓒ Ⓓ Ⓔ   79 Ⓐ Ⓑ Ⓒ Ⓓ Ⓔ   104 Ⓐ Ⓑ Ⓒ Ⓓ Ⓔ
5 Ⓐ Ⓑ Ⓒ Ⓓ Ⓔ   30 Ⓐ Ⓑ Ⓒ Ⓓ Ⓔ   55 Ⓐ Ⓑ Ⓒ Ⓓ Ⓔ   80 Ⓐ Ⓑ Ⓒ Ⓓ Ⓔ   105 Ⓐ Ⓑ Ⓒ Ⓓ Ⓔ
6 Ⓐ Ⓑ Ⓒ Ⓓ Ⓔ   31 Ⓐ Ⓑ Ⓒ Ⓓ Ⓔ   56 Ⓐ Ⓑ Ⓒ Ⓓ Ⓔ   81 Ⓐ Ⓑ Ⓒ Ⓓ Ⓔ   106 Ⓐ Ⓑ Ⓒ Ⓓ Ⓔ
7 Ⓐ Ⓑ Ⓒ Ⓓ Ⓔ   32 Ⓐ Ⓑ Ⓒ Ⓓ Ⓔ   57 Ⓐ Ⓑ Ⓒ Ⓓ Ⓔ   82 Ⓐ Ⓑ Ⓒ Ⓓ Ⓔ   107 Ⓐ Ⓑ Ⓒ Ⓓ Ⓔ
8 Ⓐ Ⓑ Ⓒ Ⓓ Ⓔ   33 Ⓐ Ⓑ Ⓒ Ⓓ Ⓔ   58 Ⓐ Ⓑ Ⓒ Ⓓ Ⓔ   83 Ⓐ Ⓑ Ⓒ Ⓓ Ⓔ   108 Ⓐ Ⓑ Ⓒ Ⓓ Ⓔ
9 Ⓐ Ⓑ Ⓒ Ⓓ Ⓔ   34 Ⓐ Ⓑ Ⓒ Ⓓ Ⓔ   59 Ⓐ Ⓑ Ⓒ Ⓓ Ⓔ   84 Ⓐ Ⓑ Ⓒ Ⓓ Ⓔ   109 Ⓐ Ⓑ Ⓒ Ⓓ Ⓔ
10 Ⓐ Ⓑ Ⓒ Ⓓ Ⓔ 35 Ⓐ Ⓑ Ⓒ Ⓓ Ⓔ   60 Ⓐ Ⓑ Ⓒ Ⓓ Ⓔ   85 Ⓐ Ⓑ Ⓒ Ⓓ Ⓔ   110 Ⓐ Ⓑ Ⓒ Ⓓ Ⓔ
11 Ⓐ Ⓑ Ⓒ Ⓓ Ⓔ 36 Ⓐ Ⓑ Ⓒ Ⓓ Ⓔ   61 Ⓐ Ⓑ Ⓒ Ⓓ Ⓔ   86 Ⓐ Ⓑ Ⓒ Ⓓ Ⓔ   111 Ⓐ Ⓑ Ⓒ Ⓓ Ⓔ
12 Ⓐ Ⓑ Ⓒ Ⓓ Ⓔ 37 Ⓐ Ⓑ Ⓒ Ⓓ Ⓔ   62 Ⓐ Ⓑ Ⓒ Ⓓ Ⓔ   87 Ⓐ Ⓑ Ⓒ Ⓓ Ⓔ   112 Ⓐ Ⓑ Ⓒ Ⓓ Ⓔ
13 Ⓐ Ⓑ Ⓒ Ⓓ Ⓔ 38 Ⓐ Ⓑ Ⓒ Ⓓ Ⓔ   63 Ⓐ Ⓑ Ⓒ Ⓓ Ⓔ   88 Ⓐ Ⓑ Ⓒ Ⓓ Ⓔ   113 Ⓐ Ⓑ Ⓒ Ⓓ Ⓔ
14 Ⓐ Ⓑ Ⓒ Ⓓ Ⓔ 39 Ⓐ Ⓑ Ⓒ Ⓓ Ⓔ   64 Ⓐ Ⓑ Ⓒ Ⓓ Ⓔ   89 Ⓐ Ⓑ Ⓒ Ⓓ Ⓔ   114 Ⓐ Ⓑ Ⓒ Ⓓ Ⓔ
15 Ⓐ Ⓑ Ⓒ Ⓓ Ⓔ 40 Ⓐ Ⓑ Ⓒ Ⓓ Ⓔ   65 Ⓐ Ⓑ Ⓒ Ⓓ Ⓔ   90 Ⓐ Ⓑ Ⓒ Ⓓ Ⓔ   115 Ⓐ Ⓑ Ⓒ Ⓓ Ⓔ
16 Ⓐ Ⓑ Ⓒ Ⓓ Ⓔ 41 Ⓐ Ⓑ Ⓒ Ⓓ Ⓔ   66 Ⓐ Ⓑ Ⓒ Ⓓ Ⓔ   91 Ⓐ Ⓑ Ⓒ Ⓓ Ⓔ   116 Ⓐ Ⓑ Ⓒ Ⓓ Ⓔ
17 Ⓐ Ⓑ Ⓒ Ⓓ Ⓔ 42 Ⓐ Ⓑ Ⓒ Ⓓ Ⓔ   67 Ⓐ Ⓑ Ⓒ Ⓓ Ⓔ   92 Ⓐ Ⓑ Ⓒ Ⓓ Ⓔ   117 Ⓐ Ⓑ Ⓒ Ⓓ Ⓔ
18 Ⓐ Ⓑ Ⓒ Ⓓ Ⓔ 43 Ⓐ Ⓑ Ⓒ Ⓓ Ⓔ   68 Ⓐ Ⓑ Ⓒ Ⓓ Ⓔ   93 Ⓐ Ⓑ Ⓒ Ⓓ Ⓔ   118 Ⓐ Ⓑ Ⓒ Ⓓ Ⓔ
19 Ⓐ Ⓑ Ⓒ Ⓓ Ⓔ 44 Ⓐ Ⓑ Ⓒ Ⓓ Ⓔ   69 Ⓐ Ⓑ Ⓒ Ⓓ Ⓔ   94 Ⓐ Ⓑ Ⓒ Ⓓ Ⓔ   119 Ⓐ Ⓑ Ⓒ Ⓓ Ⓔ
20 Ⓐ Ⓑ Ⓒ Ⓓ Ⓔ 45 Ⓐ Ⓑ Ⓒ Ⓓ Ⓔ   70 Ⓐ Ⓑ Ⓒ Ⓓ Ⓔ   95 Ⓐ Ⓑ Ⓒ Ⓓ Ⓔ   120 Ⓐ Ⓑ Ⓒ Ⓓ Ⓔ
21 Ⓐ Ⓑ Ⓒ Ⓓ Ⓔ 46 Ⓐ Ⓑ Ⓒ Ⓓ Ⓔ   71 Ⓐ Ⓑ Ⓒ Ⓓ Ⓔ   96 Ⓐ Ⓑ Ⓒ Ⓓ Ⓔ   121 Ⓐ Ⓑ Ⓒ Ⓓ Ⓔ
22 Ⓐ Ⓑ Ⓒ Ⓓ Ⓔ 47 Ⓐ Ⓑ Ⓒ Ⓓ Ⓔ   72 Ⓐ Ⓑ Ⓒ Ⓓ Ⓔ   97 Ⓐ Ⓑ Ⓒ Ⓓ Ⓔ   122 Ⓐ Ⓑ Ⓒ Ⓓ Ⓔ
23 Ⓐ Ⓑ Ⓒ Ⓓ Ⓔ 48 Ⓐ Ⓑ Ⓒ Ⓓ Ⓔ   73 Ⓐ Ⓑ Ⓒ Ⓓ Ⓔ   98 Ⓐ Ⓑ Ⓒ Ⓓ Ⓔ   123 Ⓐ Ⓑ Ⓒ Ⓓ Ⓔ
24 Ⓐ Ⓑ Ⓒ Ⓓ Ⓔ 49 Ⓐ Ⓑ Ⓒ Ⓓ Ⓔ   74 Ⓐ Ⓑ Ⓒ Ⓓ Ⓔ   99 Ⓐ Ⓑ Ⓒ Ⓓ Ⓔ   124 Ⓐ Ⓑ Ⓒ Ⓓ Ⓔ
25 Ⓐ Ⓑ Ⓒ Ⓓ Ⓔ 50 Ⓐ Ⓑ Ⓒ Ⓓ Ⓔ   75 Ⓐ Ⓑ Ⓒ Ⓓ Ⓔ   100 Ⓐ Ⓑ Ⓒ Ⓓ Ⓔ 125 Ⓐ Ⓑ Ⓒ Ⓓ Ⓔ

Shorthand Format Posttest

1 Ⓐ Ⓑ Ⓒ Ⓓ   3 Ⓐ Ⓑ Ⓒ Ⓓ   5 Ⓐ Ⓑ Ⓒ Ⓓ   7 Ⓐ Ⓑ Ⓒ Ⓓ   9 Ⓐ Ⓑ Ⓒ Ⓓ
2 Ⓐ Ⓑ Ⓒ Ⓓ   4 Ⓐ Ⓑ Ⓒ Ⓓ   6 Ⓐ Ⓑ Ⓒ Ⓓ   8 Ⓐ Ⓑ Ⓒ Ⓓ   10 Ⓐ Ⓑ Ⓒ Ⓓ

Stenography Performance Posttest

1	Ⓐ Ⓑ Ⓒ Ⓓ Ⓔ
2	Ⓐ Ⓑ Ⓒ Ⓓ Ⓔ
3	Ⓐ Ⓑ Ⓒ Ⓓ Ⓔ
4	Ⓐ Ⓑ Ⓒ Ⓓ Ⓔ
5	Ⓐ Ⓑ Ⓒ Ⓓ Ⓔ
6	Ⓐ Ⓑ Ⓒ Ⓓ Ⓔ
7	Ⓐ Ⓑ Ⓒ Ⓓ Ⓔ
8	Ⓐ Ⓑ Ⓒ Ⓓ Ⓔ
9	Ⓐ Ⓑ Ⓒ Ⓓ Ⓔ
10	Ⓐ Ⓑ Ⓒ Ⓓ Ⓔ
11	Ⓐ Ⓑ Ⓒ Ⓓ Ⓔ
12	Ⓐ Ⓑ Ⓒ Ⓓ Ⓔ
13	Ⓐ Ⓑ Ⓒ Ⓓ Ⓔ
14	Ⓐ Ⓑ Ⓒ Ⓓ Ⓔ
15	Ⓐ Ⓑ Ⓒ Ⓓ Ⓔ
16	Ⓐ Ⓑ Ⓒ Ⓓ Ⓔ
17	Ⓐ Ⓑ Ⓒ Ⓓ Ⓔ
18	Ⓐ Ⓑ Ⓒ Ⓓ Ⓔ
19	Ⓐ Ⓑ Ⓒ Ⓓ Ⓔ
20	Ⓐ Ⓑ Ⓒ Ⓓ Ⓔ
21	Ⓐ Ⓑ Ⓒ Ⓓ Ⓔ
22	Ⓐ Ⓑ Ⓒ Ⓓ Ⓔ
23	Ⓐ Ⓑ Ⓒ Ⓓ Ⓔ
24	Ⓐ Ⓑ Ⓒ Ⓓ Ⓔ
25	Ⓐ Ⓑ Ⓒ Ⓓ Ⓔ
26	Ⓐ Ⓑ Ⓒ Ⓓ Ⓔ
27	Ⓐ Ⓑ Ⓒ Ⓓ Ⓔ
28	Ⓐ Ⓑ Ⓒ Ⓓ Ⓔ
29	Ⓐ Ⓑ Ⓒ Ⓓ Ⓔ
30	Ⓐ Ⓑ Ⓒ Ⓓ Ⓔ
31	Ⓐ Ⓑ Ⓒ Ⓓ Ⓔ
32	Ⓐ Ⓑ Ⓒ Ⓓ Ⓔ
33	Ⓐ Ⓑ Ⓒ Ⓓ Ⓔ
34	Ⓐ Ⓑ Ⓒ Ⓓ Ⓔ
35	Ⓐ Ⓑ Ⓒ Ⓓ Ⓔ
36	Ⓐ Ⓑ Ⓒ Ⓓ Ⓔ
37	Ⓐ Ⓑ Ⓒ Ⓓ Ⓔ
38	Ⓐ Ⓑ Ⓒ Ⓓ Ⓔ
39	Ⓐ Ⓑ Ⓒ Ⓓ Ⓔ
40	Ⓐ Ⓑ Ⓒ Ⓓ Ⓔ
41	Ⓐ Ⓑ Ⓒ Ⓓ Ⓔ
42	Ⓐ Ⓑ Ⓒ Ⓓ Ⓔ
43	Ⓐ Ⓑ Ⓒ Ⓓ Ⓔ
44	Ⓐ Ⓑ Ⓒ Ⓓ Ⓔ
45	Ⓐ Ⓑ Ⓒ Ⓓ Ⓔ
46	Ⓐ Ⓑ Ⓒ Ⓓ Ⓔ
47	Ⓐ Ⓑ Ⓒ Ⓓ Ⓔ
48	Ⓐ Ⓑ Ⓒ Ⓓ Ⓔ
49	Ⓐ Ⓑ Ⓒ Ⓓ Ⓔ
50	Ⓐ Ⓑ Ⓒ Ⓓ Ⓔ
51	Ⓐ Ⓑ Ⓒ Ⓓ Ⓔ
52	Ⓐ Ⓑ Ⓒ Ⓓ Ⓔ
53	Ⓐ Ⓑ Ⓒ Ⓓ Ⓔ
54	Ⓐ Ⓑ Ⓒ Ⓓ Ⓔ
55	Ⓐ Ⓑ Ⓒ Ⓓ Ⓔ
56	Ⓐ Ⓑ Ⓒ Ⓓ Ⓔ
57	Ⓐ Ⓑ Ⓒ Ⓓ Ⓔ
58	Ⓐ Ⓑ Ⓒ Ⓓ Ⓔ
59	Ⓐ Ⓑ Ⓒ Ⓓ Ⓔ
60	Ⓐ Ⓑ Ⓒ Ⓓ Ⓔ
61	Ⓐ Ⓑ Ⓒ Ⓓ Ⓔ
62	Ⓐ Ⓑ Ⓒ Ⓓ Ⓔ
63	Ⓐ Ⓑ Ⓒ Ⓓ Ⓔ
64	Ⓐ Ⓑ Ⓒ Ⓓ Ⓔ
65	Ⓐ Ⓑ Ⓒ Ⓓ Ⓔ
66	Ⓐ Ⓑ Ⓒ Ⓓ Ⓔ
67	Ⓐ Ⓑ Ⓒ Ⓓ Ⓔ
68	Ⓐ Ⓑ Ⓒ Ⓓ Ⓔ
69	Ⓐ Ⓑ Ⓒ Ⓓ Ⓔ
70	Ⓐ Ⓑ Ⓒ Ⓓ Ⓔ
71	Ⓐ Ⓑ Ⓒ Ⓓ Ⓔ
72	Ⓐ Ⓑ Ⓒ Ⓓ Ⓔ
73	Ⓐ Ⓑ Ⓒ Ⓓ Ⓔ
74	Ⓐ Ⓑ Ⓒ Ⓓ Ⓔ
75	Ⓐ Ⓑ Ⓒ Ⓓ Ⓔ
76	Ⓐ Ⓑ Ⓒ Ⓓ Ⓔ
77	Ⓐ Ⓑ Ⓒ Ⓓ Ⓔ
78	Ⓐ Ⓑ Ⓒ Ⓓ Ⓔ
79	Ⓐ Ⓑ Ⓒ Ⓓ Ⓔ
80	Ⓐ Ⓑ Ⓒ Ⓓ Ⓔ
81	Ⓐ Ⓑ Ⓒ Ⓓ Ⓔ
82	Ⓐ Ⓑ Ⓒ Ⓓ Ⓔ
83	Ⓐ Ⓑ Ⓒ Ⓓ Ⓔ
84	Ⓐ Ⓑ Ⓒ Ⓓ Ⓔ
85	Ⓐ Ⓑ Ⓒ Ⓓ Ⓔ
86	Ⓐ Ⓑ Ⓒ Ⓓ Ⓔ
87	Ⓐ Ⓑ Ⓒ Ⓓ Ⓔ
88	Ⓐ Ⓑ Ⓒ Ⓓ Ⓔ

SHORTHAND

Introductory Pretest and Answers

Shorthand Format Pretest

Directions: For each of the following questions, select the choice which best answers the question or completes the statement. Mark the answer sheet with the letter of that answer.

Allow 2 minutes for this pretest.

1. If dictation is taken from more than one person, the best way to indicate this is to
   - (A) Let your memory do the work.
   - (B) Place the dictator's initials at the close of each letter.
   - (C) Have a separate book for each person.
   - (D) Use a separate page for each person.

2. When taking dictation, which of the following should you *not* write in longhand?
   - (A) The name of the person to whom you are sending the letter.
   - (B) The street address, city, and state.
   - (C) Unusual words or trade names.
   - (D) The writer's name.

3. Which of the following is *not* a good way to achieve professional growth on your job?
   - (A) Attend seminars.
   - (B) Read secretarial journals and magazines.
   - (C) Limit your interests to a few topics.
   - (D) Take a professional secretarial examination.

4. After you have transcribed a letter and typed it up, and before you remove the page from the typewriter or print it out from the word processor, what should you do?
   - (A) Ask the dictator to dictate the letter again.
   - (B) Ask another individual to read your notes to you.
   - (C) Read the letter for errors.
   - (D) Use the spell check and then print it out.

5. What is the term that means a series of rules and regulations which show the correct way to perform an office task?
   - (A) Work simplification.
   - (B) Activity list.
   - (C) Flow chart.
   - (D) Procedure.

6. When taking Gregg shorthand, which of the following would not be used?
   - (A) Brief forms.
   - (B) Phrases.
   - (C) Dark and light lines.
   - (D) High-frequency words.

7. If you are left-handed, which of the following is the best practice for you to follow on a ruled shorthand pad?
   - (A) Write down the right column, then go up to the left column.
   - (B) Write down the left column, then go up to the right column.
   - (C) Write straight across the page.
   - (D) Write from the back of the notebook forward.

8. When taking notes of a meeting, lecture, etc., it is important that you have an efficient notetaking technique. Of the following, which is *not* an efficient technique?
   - (A) Listen carefully.
   - (B) Edit your notes.
   - (C) Take down notes verbatim.
   - (D) Take down only the main points and important details.

9. When you have finished transcribing a letter from your shorthand notes, the best thing you should do is which of the following?
   (A) Tear out the page and dispose of it.
   (B) File it for future reference.
   (C) Make a photocopy of it for proofreading and editing the letter.
   (D) Draw a diagonal line through it.

10. Of the following which is *not* a term familiar to the secretarial field?
   (A) Character.
   (B) Amanuensis.
   (C) Electronic filing.
   (D) Orphaning.

END OF PRETEST

Answer Key for Pretest

1. B	3. C	5. D	7. A	9. D
2. D	4. C	6. C	8. C	10. D

Stenography Performance Pretest

Directions for the Dictator: Dictate at the rate of 80 words a minute. Do not dictate the punctuation except for periods. Dictate with the expression the punctuation requires. Use a watch with a second hand or a stopwatch to maintain the proper speed.

Person dictating is allowed 3 minutes for this pretest.

Exactly on a minute, start dictating:	Finish reading each group of lines at the number of seconds indicated below.
More than 14 million people work in clerical jobs.(Period) Many keep records and do other office paperwork.(Period)	15 seconds
Others handle communications, operate office machines, ship and receive merchandise, and ring sales on cash	30 seconds
registers. (Period) Workers in clerical jobs have a wide variety of skills and experience. (Period) They include highly	45 seconds
skilled title searchers in real estate firms and executive secretaries in business offices as well	1 minute
as relatively basic messengers and file clerks. (Period) Despite the diversity of jobs and duties, much clerical	15 seconds
employment is concentrated in just a few familiar jobs. (Period) Roughly one of every five clerical workers	30 seconds
is a secretary or stenographer; while one in ten is a bookkeeper. (Period) While administrative support	45 seconds
jobs are located in virtually all industries, they are concentrated in the fast-growing service, trade, and	2 minutes

finance sectors.(Period) Because of this concentration, these jobs are expected to grow more rapidly than the average	15 seconds
for all occupations.(Period) Employers prefer to hire high school graduates for clerical positions. (Period) They look	30 seconds
for people who understand what they read, know basic spelling and grammar rules, and can use arithmetic. (Period) The	45 seconds
ability to type and do neat, accurate paperwork is required for nearly all entry-level positions. (Period)	3 minutes

After dictating the passage: Pause for 15 seconds to permit the stenographer to complete his/her notes. The stenographer should then proceed to follow the transcription instructions given next. S/he should not be permitted to look back at the dictated passage which you have just read.

Transcription

Directions for the Stenographer: The transcript given below is part of the material that was dictated to you, except that many of the words have been left out. From your *notes* you must decide what the missing words are. You are to do the following:

1. Compare your notes with the transcript. When you come to a blank space, decide what word belongs there.

2. Look at the alphabetic word list to find the missing word. If you find the missing word there, note what letter, (A), (B), (C), or (D) is printed beside it. Write that letter in the blank space in your transcript.

3. If the missing word does not appear in the alphabetic word list, mark (E) in the blank space on your transcript.

4. After you have marked all the blank spaces in the transcript, transfer your answers to the answer sheet provided.

Allow 30 minutes for this part of the test.

Alphabetic Word List

Write (E) if the answer is *not* listed.

also—A
also in—C
business—C
busy—D
clerks—A
clerical—A
communications—D
county—B
executive—D
experience—A
governing—D
governmental—C
had been—B
has been—D
messengers—A
merchandise—D
million—C
office—A

offering—C
officials—D
others—C
paperwork—D
people—A
persons—C
real estate—D
record—B
records—A
searchers—C
skilled—B
skills—D
stenographers—D
stenos—A
their—D
there—B
tied—A
trillion—B

Transcript

More than 14 __ __ work in __ jobs. Many keep __ and
        1 2   3   4

do other __ __ . __ handle __ , operate __ machines,
        5 6 7   8   9

ship and receive __ , and ring sales on __ registers.
               10   11

Workers in __ jobs have a wide variety of __ and
           12   13

__ .
14

CONTINUE TO THE NEXT PAGE WITHOUT WAITING FOR A SIGNAL.

Alphabetic Word List

Write (E) if the answer is *not* listed.

administration—B
administrative—A
all—B
always—C
basic—A
basically—D
business—C
businesses—A
clerk—C
clerks—A
concentrate—D
concentrated—C
concentration—B
diversity—B
diversified—C
duties—B
duty—D
executive—D
family—B
familiar—A
fast-developing—A
fast-growing—B
fine—C
finance—C
financial—D
financially—B
in a—B
in just—A

located—A
location—B
messenger—B
messages—A
once—B
one in five—D
one in ten—C
real estate—D
researcher—A
researchers—B
researching—C
service—B
services—A
searchers—C
searching—A
secretary—C
stenographer—A
stenography—B
skilled—B
skills—D
support—D
supporting—A
ten—B
tenth—C
twenty—A
worker—B
workers—D
working—A

Transcript

They include highly ___ title ___ in ___ firms and ___
                 15   16   17   18

secretaries in ___ offices as well as relatively ___ ___
              19   20 21

and file ___ . Despite the ___ of ___ and ___ , much ___
        22   23   24   25   26

___ is ___ ___ a few ___ jobs. Roughly ___ every five
27   28 29   30   31

___ ___ is a ___ or ___ ; while ___ is a ___ . While
32 33   34   35   36   37   38

___ jobs are ___ in ___ ___ ___ , they are ___ in the ___
39   40   41 42 43   44   45

___ , trade, and ___ ___ .
46   47 48

CONTINUE TO THE NEXT PAGE WITHOUT WAITING FOR A SIGNAL.

Alphabetic Word List

Write (E) if the answer is not listed.

ability—D

all—B

almost—C

are—B

are suppose—C

basic—A

basically—B

clerk—B

clerical—A

concentrate—B

concentration—C

employees—A

employers—C

graduate—D

graduates—B

grammar—C

jobs—D

look at—B

look for—B

more rapidly—C

more recent—B

nearly—A

neat—C

occupations—D

of this—A

of these—B

of those—C

paper—C

paperwork—D

position—A

positions—C

prefer—B

require—C

required—B

spelling—B

type—B

typewriter—C

understand—C

use—A

who—C

Transcript

Because ___ ___ , these ___ ___ to grow ___ than the
    49 50   51 52   53

___ for ___ ___ . ___ ___ to hire ___ ___ for ___ ___ .
54   55 56 57 58   59 60   61 62

They ___ people ___ ___ what they ___ , know ___ ___
    63   64 65   66   67 68

and ___ ___ , and can ___ ___ . The ___ to ___ and do
   69 70   71 72   73   74

___ , ___ ___ is ___ for ___ all ___ ___ .
75   76 77   78   79   80 81

WHEN TIME IS UP, TRANSFER YOUR TRANSCRIPT ANSWERS TO THE
ANSWER SHEET.

END OF PRETEST

Answer Key for Pretest

1.	C	18.	D	34.	C	50.	C	66.	E
2.	A	19.	C	35.	A	51.	D	67.	A
3.	A	20.	A	36.	C	52.	E	68.	B
4.	A	21.	E	37.	E	53.	C	69.	C
5.	A	22.	A	38.	A	54.	E	70.	E
6.	D	23.	B	39.	D	55.	E	71.	A
7.	C	24.	E	40.	A	56.	D	72.	E
8.	D	25.	B	41.	E	57.	C	73.	D
9.	A	26.	E	42.	B	58.	B	74.	B
10.	D	27.	E	43.	E	59.	E	75.	C
11.	E	28.	C	44.	C	60.	B	76.	E
12.	A	29.	A	45.	B	61.	A	77.	D
13.	D	30.	A	46.	B	62.	C	78.	B
14.	A	31.	E	47.	C	63.	B	79.	A
15.	B	32.	E	48.	E	64.	C	80.	E
16.	C	33.	D	49.	A	65.	C	81.	C
17.	D								

Study Hints

A stenography performance test usually involves several distinct operations.

1. Taking dictation delivered by the monitor for a number of minutes at a set speed.

2. Transcribing your shorthand notes accurately by typing them, writing them, or transferring them.

3. Answering questions based on the dictated passage, transferring the answers to a separate answer sheet; and, thus, demonstrating that the shorthand notes could be transcribed accurately—if need be.

In most stenographic examinations, dictation passages are read at the rate of 80 words a minute (wpm), except for such specialized positions as reporting stenographer and shorthand reporter. Most examinations require nothing much more than an ability to take dictation at the rate of 80 wpm and to transcribe the material accurately.

Different methods are used in scoring tests. In some cases, you are required to type the notes from the taken dictation. In other examinations, however, a transcript booklet is used. The transcript booklet gives you parts of the dictated passage, but leaves blank spaces where many of the words belong. With adequate shorthand notes, you can readily insert the omitted words that belong in the blank spaces.

An alphabetic *word list* is given with each word designated by a specific letter. You are instructed to mark the letter of the missing word in the transcript. After all blanks in the transcript booklet have been so marked, you are given extra time to transfer the transcript answers to a special answer sheet. In federal examinations, for example, only the answer sheet is scored—not the dictation notes nor the answers in the transcript booklet. It is, therefore, essential for you to understand the procedure and to achieve accuracy in marking the special answer sheet. Answers misplaced or improperly marked can severely lower an examination score.

This section has been prepared for two reasons:

1. To provide material for dictation which will help you improve your speed and accuracy in:

Taking dictation.
Reading your notes.
Transcribing your notes.

2. To provide you with a method of diagnosing your errors and correcting them.

Many good habits in addition to a knowledge of and skill in writing outlines need to be developed if you are to write efficiently. Some of these are:

1. Improve your penmanship.

2. Write down any changes, special instructions, names, etc. that are dictated; don't trust your memory.

3. Don't attempt to erase anything. Draw a line through any errors and continue.

4. Practice taking dictation by taking down speeches, newscasts, and informal talks while watching television or listening to the radio.

5. Keep a stenography pad by the telephone and practice writing down conversations in shorthand.

6. Attend conferences, seminars, meetings, etc., to practice your shorthand. Read it back later for accuracy, completeness, and insert all marks of punctuation, capitalization, word division, number usage, and abbreviations.

7. An important skill which aids in the mastery of shorthand is what is known as *word carrying ability*.

— Enlist the aid of a friend or teacher to read a short sentence and then ask to have it repeated. The length of the dictated sentences should be gradually increased.

— Dictators should dictate a short paragraph, allowing you to begin writing as soon as the dictation begins. However, they should dictate faster than you can write and you should continue to write after the dictation stops.

Rules for Giving and Taking Dictation

In taking the following stenographic tests at home, get a friend or teacher to dictate the passages at the required speed in the test directions. The dictation material presented in these pages is similar to the passages read in the actual examination; and, together with the transcript tests following, will familiarize you with the actual test conditions. Since the transcript portion of the examination is so important, you must understand the exact procedures. In reading the passages to you, your friends or teachers must *adhere* to the dictation rules. They are as follows:

1. Dictators or teachers should read the passage through a number of times to themselves until they have its contents well in mind.

    Dictators should read the selection over a few times before dictating so they may gain an idea of how to maintain a steady and predetermined dictation speed.

    They should dictate in a firm, loud voice. Since they have gained some acquaintance with the paragraph, they should read with expression. They should fully comprehend the ideas in what they are reading and should read the passage with the expression the punctuation indicates.

2. At definite intervals throughout the passage, consecutive numbers have been inserted to help dictators determine whether they are reading at the desired speed. These numbers are *not* to be read as part of the dictation. Each consecutive number represents a timed interval in the dictation test. Furnish the dictator with a stop watch or a watch that shows the seconds clearly.

3. When dictators read the passage aloud to themselves within the designated time intervals and in a coordinated and even manner, then they are ready to begin dictating.

4. Remember, dictators must maintain the same speed throughout the reading.

5. Dictators should not dictate punctuation marks, except periods. However, they should read the passage with the expression the punctuation indicates.

Note: In the actual examination, you are not permitted to read the dictation and transcript material in advance. Therefore, you must not do so at home. After a passage has been dictated, you are allowed 15 seconds to complete your notes. You should then turn to the transcription test for the passage. Read and carefully follow the directions. Answer the transcript questions and mark the answer sheet accordingly. Do this for each test. In studying follow all directions precisely, especially the time limits.

Diagnosis of Stenographic Errors

Grade the transcription of each exercise immediately after completion. One diagnostic method for this purpose is called "Postem Scoring." "Postem" is derived from "post 'em" and is a key expression for remembering the typical kinds of errors which are made in transcription. For example:

P   The number of errors which were made in punctuation, capitalization, and paragraphing.
O   The number of omitted words.
S   The number of substituted, transposed, or added words.
T   The number of typographical errors.

E   The number of obvious erasures.
M   The number of misspelled words.

This kind of scoring is achieved by proofreading. Reserve 5 or more minutes at the end of each transcription period. Read aloud the correct copy.

Postem scoring is diagnostic; that is, it reveals the total number of each kind of error which has been made. Postem scoring also demonstrates that errors in typing, spelling, punctuation, grammar, word division, numbers, format, capitalization, erasures, abbreviations, and omissions account for most of the errors which are made in transcription.

Tests and Answers

The answer key will be found at the end of these practice tests.

Shorthand Format Questions

Shorthand Format Test 1

Directions: For each of the following questions, select the choice which best answers the question or completes the statement. Mark the answer sheet with the letter of that answer.

Allow 2 minutes for this test.

1. The individual who performs the typing and transcribing functions frequently is called a(n)
   (A) administrative secretary.
   (B) correspondence secretary.
   (C) word processing secretary.
   (D) managing secretary.

2. Of the following items, which is the greatest advantage of grouping similar tasks?
   (A) You can work at more rapid speeds.
   (B) You can save time and energy.
   (C) You can correct your errors at a later date.
   (D) You can develop new procedures.

3. The major role of a secretary is to
   (A) handle repetitive tasks.
   (B) keep up to date with new office equipment.
   (C) be a support to management.
   (D) keep up to date with secretarial changes.

4. What is the major advantage of an office layout arrangement?
   (A) Improvement of work flow.
   (B) Improvement of telephone communications.
   (C) Improvement of handling nonrepetitive projects.
   (D) None of the above.

5. When applying for a new position, it is important that you prepare a letter of application. Of the following, what should it contain?
   (A) Job you are applying for.
   (B) Introduction of yourself.
   (C) Your qualifications.
   (D) All of the above.

6. Which of the following should be included in the heading of the second page of a letter?
   (A) The address.
   (B) The page number.
   (C) The date the letter was received.
   (D) The subject.

7. On a standard-size postcard, what is the minimum side margins you should leave?
   (A) ½ inch.
   (B) ¼ inch.
   (C) ¾ inch.
   (D) ⅝ inch.

8. High-level executive correspondence differs somewhat from routine business correspondence in that high-level official correspondence is more formal. Of the following, which is more appropriate for use by the executive correspondences?
   (A) No punctuation after the salutation.
   (B) No punctuation after the complimentary close.
   (C) Reference initials and enclosure are omitted.
   (D) Blocked style is used.

9. Letters have three types of punctuation styles. The most popular form is mixed punctuation. This style requires
   (A) punctuation after the salutation and signature line.
   (B) punctuation after the salutation and complimentary close.
   (C) punctuation after all special lines.
   (D) punctuation after the date, closing, signature, and reference initials.

10. A postscript is often used at the end of a letter. Which of the following is *not* a correct usage of the postscript?
    (A) Type ''PS:''
    (B) Type ''PS.''
    (C) Type ''PPS:''
    (D) Type ''P.P.S.''

END OF TEST

Shorthand Format Test 2

Allow 2 minutes for this test.

1. If the same interoffice memo is to be sent to ten people, of the following, which is the best method to be used?
   (A) Send a separate memo to each person with his/her name typed in the ''TO:'' position.
   (B) In the ''TO:'' position, type the word ''Distribution'' and type the names of the individuals at the end of the memo.
   (C) Send a separate memo to each person with a c notation at the bottom of the page with each person's name.
   (D) Type one memo, photocopy the memo, and write each persons name in the ''TO:'' position.

2. If an interoffice memo contains more than one page, the second page should include which of the following?
   (A) Use a memo form, type ''Continued'' on line 3.
   (B) Use a memo form, type ''Page 2'' on line 7 and fill in all the guide word information.
   (C) Use plain paper and type in all the guide word information and mark ''Page 2'' on line 3.
   (D) Use plain paper and type the person's name, date, and page number on line 7.

3. Which of the following complimentary closings is incorrectly used?
   (A) Sincerely yours,
   (B) Very cordially yours,
   (C) Respectively yours,
   (D) Cordially,

4. When you are removing the contents from an envelope, what should you be aware of?
   (A) The return address on the letter.
   (B) The return address on the envelope.
   (C) Enclosures.
   (D) Dates are on both the letter and envelope.

5. Where is the proper placement of enclosure notations on a letter?
   (A) The line below the enclosure notation.
   (B) The line below the copy notation.
   (C) The line below the postscript.
   (D) After the inside address.

6. Which of the following is *not* part of an interoffice memo?
   (A) Date.
   (B) Subject.
   (C) Salutation.
   (D) From.

7. Which of the following is *not* a common type of typewriter?
   (A) Variable typewriter.
   (B) Varityper.
   (C) Justowriter.
   (D) Automatic typewriter.

8. Which of the following is the most common business stationery size?
   (A) Baronial.
   (B) Monarch.
   (C) Government.
   (D) Standard.

9. What is the major advantage of using a window envelope over a regular envelope?
   (A) They cost less.
   (B) The postal rate is cheaper.
   (C) Saves addressing the envelope.
   (D) The address is easier to understand.

10. If you are falling behind the dictator's dictation, which of the following should you do?
    - (A) Don't interrupt the dictator.
    - (B) Continue taking as much as you can and fill in the gaps later.
    - (C) Alert the dictator that you are behind.
    - (D) Drop your pen or pad so the dictator will pause.

END OF TEST

Answer Key for Practice Exercises

Shorthand Format Test 1

1. B	3. C	5. D	7. A	9. B
2. B	4. A	6. B	8. C	10. D

Shorthand Format Test 2

1. B	3. C	5. A	7. A	9. C
2. D	4. C	6. C	8. D	10. C

Stenography Performance Test

Stenography Performance Test 1

Person dictating is allowed 3 minutes 15 seconds for this part.

Directions for the Dictator: Dictate at the rate of 80 words a minute. Do not dictate the punctuation except for periods. Dictate with the expression the punctuation requires. Use a watch with a second hand or a stopwatch to maintain the proper speed.

Exactly on a minute, start dictating

Finish reading each group of lines at the number of seconds indicated below.

The advantages of a good education are appreciated by almost everyone in this country, and

15 seconds

good colleges and technical schools are found in every state. (Period) Some young people prepare themselves for work which

30 seconds

does not require a college degree and either do not go on to college at all or take only courses of

45 seconds

special interest to them. (Period) Those who do wish to continue their education after high school often find that they can

1 minute

hold full-time jobs during the day and go to school at night. (Period) Washington, for example, is a city whose universities	15 seconds
are open both throughout the day and in the evening. (Period) Classes after office hours are popular	30 seconds
with government employees, many of whom earn degrees in this way. (Period) Many students are preparing for the foreign	45 seconds
service or for careers in law or teaching. (Period) Others are young scientists who began in government research	2 minutes
just out of college and are going to school to obtain broader knowledge that will help them to advance. (Period) There are	15 seconds
many stenographers and clerks who have come to the city from all parts of the United States. (Period) Some of these young	30 seconds
people return home after college and practice law, run their own businesses, or work in the field offices and	45 seconds
laboratories of the government. (Period) Those who prefer to stay in Washington often rise to positions of	3 minutes
importance as secretaries or as specialists in various lines of work such as accounting, law, or management. (Period)	15 seconds

After dictating the passage: Pause for 15 seconds to permit the stenographer to complete his/her notes. The stenographer should then proceed to follow the transcription instructions given next. She/he should not be permitted to look back at the dictated passage which you have just read.

Transcription

Directions for the stenographer: The transcript given below is part of the material that was dictated to you, except that many of the words have been left out. From your *notes* you must decide what the missing words are. You are to do the following:

1. Compare your notes with the transcript. When you come to a blank space, decide what word belongs there.

2. Look at the alphabetic word list to find the missing word. If you find the missing word there, note

what letter, (A), (B), (C), or (D) is printed beside it. Write that letter in the blank space in your transcript.

3. If the missing word does not appear in the alphabetic word list, mark (E) in the blank space on your transcript.

4. After you have marked all the blank spaces in the transcript, transfer your answers to the answer sheet provided.

Allow 30 minutes for this part of the test.

Alphabetic Word List

Write (E) if the answer is *not* listed.

advantages—C
and—C
appeal—C
appreciated—A
are—A
are found—D
but—D
by—B
classes—D
college—C
continue—D
country—C
degree—D
do—D
education—D
either—A
everywhere—C
for—A
go—B
interest—B

only—A
people—C
prefer—D
prepare—C
recognize—B
request—A
require—D
scholars—C
schools—B
separate—C
special—B
specific—A
state—B
technical—D
themselves—D
they—C
this—D
to—D
to college—B
training—A

Transcript

The __ of a good __ __ __ by almost __ in __ __ , and
   1   2 3 4   5   6 7

good colleges __ __ __ __ in __ __ . Some young
               8 9 10 11   12 13

__ __ __ __ work __ does not __ a __ __ and __
14 15 16 17   18   19 20 21   22

__ __ __ on __ at all or take __ __ of __ __ to
23 24 25   26   27 28   29 30

them.

CONTINUE ON TO THE NEXT PAGE WITHOUT WAITING FOR A SIGNAL.

Alphabetic Word List

Write (E) if the answer is not listed.

after—C

and—C

at night—D

believe—C

both—A

college—C

colleges—B

complete—C

continue—D

day—C

daytime—A

degrees—C

desire—C

do—D

during—C

earn—D

earning—A

education—D

either—A

employees—B

employers—D

even—D

find—B

first-rate—C

government—A

got—D

go—B

great—D

high school—D

hours—B

in the—A

many—A

most—A

offered—A

office—D

often—B

popular—A

preferred—B

prepared—D

seek—B

sought—B

the—C

their—B

them—B

think—A

throughout—D

to school—C

to work—A

training—A

universities—A

where—D

whose—C

wish—A

with—A

work—C

year—A

Transcript

Those who ___ ___ to ___ ___ ___ after ___ ___ ___ that
       31 32   33 34 35   36 37 38

they can hold ___ jobs ___ ___ ___ and ___ ___ ___ .
         39   40 41 42   43 44 45

Washington, for example, is a city ___ ___ are ___ ___
                    46 47   48 49

___ the day and ___ ___ . Classes ___ ___ ___ are ___
50   51 52   53 54 55   56

with ___ ___ , ___ of ___ ___ ___ in this way.
    57 58   59   60 61 62

CONTINUE ON TO THE NEXT PAGE WITHOUT WAITING FOR A SIGNAL.

Alphabetic Word List

Write (E) if the answer is *not* listed.

all—B	obtain—A
and—C	or—B
are—B	out of—A
assure—B	prepare—C
at night—D	prepared—D
began—A	preparing—A
beginning—C	research—B
broader—B	reserves—C
came—D	schools—B
careers—C	scientists—A
classes—D	secretaries—A
clerks—A	service—D
college—C	standards—D
come to—A	state—B
degrees—C	states—D
find—B	students—A
forest—C	surface—A
going—D	teaching—B
help—D	the city—D
in—C	them—B
in law—B	they—C
just—D	to—D
many—C	to school—C
men—A	typists—D
more—D	will—A

Transcript

Many ___ ___ ___ for the ___ ___ or for ___ ___ or ___ .
    63 64 65   66 67   68 69   70

Others are ___ ___ who ___ ___ government ___ ___ ___
    71 72   73 74   75 76 77

___ and are ___ ___ to ___ ___ ___ that will ___ ___ ___
78   79 80   81 82 83   84 85 86

advance. There are ___ ___ ___ ___ who have ___ ___
    87 88 89 90   91 92

from ___ ___ of the United States.
   93 94

CONTINUE ON TO THE NEXT PAGE WITHOUT WAITING FOR A SIGNAL.

Alphabetic Word List

Write (E) if the answer is *not* listed.

activity—B	officers—B
after—C	often—B
assistants—D	out of—A
begin—B	own—D
businesses—A	people—C
career—A	positions—A
college—C	practice—A
field—D	prefer—D
government—A	prepare—C
graduates—B	right—B
hold—C	run—D
home—D	scientists—D
importance—C	special—B
in—C	specialists—C
in the—A	state—B
including—C	students—A
interest—B	such—A
kinds—D	that are—B
lines—A	their—B
local branches—B	these—A
may—D	to school—C
of—D	to stay—A
of their—C	to work—A
offices—C	who—C
	work—C

Transcript

Some of __ __ __ return __ __ __ and __ __ ,
    95 96 97   98 99 100   101 102

run __ __ __ , or __ __ __ __ and __
    103 104 105   106 107 108 109   110

__ the __ . Those __ __ __ in Washington
111   112   113 114 115

__ rise to __ __ __ as secretaries or as __ __
116   117 118 119   120 121

__ __ of __ __ as __ , law, or management.
122 123   124 125   126

WHEN TIME IS UP, TRANSFER YOUR TRANSCRIPT ANSWERS TO THE
ANSWER SHEET.

END OF TEST

Stenography Performance Test 2

Person dictating is allowed 3 minutes 15 seconds for this part.

Directions for the Dictator: Dictate at the rate of 80 words a minute. Do not dictate the punctuation except for periods. Dictate with the expression the punctuation requires. Use a watch with a second hand or a stopwatch to maintain the proper speed.

Exactly on a minute, start dictating

Finish reading each group of lines at the number of seconds indicated below.

The number enrolled in shorthand classes in the high schools has shown a marked increase.(Period) Today this subject is one of

15 seconds

the most popular offered in the field of business education.(Period) When shorthand was first taught, educators claimed

30 seconds

that it was of value mainly in sharpening the powers of observation and discrimination.(Period) However,	45 seconds
with the growth of business and the increased demand for office workers, educators have come to realize the importance	1 minute
of stenography as a vocational tool.(Period) With the differences in the aims of instruction came changes in the grade	15 seconds
placement of the subject.(Period) The prevailing thought has always been that it should be offered in high school.(Period)	30 seconds
When the junior high school first came into being, shorthand was moved down to that level with little change in the manner in which	45 seconds
the subject was taught.(Period) It was soon realized that shorthand had no place there because the training had lost its vocational utility	2 minutes
by the time the student could graduate.(Period) Moreover, surveys of those with education only through junior high school seldom found them at work as	15 seconds
stenographers.(Period) For this reason shorthand was returned to the high school level	30 seconds
and is offered as near as possible to the time of graduation so that the skill will be retained when the student	45 seconds
takes a job.(Period) Because the age at which students enter office jobs has advanced, there is not a tendency to	3 minutes
upgrade business education into the junior college.(Period)	15 seconds

After dictating the passage: Pause for 15 seconds to permit the stenographer to complete his/her notes. The stenographer should then proceed to follow the transcription instructions given next. She/he should not be permitted to look back at the dictated passage which you have just read.

Transcription

Directions for the stenographer: The transcript given below is part of the material that was dictated to you, except that many of the words have been left out. From your *notes* you must decide what the missing words are. You are to do the following:

1. Compare your notes with the transcript. When you come to a blank space, decide what word belongs there.

2. Look at the alphabetic word list to find the missing word. If you find the missing word there, note what letter, (A), (B), (C), or (D) is printed beside it. Write that letter in the blank space in your transcript.

3. If the missing word does not appear in the Alphabetic Word List, mark (E) in the blank space on your transcript.

4. After you have marked all the blank spaces in the transcript, transfer your answers to the answer sheet provided.

Allow 30 minutes for this part of the test.

Alphabetic Word List

Write (E) if the answer is *not* listed.

administration—C

observation—B

along the—B

observing—A

area—A

offered—C

at first—A

of value—C

claimed—C

open—A

classes—B

popular—B

concluded—D

power—B

could be—D

powers—D

courses—C

practical—A

decrease—D

shaping—A

discriminating—C

sharpen—B

discrimination—D

shorthand—D

education—B

shown—C

enrolled—D

stenography—B

entering—A

study—C

field—D

subject—A

first—D

taught—D

given—B

that—C

great—C

the—D

increase—A

these—B

in the—D

this—A

known—D

thought—B

line—C

to be—A

mainly—B

training—D

marked—B

valuable—A

mostly—D

vast—A

Transcript

The number __ in shorthand __ __ high schools has __
　　　　　1　　　　　　　　　2　　3　　　　　　　　4

a __ __ . Today __ __ is one of the most __ __ __ __
　5　6　　　　　　7　8　　　　　　　　　　　　9　10　11　12

of business __ . When __ __ __ __ , educators __
　　　　　　13　　　　　　14　15　16　17　　　　　　　18

that it __ __ __ in __ __ __ of __ and __ .
　　　　19　20　21　　　22　23　24　　25　　26

CONTINUE ON TO THE NEXT PAGE WITHOUT WAITING FOR A SIGNAL.

Alphabetic Word List

Write (E) if the answer is *not* listed.

a change—D
administration—C
aims—A
always been—A
begun—D
businesses—A
came—D
changes—B
come—C
defects—B
demand—B
demands—A
differences—D
education—B
educators—D
for—D
given—B
grade—C
grading—B
has—C
had—B
have come—A
high school—B
increased—D
increasing—C
institutions—D
instruction—C
it—B

offered—C
office—A
official—C
often been—B
ought to be—B
place—B
placement—D
prevailing—B
rule—D
schools—D
shorthand—D
should be—A
significance—C
stenography—B
study—C
subject—A
thinking—C
this—A
thought—B
tool—B
to realize—B
to recognize—B
valuable—A
vocational—C
when the—D
with—A
without—C
workers—C

Transcript

However, ___ the growth of ___ and the ___ ___ for ___
      27   28   29 30   31

___ , ___ have ___ ___ the ___ of ___ ___ a ___ ___ .
32   33   34 35   36   37 38   39 40

With the ___ in the ___ of ___ ___ ___ in the ___ ___ of
        41   42   43 44 45   46 47

the ___ . The ___ ___ ___ ___ that ___ ___ ___ in ___ .
   48   49 50 51 52   53 54 55   56

CONTINUE ON TO THE NEXT PAGE WITHOUT WAITING FOR A SIGNAL.

Alphabetic Word List

Write (E) if the answer is *not* listed.

became—B
because—B
came—D
change—A
changed—C
could—C
could be—D
date—D
first—D
graduate—D
graduated—B
had little—C
had no—A
here—D
high—C
into being—A
into business—C
junior high—D
less—B
lessened—C
level—C
little—A
lost—D
manner—B
method—C

moved—C
moved down—B
occupational—B
recognized—A
shorthand—D
since—C
soon—C
stenography—B
student—A
students—C
study—C
subject—A
taught—D
that—D
the—D
their—A
there—B
this—A
time—B
training—D
usefulness—B
utility—C
vocational—C
which—A

Transcript

When the ___ school ___ ___ ___ , ___ was ___ to ___
     57   58 59 60   61   62   63

___ with ___ ___ in ___ ___ ___ the ___ was ___ . It was
64   65 66   67 68 69   70   71

___ ___ that ___ ___ place ___ ___ the ___ had ___ ___
72 73   74 75   76 77   78   79 80

___ ___ by the ___ the ___ ___ ___ .
81 82   83   84 85 86

CONTINUE ON TO THE NEXT PAGE WITHOUT WAITING FOR A SIGNAL.

Alphabetic Word List

Write (E) if the answer is *not* listed.

advanced—A

age—A

as far as—C

at which—D

at work—A

be—B

date—D

education—B

enter—D

found—D

graduating—A

graduation—C

has—C

high school—B

in—A

in order—D

increased—D

into—B

job—B

junior high—D

level—C

may be—C

near as—A

nearly as—C

offered—C

often—B

only—B

possible—D

rarely—D

reason—B

reasons—D

retained—B

school—A

secretaries—D

secures—D

seldom—C

showed—A

so—A

stenographers—C

studies—B

surveys—A

takes—A

taught—D

that—C

there—B

this—A

through—D

time—B

training—D

undertake—A

until—A

upgrade—D

when—C

which—A

will—B

would—D

working—B

Transcript

Moreover, __ of __ with __ __ __ __ school __
$\quad$ 87 $\quad$ 88 $\quad\quad\quad$ 89 $\;$ 90 $\;$ 91 $\;$ 92 $\quad\quad$ 93

__ them __ as __ . For __ __ , shorthand was __
94 $\quad\quad$ 95 $\quad$ 96 $\quad\quad\quad$ 97 $\;$ 98 $\quad\quad\quad\quad\quad\quad$ 99

to the __ __ and is __ as __ __ to the __ of
$\quad\quad$ 100 $\;$ 101 $\quad\quad\quad$ 102 $\quad$ 103 $\;$ 104 $\quad\quad$ 105

__ __ __ the skill __ __ __ __ the student
106 $\;$ 107 $\;$ 108 $\quad\quad\quad$ 109 $\;$ 110 $\;$ 111 $\;$ 112

__ a __ . Because the __ __ students __ office
113 $\;\;$ 114 $\quad\quad\quad\quad\quad$ 115 $\;$ 116 $\quad\quad\quad$ 117

__ __ __ , there is __ a __ to __ __ educa-
118 $\;$ 119 $\;$ 120 $\quad\quad\quad$ 121 $\quad$ 122 $\quad$ 123 $\;$ 124

tion __ the junior college.
$\quad$ 125

WHEN TIME IS UP, TRANSFER YOUR TRANSCRIPT ANSWERS TO THE ANSWER SHEET.

END OF TEST

Answer Key for Practice Tests

Stenography Performance Test 1

1.	C	27.	A	52.	E	77.	A	102.	E
2.	D	28.	E	53.	C	78.	C	103.	B
3.	A	29.	B	54.	D	79.	D	104.	D
4.	A	30.	B	55.	B	80.	C	105.	A
5.	E	31.	D	56.	A	81.	A	106.	C
6.	D	32.	A	57.	A	82.	B	107.	A
7.	C	33.	D	58.	B	83.	E	108.	D
8.	C	34.	B	59.	A	84.	D	109.	C
9.	D	35.	D	60.	E	85.	B	110.	E
10.	B	36.	D	61.	D	86.	D	111.	D
11.	D	37.	B	62.	C	87.	C	112.	A
12.	E	38.	B	63.	A	88.	E	113.	C
13.	B	39.	E	64.	B	89.	C	114.	D
14.	C	40.	C	65.	A	90.	A	115.	A
15.	C	41.	C	66.	E	91.	A	116.	B
16.	D	42.	C	67.	D	92.	D	117.	A
17.	A	43.	B	68.	C	93.	B	118.	D
18.	E	44.	C	69.	B	94.	E	119.	C
19.	D	45.	D	70.	B	95.	A	120.	C
20.	C	46.	C	71.	E	96.	E	121.	C
21.	D	47.	A	72.	A	97.	C	122.	E
22.	A	48.	E	73.	A	98.	D	123.	A
23.	D	49.	A	74.	C	99.	C	124.	C
24.	E	50.	D	75.	B	100.	C	125.	A
25.	B	51.	A	76.	D	101.	A	126.	E
26.	B								

Stenography Performance Test 2

1.	D	20.	C	39.	C	58.	D	77.	B
2.	B	21.	B	40.	B	59.	D	78.	D
3.	D	22.	E	41.	D	60.	A	79.	D
4.	C	23.	D	42.	A	61.	D	80.	E
5.	B	24.	D	43.	C	62.	B	81.	C
6.	A	25.	B	44.	D	63.	D	82.	C
7.	A	26.	D	45.	B	64.	C	83.	B
8.	A	27.	A	46.	C	65.	A	84.	A
9.	B	28.	E	47.	D	66.	A	85.	C
10.	C	29.	D	48.	A	67.	D	86.	D
11.	D	30.	B	49.	B	68.	B	87.	A
12.	D	31.	A	50.	B	69.	E	88.	E
13.	B	32.	C	51.	C	70.	A	89.	B
14.	D	33.	D	52.	A	71.	D	90.	B
15.	E	34.	C	53.	B	72.	C	91.	D
16.	D	35.	B	54.	A	73.	E	92.	D
17.	D	36.	E	55.	C	74.	D	93.	C
18.	C	37.	B	56.	B	75.	A	94.	D
19.	E	38.	E	57.	D	76.	B	95.	A

96.	C	102.	C	108.	C	114.	B	120.	A
97.	A	103.	A	109.	B	115.	A	121.	E
98.	B	104.	D	110.	B	116.	D	122.	E
99.	E	105.	B	111.	B	117.	D	123.	D
100.	B	106.	C	112.	C	118.	E	124.	E
101.	C	107.	A	113.	A	119.	C	125.	B

Posttest and Answers

Shorthand Format Questions

Directions: For each of the following questions, select the choice which best answers the question or completes the statement. Mark the answer sheet with the letter of that answer.

Allow 2 minutes for this part of the test.

1. Of the following, which is the best definition of a secretary image?
   (A) A mental conception held in common by members of a group and symbolic of a basic attitude and orientation.
   (B) Confident and with the ability to handle stressful situations calmly.
   (C) Able to see problems ahead of time, but can figure out how to deal with them when they occur.
   (D) Able to reflect excellence.

2. Of the following, which is the best definition of a secretary?
   (A) One employed to arrange material in order for reference.
   (B) One employed only to handle documents used by a supervisor.
   (C) One employed to handle correspondence and manage routine and detail work for a superior.
   (D) Person who makes appointments and handles correspondence.

3. Of the following, which is the best definition of communications?
   (A) Extra severance pay for dismissed business managers.
   (B) A computer able to perform a couple of functions simultaneously.
   (C) Working hard to do a task well.
   (D) The use of computers in communications.

4. Another up-to-date terminology for coaching, training, and sponsoring individuals in the organization and helping them to advance their careers is called
   (A) Development.
   (B) Mentoring.
   (C) Networking.
   (D) Trendsetting.

5. The copies that you prepare should be professionally printed. Most likely you would use a
   (A) Stencil machine.
   (B) Spirit duplicating machine.
   (C) Phototypesetting machine.
   (D) Xerography machine.

6. The standard letter-sized filing cabinet requires which of the following?
   (A) 3 to 5 square feet.
   (B) 4 to 6 square feet.
   (C) 5 to 7 square feet.
   (D) 8 to 10 square feet.

7. New technologies' primary use of both data and word processing is
   (A) to get the work done as soon as possible.
   (B) to produce more information quickly.
   (C) to create fewer employee positions.
   (D) to use only one piece of equipment and to cut down costs.

8. Of the following, which is the most efficient method of producing catalogs, reports, form letters, etc., using a variety of print styles and colors?
   (A) Diazo process.
   (B) Typewriter.
   (C) Duplicator.
   (D) Offset composer.

9. Of the following which would *not* be the most effective task if you have to use a typewriter?
   (A) Envelopes.
   (B) Rolodex cards.
   (C) One-time forms.
   (D) Lengthy reports.

10. Which term means an active, systematic process of meeting individuals or exchanging information to get ahead or to get things done?
    (A) Networking.
    (B) Information.
    (C) Reciprocal.
    (D) Mentoring.

Answer Key for Posttest

1. A	3. D	5. D	7. B	9. D
2. C	4. B	6. C	8. D	10. A

Stenography Performance Posttest

Person dictating is allowed 3 minues for this part.

Directions for the dictator: Dictate at the rate of 80 words a minute. Do not dictate the punctuation except for periods. Dictate with the expression the punctuation requires. Use a watch with a second hand or a stop watch to maintain the proper speed.

Exactly on a minute, start dictating:

Finish reading each group of lines at the number of seconds indicated below.

Have you ever heard of the Support Specialist Program offered by New Jersey State Department of Personnel?	15 seconds
The Support Specialist Program is designed as a comprehensive training program which will help the participant	30 seconds
understand his or her role and function as a member of a working unit. (Period) The Program is not an "end	45 seconds
all."(Period) There is no closure to the Program; it is hoped that the individuals will continue to build upon	1 minute
their careers through further education and development.(Period) The number of areas treated in the Program	15 seconds
is limited to allow sufficient time to adequately cover material considered essential	30 seconds
for each.(Period) Anyone finding certain areas of particular interest will be encouraged to pursue them	45 seconds
more fully through a careful selection of relevant elective programs. (Period) The classroom sessions are heavily	2 minutes
supported by practice exercises in the application of the concepts. (Period) The desired outcome is not only	15 seconds
to impart information, but also to allow for the practical application of the theories through outside	30 seconds
readings, in-basket exercises, case studies, and projects.(Period) Classroom instruction and outside exercises	45 seconds
will not be dogmatic but will seek to give opposing viewpoints from experts in the various areas. (Period)	3 minutes

After dictating the passage: Pause for 15 seconds to permit the stenographer to complete his/her notes. The stenographer should then proceed to follow the transcription instructions given next. She/he should not be permitted to look back at the dictated passage which you have just read.

Transcription

Directions for the stenographer: The transcript given below is part of the material that was dictated to you, except that many of the words have been left out. From your *notes* you must decide what the missing words are. You are to do the following:

1. Compare your notes with the transcript. When you come to a blank space, decide what word belongs there.

2. Look at the alphabetic word list to find the missing word. If you find the missing word there, note what letter, A, B, C, or D is printed beside it. Write that letter in the blank space in your Transcript.

3. If the missing word does not appear in the alphabetic word list, mark E in the blank space on your transcript.

4. After you have marked all the blank spaces in the transcript, transfer your answers to the answer sheet provided.

Allow 30 minutes for this part of the test.

Alphabetic Word List

Write (E) if the answer is *not* listed.

aid—A	member—D
build—B	New Jersey—A
building—C	New York—B
careers—C	offered—C
comprehensive—B	offering—D
continue—B	office—C
continuing—C	offices—A
course—C	participant—A
department—B	participants—B
designed—C	personal—B
education—A	personnel—A
enclosure—D	program—D
end—B	programming—C
end all—C	role—A
ever—D	roles—B
every—C	special—C
function—C	specialist—B
functions—A	support—A
further—D	supports—C
future—C	understand—C
hear—A	understood—D
heard—D	work—C
help—D	workers—D
hoped—B	working—B
individual—A	you—C
individuals—C	your—B

Transcript

Have __ __ __ of the __ __ Program __ by __ State __ of
   1 2 3   4 5   6   7   8

__ ? The __ __ __ is __ as a __ training __ which
9   10 11 12   13   14   15

will "__" the __ __ his or her __ and __ as a __ of
   16   17 18   19   20   21

a __ unit. The __ is not an __ . There is no __ to the
  22   23   24   25

__ ; it is __ that the __ will __ to __ upon their __
26   27   28   29   30   31

through __ __ and __ .
        32 33   34

CONTINUE ON TO THE NEXT PAGE WITHOUT WAITING FOR A SIGNAL.

Alphabetic Word List

Write (E) if the answer is *not* listed.

adequate—C
adequately—D
anybody—C
anyone—A
area—A
areas—B
careful—B
carefully—D
certain—B
class—C
classroom—B
concepts—D
considerable—B
considered—C
elect—B
elective—C
encourage—C
encouraged—B
essential—B
exercises—A
full—A
fully—C
heavily—D
heavy—A
interest—D

interesting—C
limited—B
material—B
materials—C
needed—A
number—C
numbers—D
practiced—C
program—D
pursue—A
related—B
relevant—A
select—A
selection—D
sufficient—C
support—B
supported—C
to allow—A
to let—B
treated—A
though—B
through—C
year—D
yearly—A

Transcript

The ___ of ___ ___ in the ___ is ___ ___ ___ time to ___
    35   36 37   38   39 40 41   42

cover ___ ___ ___ for each. ___ finding ___ ___ of ___
     43 44 45   46   47 48   49

___ will be ___ to ___ them more ___ ___ a ___ ___ of
50   51   52   53 54   55 56

___ ___ programs. The ___ ___ are ___ ___ by ___ ___ in
57 58   59 60   61 62   63 64

the ___ of the ___ .
    65   66

CONTINUE ON TO THE NEXT PAGE WITHOUT WAITING FOR A SIGNAL.

Alphabetic Word List

Write (E) if the answer is not listed.

also—A
applicant—B
application—D
applicants—A
case—B
desire—A
desired—B
dogmatic—C
experts—D
impart—C
impartial—B
inform—C
information—D
opposing—C
outcome—A

outside—B
practical—D
practice—C
projects—D
projections—A
readings—A
seed—A
theories—C
though—B
through—A
to allow—A
to let—C
to meet—C
various—B

Transcript

The ___ ___ is not only to ___ ___ , but ___ ___ for the
   67 68   69 70   71 72

___ ___ of the ___ through ___ ___ , ___ exercises, ___
73 74   75   76 77 78   79

studies, and ___ . Classroom ___ and ___ exercises will
     80   81   82

not be ___ but will ___ to give ___ ___ from ___ in the
    83   84   85 86   87

___ areas.
88

WHEN TIME IS UP, TRANSFER YOUR TRANSCRIPT ANSWERS TO THE

ANSWER SHEET.

END OF POSTTEST

Answer Key for Posttest

1. C	19. A	37. A	55. B	72. A
2. D	20. C	38. D	56. D	73. D
3. D	21. D	39. B	57. A	74. D
4. A	22. B	40. A	58. C	75. C
5. B	23. D	41. C	59. B	76. B
6. C	24. C	42. D	60. E	77. A
7. A	25. E	43. B	61. D	78. E
8. B	26. D	44. C	62. C	79. B
9. A	27. B	45. B	63. E	80. D
10. A	28. C	46. A	64. A	81. E
11. B	29. B	47. B	65. E	82. B
12. D	30. B	48. B	66. D	83. C
13. C	31. C	49. E	67. B	84. E
14. B	32. D	50. D	68. A	85. C
15. D	33. A	51. B	69. C	86. E
16. D	34. E	52. A	70. D	87. D
17. A	35. C	53. C	71. A	88. B
18. C	36. B	54. C		

BOOKS FOR JOB HUNTERS

CAREERS / STUDY GUIDES

Airline Pilot
Allied Health Professions
Federal Jobs for College Graduates
Federal Jobs in Law Enforcement
Getting Started in Film
How to Pass Clerical Employment Tests
How You Really Get Hired
Law Enforcement Exams Handbook
Make Your Job Interview a Success
Mechanical Aptitude and Spatial Relations Tests
Mid-Career Job Hunting
100 Best Careers for the Year 2000
Passport to Overseas Employment
Travel Agent

RESUME GUIDES

The Complete Resume Guide
Resumes for Better Jobs
Resumes That Get Jobs
Your Resume: Key to a Better Job

AVAILABLE AT BOOKSTORES EVERYWHERE

PRENTICE HALL